FILTHY RICH
POLITICIANS

FILTHY RICH
POLITICIANS

*The Swamp Creatures,
Latte Liberals, and Ruling-Class
Elites Cashing In on America*

MATT K. LEWIS

**CENTER
STREET**

Nashville • New York

Cover design by Micah Kandros
Author photograph by Richele Cole Burch
Cover copyright © 2023 by Hachette Book Group, Inc.

Center Street
Hachette Book Group
1290 Avenue of the Americas, New York, NY 10104
centerstreet.com
twitter.com/centerstreet

First edition: July 2023

Center Street is a division of Hachette Book Group, Inc. The Center Street name and logo are trademarks of Hachette Book Group, Inc.

The publisher is not responsible for websites (or their content) that are not owned by the publisher.

The Hachette Speakers Bureau provides a wide range of authors for speaking events. To find out more, go to hachettespeakersbureau.com or email HachetteSpeakers@hbgusa.com.

Center Street books may be purchased in bulk for business, educational, or promotional use. For information, please contact your local bookseller or the Hachette Book Group Special Markets Department at special.markets@hbgusa.com.

Library of Congress Cataloging-in-Publication Data

Names: Lewis, Matt K., author.
Title: Filthy-rich politicians : the swamp creatures, latte liberals, and ruling-class elites cashing in on America / Matt K. Lewis.
Description: First edition. | Nashville : Center Street, [2023] | Includes index.
Identifiers: LCCN 2023003963 | ISBN 9781546004417 (hardcover) | ISBN 9781546004431 (ebook)
Subjects: LCSH: Transparency in government—United States. | Elite (Social sciences)—United States. | Rich people—Finance, Personal—United States. | Social networks—Economic aspects—United States. | United States—Officials and employees—Supplementary income. | United States—Officials and employees—Salaries, etc.
Classification: LCC JK468.S4 L49 2023 | DDC 352.8/80973—dc23/eng/20230216
LC record available at https://lccn.loc.gov/2023003963

ISBNs: 9781546004417 (hardcover), 9781546004431 (ebook)

Printed in the United States of America

LSC-C

Printing 1, 2023

To my wife, Erin, who brings me sunshine
and makes it rain

Contents

Foreword

I'm a populist writer on the left, and Matt Lewis is a center-right journalist. So why am I writing the foreword to his new book? What you are about to read should greatly concern people on the left (like me) and the right (like Matt). Anyone who cares about America should pay close attention.

Don't be fooled by the readability of this book, which has the juiciness of a gossipy tell-all and the pacing of a mystery novel. It is a serious work on an important topic told in a compelling way.

Matt is that rare creature who has experienced the upper echelons of the American elites—which now includes journalists and politicians—as an outsider and yet managed to retain his sense of humor.

Discovering just how tightly the elites police their ranks to keep out people like Matt has made many young people bitter. Matt has rejected the rage and envy that afflict those who realize that, more often than not, you have to come from money to make it in America. That's true regardless of whether you want to be a journalist or a politician.

That's where this book comes from: a man of humble beginnings who has made it in an industry that hates people like him, and yet has kept his humility, humor, and deep love of middle America.

Matt's book is not just about how much money people make once they become politicians; it's about how many of our elected officials come from money. His work underscores my own investigation into the wealth powering our journalistic caste. Many jobs that used to be working-class trades have now become the exclusive privilege of the rich or nearly rich, changing our public discourse from one that was answerable to the public to one that is answerable to the elites.

Matt brings a light touch to this infuriating topic and an appreciation for the absurdity of what our political and economic systems have done to our country. He has a healthy skepticism toward the new populists on both sides of the political aisle who act like they speak for the working class while burnishing their elite credentials; though Matt is a conservative, he is scathing of right-wing Ivy League populists and latte liberals alike.

In other words, Matt is one of the few people who could have told this story in a way that anyone can hear it. While he is relentless in exposing how politics has become both fueled by and an engine for extreme wealth, he is never bitter, angry, or cruel.

At the end of the day, this book treats a serious topic in a fun, light-hearted way. My hope is that this book also exposes the shameless exploitation of the American public by elites in today's society.

Batya Ungar-Sargon,
November 2022

Introduction

I'm not a businessman. I'm a business, man.

—Jay-Z[1]

Let me start by putting my maxed-out credit cards on the table.

We hear about the role money plays in politics all the time, but back in the mid-2000s, the very peak of "the aughts," I had a front-row seat in full view of the action. This was before I was a television commentator, before I wrote columns discussing politics, and before I had my own podcast. Come to think of it, it was before podcasts even existed.

I was about seven years into my political career at that point, and I had just finished managing an innovative, well-run (though ultimately losing) congressional campaign. I was back in Washington, DC, eager to apply the skills I had learned on the campaign trail to my new job as a political professional—what some news outlets might call an "operative." I took some consulting jobs for issue advocacy and corporate communications.

It sounds fancy, doesn't it? When you hear "political operative," you might imagine James Carville, Paul Begala, Lee Atwater, Karl Rove, or George Stephanopoulos (before he started hosting bubble-gum morning infotainment shows). You know the type: polished, cunning, and always thinking two or three moves ahead on the three-dimensional chessboard that only they can see.

I worked for some people who were like those guys. But as I found out quickly, I *wasn't* one of them.

It turns out that people don't come knocking down your door when you run an innovative, well-run (though ultimately losing) campaign—mostly because they focus on the "ultimately losing" part. So the consulting gigs I got became very important to support my twin goals of (1) not starving and (2) not sleeping on the street.

It all hit home when I did a project for the princely sum of $1,000. I'm only half joking by calling it princely—back then, that G was important to me. It was rent, food, a car payment, and a minimum payment on a credit card. Today, $1,000 is still important to me, but I *needed* it back then.

The problem? My client wasn't going to pay me until *they* got paid by their client. So I was waiting on not just one but two corporate accounting departments. If you've ever dealt with people in corporate accounting, you know what I'm talking about. If you haven't, this is every bit the slog you're imagining.

Weeks went by without payment. Then a whole month. My seasoned political operative clients absorbed the delay just fine. Me? I floated checks that would bounce so hard I'm surprised OSHA didn't require special eyewear for anyone who handled them. And when they bounced, that meant overdraft fees—$35 per *boing!* When my client finally did pay, that $1,000 ended up costing me well over $300.

The situation was nerve-racking and a little embarrassing. But then again, most people know exactly where I'm coming from. According to a January 2022 survey by the consumer financial services company Bankrate, more than half (56 percent) of American families can't afford an emergency expense of $1,000.[2]

Shortly afterward, I left the campaign operative world for good. It might say something about my penchant for punishment that I opted for the notoriously low-paying industry that is news media.

I never got rich in politics, but plenty of others sure do. And I'm not talking about the savvy, expert political operatives who can charge way more than $1,000 for their consulting expertise. I'm talking about the people who hire them: *politicians.*

$$$

I'm not trying to stoke class warfare. I'm not interested in a revolution to overthrow the bourgeoisie or anyone else. To paraphrase conservative political theorist Russell Kirk's defense of President Dwight D. Eisenhower, *I'm not a Communist. I'm a golfer.* (Okay, I'm not a golfer, but I *am* a center-right columnist. And my wife *is* a Republican fund-raiser, so that basically qualifies me for any country club in America—well, maybe not Trump National.) I'm not big on socialism, and my church warns against envy and covetousness (then again, they also warn against drunkenness).

On the other hand, I know what it's like to struggle, man. My nail-biting experience over $1,000 isn't the only time I've been in a pinch. I've been rich, and I've been poor. And as Mrs. George S. Kaufman (or Mae West or Sophie Tucker) once observed, "Rich is better."

Okay, *poor* might be a stretch. *Rich* might be, too, depending on your standards. But I've spanned a pretty wide gamut. I'm the son of a prison guard (my dad worked as a correctional officer for about thirty years in Hagerstown, Maryland) who talks politics on TV and is on texting terms with some of the biggest names in politics and journalism. My mom was a homemaker who also babysat. Interestingly, she did a stint proofreading for the Doubleday book publishing company in Smithsburg, Maryland. Maybe that's how I inherited this writing bug.

People probably don't realize how rural parts of western Maryland were then (and still are today). When I was a kid in Wolfsville Elementary School (about seven miles from the presidential retreat at Camp David) in Frederick County, Maryland, my teacher would ask us what we wanted to be when we grew up. The number one answer was a farmer, and the number two answer was a truck driver. (I was a rebel. I wanted to play for the Baltimore Orioles.) At least I had indoor plumbing. That was not true for one of my classmates (a distant cousin), who used an outhouse until we were in middle school.

I went to Frederick Community College in Maryland, before graduating with a BS degree (an apt abbreviation) in political science from Shepherd College (now Shepherd University) in West Virginia. During that time, I worked at restaurants and an Amoco gas station while also playing in a rock band. No wonder it took me six years to graduate!

I was a newly minted middle-class kid, and a college degree was supposed to mean people would beat down my door to hire me, right? Mind you, this was in the spring of 1998 when President Bill Clinton and Federal Reserve chairman Alan Greenspan had the economy *humming*. I actually believed that you found a job by looking at the help wanted ads in the back of the *Frederick News-Post*. Even before Craigslist and the internet, everyone knew that route was for suckers. But I didn't get the memo. So I ended up in a trainee program to manage a Roy Rogers fast-food restaurant. ("If you've got time to lean, you've got time to clean.")

Rich people absorb money skills by osmosis (as anyone who has read *Rich Dad Poor Dad* by Robert T. Kiyosaki can attest), and networking was one of those skills. Many privileged Americans are exposed to networking from birth. Your dad has friends who are doctors and lawyers. They're on his Christmas card list. He does them favors, and they do him favors (like give you your first job). But I had to resort to reading a book about it in 1999 at the age of twenty-five (it was called *Dig Your Well Before You're Thirsty: The Only Networking Book You'll Ever Need* by Harvey Mackay).

By that time, a fortuitous series of events had led me to intern at a conservative nonprofit called the Leadership Institute in Arlington, Virginia. Eventually, I was able to land my first real job there. A young staffer took pity on me and hired me, even though I was (to put it charitably) a mess. I'll never forget the time he told me in an elevator, "Lewis, you don't button all the buttons on your blazer."

Until then, nobody had bothered to tell me that you only button the top button on a two-button blazer and that you never button all *three* buttons. According to *Esquire*, "The three-button suit comes with a simple rule: 'sometimes, always, never.' It means you should sometimes fasten the top button (if you feel like it), always fasten the middle button, and never button the third."[3] This raises the question: why are they all there if you don't button them all? "So you can spot the rubes" is my only possible answer.

From time to time, people are a bit taken aback by my humble background, mainly because I tried to conceal it. There's an old country song by Don Williams called "Good Ole Boys Like Me," where the narrator sings that he "learned to talk like the man on the six o'clock news." I was a bit like that. In fact, my wife (who actually grew up in West Virginia) worked to help me pronounce words correctly. (I used to say "krick" instead of "creek," "collar" instead of "color," and "motorsickle" instead of "motorcycle.")

Why did I change? Partly because I *had to* if I was going to be taken seriously in my chosen career. It's ironic that sometimes the privileged kids have the luxury of remaining authentic, while strivers have to conform and risk losing their uniqueness. (Rich people are eccentric, while the rest of us are "crazy.")

After I'd elbowed my way into journalism (after parlaying running political campaigns into conservative blogging, and blogging into writing political columns), my colleagues and competitors tended to be young people who had been educated in prep schools and/or the Ivy League, with all the attendant interests and hobbies.

Here's one example. While working at the Daily Caller in the early 2010s, I received a tip that a member of a very prominent liberal family had wrecked a boat, and it was causing an ecological disaster. I tracked down the liberal scion, who conceded that he had scuttled the vessel. But the spillage was very minimal. "Does anyone there know anything about sailing?" he asked over the phone. Well, unless you were talking about a bass boat, I sure as hell didn't. But I walked into the bullpen area of the Daily Caller, where all the young staff congregated, and asked, "Does anyone here know about yachting or sailing?" About ten hands shot up. People who assume the Daily Caller is a right-wing tabloid looking for "gotcha" journalism might be surprised to learn that this prominent liberal family member persuaded one of our many nautical experts that this was, in fact, not a big deal. We abandoned ship and spiked the story.

The point is, my office was full of people with extensive sailing experience. Apparently, William F. Buckley Jr. wasn't the only conservative who sailed through life. But there's a serious point to be made here. It's worth considering what it means when only a rich person can afford to be a journalist (or a politician). It's also worth considering how this affects our news (or laws).

I had much to learn, but those lessons were starting to pay off. By 2016, I had a book deal, a cable TV news contract, and a speaker's bureau gig.

And a mountain of debt.

I used to find it absurd that rich and famous people like Willie Nelson got in trouble with the IRS, but I can attest that bad accountants can mess you up. People also have no idea how hard it is to pay off tens of thousands of dollars in taxes. The more you earn to pay off the taxes, the more they tax. It's a vicious cycle. And you can't declare bankruptcy to get out of paying most tax debt, either. (The government always gets its money.)

While my journalism career flourished, my wallet deflated. Donald Trump was ever-present during this time, and I took a bit of comfort from a story Ivanka Trump told about her dad. "I remember once my father and I were walking down Fifth Avenue and there was a homeless person sitting right outside of Trump Tower and I remember my father pointing to him and saying, 'You know, that guy has $8 billion more than me,' because he was in such extreme debt at that point, you know?" she said.[4]

On a much, *much* smaller scale, I could identify with Trump.

At the same time, my provincial background continued to occasionally prove embarrassing. A few years ago when I was in New York to do a TV spot, I grabbed a beer with a sophisticated journalist friend at a sushi bar near Central Park. Being unsophisticated, I don't eat raw fish, but my colleague explained she was ordering edamame (aka soybeans). I didn't realize you *weren't supposed to eat the pods.* There is no genteel way to extricate yourself or save face when you are in the middle of Manhattan trying to hold a conversation while sputtering out chewed-up chunks of soybean pod.

This wasn't as consequential as President Gerald Ford munching on a tamale husk at the Alamo or John Kerry asking for Swiss cheese on his cheesesteak at Pat's King of Steaks in South Philly. But it was, shall we say, a faux pas. You can take the boy out of the country, but you can't take the country out of the boy.

The Lord works in mysterious ways. Partially to economize, my wife and I decided to move to West Virginia—a state that is governed by a colorful coal-mining magnate named Jim Justice, allegedly the state's only billionaire—just before COVID-19 slammed into the region (and Justice collected a $2,400 coronavirus stimulus check, as *ProPublica* reported).[5] Soon thereafter, massive protests exploded in Washington, DC, as a result of George Floyd's murder.

While the amenities that make DC a great place to call home shut down, we flourished in the Mountain State. That move turned out to be a blessing. We found a church, and I started coaching Little League. We were closer to family, including my mom, who lives in Pennsylvania (the Bob Evans in Hagerstown, Maryland, is just a forty-five-minute drive for either of us). I was also once again around the kinds of folks that I grew up with (swap the Reagan-Bush yard signs for MAGA ones). For someone who writes about conservative culture and politics, the ability to live alongside rural Americans gives me much-needed perspective.

If you're wondering why I'm talking so much about myself in a book that is supposed to focus on rich politicians, it's simply to make this point:

I'm not predisposed to love or hate the rich. My position on money could be summed up by Tim McGraw: "I like it, I love it, I want some more of it!"[6]

I know what it's like to be broke, and I can appreciate the anger and bitterness that come from watching decadent elites get rich from things like inherited wealth, stock tips, real estate, and revenue that gets taxed at a lower rate than their employees' paychecks.

At the same time, my faith and my political philosophy tell me that it's wrong and counterproductive to let envy or bitterness control you. We each have an individual responsibility to avoid falling prey to jealousy or negativity.

We live in a fallen world, and there is no perfect civilization. The blessings we have here in America are precious, and my goal is to conserve them. But this is contingent on America remaining a place where, if you work hard and play by the rules, you can get ahead in life. No matter where you are on the spectrum of class or wealth, you should support preserving this premise. Even (especially) the richest among us should want to mitigate the chances of a mob showing up at their front door with pitchforks and flaming torches. Far better for them to show up with well-typed résumés.

My experience living in rural America has come in handy these last few years. Populism has been on the rise, and it has become fashionable—both on the left and the right—to criticize the moneyed class. (On the left, the targets tend to be corporate overlords and Washington power players; on the right, it is woke corporations and highly educated cosmopolitan elites.) At the very least, it has allowed me to understand their good faith critiques and concerns, even if some populist rhetoric and policies conflict with my vision.

For better or worse, we now live in a populist era. We see this on the left, with politicians like Elizabeth Warren and Alexandria Ocasio-Cortez, and on the right, with commentators like my former boss Tucker Carlson and rookie politicians like Senator J. D. Vance (R-OH).

For the Left, populism is old hat. For the Right, it's something new (at least in my lifetime). As a conservative who came of age in the Reagan era, I have generally found populism, which tends to require victims and oppressors, to be potentially dangerous. But like every great movement, it contains kernels of truth that cannot be ignored. America's elites *have*, to a large extent, abdicated their responsibility to our nation.

If American conservatism is about conserving liberal democracy (an increasingly controversial premise), then average citizens must retain faith in the system, and elites must work hard to earn their place in the pecking order. When people begin to believe that liberal democracy is a façade, that the system is rigged and it's all just a thin veneer hiding corrupt politicians, they feel like suckers for endorsing it. And eventually, they stop. They lose faith in norms, customs, and institutions, and they are tempted to turn to more radical and corrupt forms of government. This lack of trust in elites and institutions eventually leads to a breakdown of democracy.

I don't disdain wealthy people, and I don't begrudge politicians who are making a decent living. What is more, I think it is admirable when wealthy people want to dedicate their lives to pursuits that transcend self-indulgent activities.

Capitalism has lifted more people out of poverty than any other system in the world. I do not hate the rich. But I love America. And one of the ways we can lose it is when the public stops trusting institutions, leaders, and elites.

The truth is, in many cases, they no longer deserve our trust. Many complicated reasons for this exist.

Some of them have to do with money.

So why am I writing about this? In a way, I'm working backward. My last book explored the rise of populist nationalism on the right. While America's political elites were too weak and impotent to squash a populist uprising, they were also too decadent to head it off by addressing some of its legitimate concerns. After years of giving the masses beer and football (our generation's version of bread and circuses), our elites started feeding them oxy and fentanyl (or, at the very least, turned a blind eye to it).

Normal people are having a hard time making ends meet. And our political elites just keep getting richer.

The big question is, what (if anything) should we do about that? The first step is transparency. This book will help with that.

Chapter 1

The Ruling Class

Let me tell you about the very rich. They are different from you and me.

—F. Scott Fitzgerald[1]

A viral Facebook post grabbed my normally short attention span recently and wouldn't let go. It alleges that the percentage of millionaires in Congress is 50 percent, while the overall percentage in the United States is 1 percent. The post concludes with this zinger of a question: "[T]ell me again how you become a multimillionaire earning $174,000 [the current salary for rank-and-file House and Senate Members] annually?"[2] It's a good question. So good, in fact, that I decided to write a book about it.

Facebook (as usual) got some of its details wrong (the percentage of millionaires in the US is somewhere around 6 to 8 percent, as financial writer Dan Burrows noted),[3] but the point remains largely cogent.[4] A huge financial disparity exists between our leaders and our neighbors (and, more disturbingly, ourselves).[5] Even if members of Congress were simply living off their $174,000 annual salary (they're not), the average American salary in 2021 was just $56,260, according to the Bureau of Labor Statistics.[6] But, as Facebook correctly pointed out, more than half of the members of Congress *are* millionaires.[7] The median net worth of a member of Congress is something like twelve times greater than the net worth of the median American household.[8]

Some portion of this disparity can be chalked up to selection bias: members of Congress tend to be disproportionately older (older people tend to have accrued more wealth), whiter,[9] and (increasingly) more highly educated than the US population overall.[10]

But the question remains: *Why are so many people in Congress so damn rich, and how did they get that way?*[11]

Affluent parents (and grandparents), marrying rich, inside info on the stock market, and (yes) car dealerships are often part of the story. A few of these folks even created businesses that *earned* them money.

But here's one thing on which we can probably all agree: America's public servants are supposed to be *public servants*. The elites who founded this nation envisioned that they would come to Washington, do their civic duty, and skedaddle back to the farm. The fact that we have so many elderly politicians currently running America suggests this vision has been scrapped. These days, nobody wants to go back to the farm. Most members of Congress would rather "buy the farm" than go back to it.

Today, we are represented by an unsavory hybrid of plutocrats and hypocrites. In one corner are the people who leveraged their riches to win an elected position. In the other corner are the people who leveraged their elected position to grow even richer, usually through completely legal means and often while decrying things like income inequality. As the cliché goes, they came to Washington to do good and stayed to do well.

$ $ $

To make matters worse, the wealth gap between average citizens and our public servants has widened dramatically in my lifetime.

According to a 2011 article in the *Washington Post*, as recently as 1975 (the year after I was born), "it wasn't nearly so unusual for a person with few assets besides a home to win and serve in Congress."[12] The article goes on to note that lawmakers "of that time included a barber, a pipe fitter and a house painter."

Of course, this phenomenon is not unique to the world of politics. In 2022, writer and director Peter Atencio noted this same trend in the world of acting.[13] For example, he described a typical actor's résumé in the 1960s and '70s: "He was an amateur boxer and truck driver before joining the merchant marines and was discovered by a producer in Cuba where he was in jail for assault." Then he compared it with the typical actor's biography today: "His dad was an investment banker and his mom was a model. He attended Yale."

The world has changed, and it's no surprise these changes would also manifest in the world of politics—a fact that may buttress the "Politics is Hollywood for ugly people" theory. The problem is that it's one thing for Americans to view movie stars as out-of-touch elites, and quite another thing for our political leaders to make us feel the same way.

Between my tenth and thirty-fifth birthdays, congressional median wealth "more than doubled," while "the wealth of the average American family declined," as the *Washington Post* reported.[14] The chasm has only widened since then. According to Ballotpedia's "Personal Gain Index," between 2004 and 2012, the average increase in net worth for the one hundred richest congressional incumbents was a whopping 114 percent per year.[15] I'm no math major, but I think that's pretty good.

Consider how this increase in wealth has correlated with the public's declining trust in our institutions. According to a 2015 Pew Research Center study, just 19 percent of people surveyed said "elected officials in Washington try hard to stay in touch with voters back home," while a whopping "77 percent say elected officials lose touch with the people quickly."[16]

These results make perfect sense. Getting elected to serve in Washington is the new version of being discovered at a pharmacy counter. And no matter how much you promise to "remember the little people," that desire only lasts so long. Remember that girl you went to high school with who got super hot over the summer? Did she hang out with you when school started in the fall? I didn't think so. People who outpace us tend to move on.

Meanwhile, "roughly three-quarters (74%) say elected officials put their own interests ahead of the country's, while just 22% say elected officials put the interests of the country first," the Pew Research Center noted in 2015.[17] And 72 percent of Americans describe politicians as "selfish."

Surveys are more likely to ask about campaign cash corrupting the elections process than about politicians themselves getting rich. But there is a clear sense that politicians keep putting their own interests ahead of citizens' interests. "Neither party is going to drain this political swamp," Pat Buchanan explained in 2000, "because to them it's not a swamp, it's a protected wetland. It's their natural habitat."[18] Pat was ahead of the curve.

A 2019 Pew Research Center study showed that of those who believe trust in the federal government has declined in the last twenty years, 36 percent cited "something related to how the U.S. government is performing...including how money has corrupted it, how corporations control it and general references to 'the swamp.'"[19]

Three years later, a Gallup survey showed that just 7 percent of Americans had a "great deal" or "quite a lot" of confidence in Congress.[20] Of all the "institutions in American society," Congress came in dead last— behind institutions like "big business," "organized labor," "the public schools," and even "television news."

As has been widely documented, trust in the government began to dramatically decline after Vietnam and Watergate.[21] Thanks, boomers! Both of these events forced Americans to reconsider how much they should trust their politicians and elites. This is to say that the financial gap between politicians and the people they serve is far from the only driver of government distrust. The trend of gazillionaire politicians only contributes to this problem.

The gap between politicians and the rest of us is only exacerbated by Americans feeling like they are barely treading water. Whether you blame automation, immigration, outsourcing—or some combination of the three—the declining number of well-paying industrial jobs has only stoked populism in America. Working people often feel underrepresented and disadvantaged. In the Biden era, the return of 1970s-era problems like inflation and violent crime have added to the sense that the wheels are coming off the political clown car.

But even during the salad days, when the US economy was doing very well and most Americans were benefiting from cheap consumer goods, we were losing ground when it came to some things like child care and home prices that were inextricably tied to the future and the American dream. "[T]he prices of the things we need most," explained the *New York Times'* Ezra Klein in 2022, "have been growing far faster than inflation."[22]

Why are American citizens less trusting of our leaders these days? One obvious reason is that our politicians live lives that are distinctly separate from the rest of us. What is more, instead of concealing it, they are flaunting it.

$ $ $

It was April 2020, and we were in the middle of the global COVID-19 pandemic lockdowns. People were scared and isolated. Businesses were shuttered. And the then speaker of the house Nancy Pelosi decided to have a video conference on *The Late Late Show with James Corden* and show off her expensive fridge and luxury ice cream. "I don't know what I would have done if ice cream had not been invented," Pelosi said.[23] This was back when the pandemic had forced TV shows essentially to become Zoom calls. There was no studio audience to guffaw, not that anyone would have. The whole thing felt cold and out of touch, especially since it coincided with Democrats briefly blocking Republican attempts to provide more money for small business (they wanted more money for hospitals and coronavirus testing—which they eventually got).

First, Republicans (as they say) pounced. "While Nancy Pelosi sits in her ivory tower in San Francisco, eating $13 dollar a pint ice cream out of her $24,000 fridge, she is cheering on Democrats for blocking coronavirus relief aid that has so far been distributed to 1.3 million small businesses that is about to run out," tweeted the Republican National Committee's rapid response director, Steve Guest.[24]

"It's so revealing that the politician [Democrats] adore most is one of the richest members of Congress. Pelosi has been so rich for so long that she can't see how tone-deaf this is. It's her normal," tweeted journalist Glenn Greenwald.[25] It also spawned outrage from average online commenters on YouTube. "Her fridge is bigger than most of [the] homeless people's tents in California," wrote one.[26]

But this wasn't just some gaffe that would quickly blow over—at least, not according to left-wing groups who pointed back to that moment after Republicans surprised everyone by gaining House seats in 2020. This happened despite Democrats winning the presidency and the US Senate that year. And although it wasn't enough to flip the House to Republicans, the losses still constituted a disappointing result for House Democrats.

"When Democratic leaders make unforced errors like showing off two sub-zero freezers full of ice cream on national television or cozy up with Wall Street executives and corporate lobbyists while Trump tells voters we are the party of the swamp, it is not surprising that we lose," read a 2020 post-election memo issued by New Deal Strategies, Justice Democrats, Sunrise Movement, and Data for Progress.[27] "We need a new generation of leadership grounded in a multiracial, working class experience and background," the memo continued.

They got what they asked for. After Democrats lost the House in 2022, Pelosi finally stepped down from leadership, paving the way for Representative Hakeem Jeffries (D-NY) to take over as House minority leader. For what it's worth, Representative Jeffries is just fifty-two. He's also the first Black congressperson to lead the House or the Senate. What is more, his estimated net worth is a paltry (for Congress, that is) $567,000.[28] In so many ways, he stands in stark contrast to Pelosi.

But Pelosi's problem isn't that she's rich. From George Washington to the present moment, America has had its fair share of rich politicians. The problem is that, unlike other times in our history, it feels like today's political leaders are completely out of touch and disconnected from the rest of us. It feels like they are putting their own needs ahead of ours. This sense drives distrust in our institutions. It drives anger.

In the coming chapters, we will delve into how we got here and how to fix it.

The bottom line is that American politics has gotten crazy and conspiratorial, in part because more and more people believe that the roulette wheel is rigged for the rich, the connected, and yes, the elected.

To be honest, *they have a point.* They always have.

Chapter 2

A Rich History: Pre$idents from Washington to Biden

No young man should go into politics if he wants to get rich or if he expects an adequate reward for his services. An honest public servant can't become rich in politics.[1]

—Harry S. Truman

Let's be real. American politicians have always differed from the rest of us—and this is especially true of our presidents. America was founded by a bunch of (admittedly brilliant) elites. But they didn't all come from uber-privileged backgrounds. John Adams, our second president, came from a "comfortable, but not wealthy, Massachusetts farming family," according to the University of Virginia's Miller Center.[2] Other Founders came from more humble backgrounds. PolitiFact notes that Benjamin Franklin "was the son of a man who made soap and candles, which Encyclopedia Britannica terms 'one of the lowliest of the artisan crafts' at the time."[3] And these days, every student knows that Alexander Hamilton was the "bastard, orphan, son of a whore"...who was "dropped in the middle of a forgotten spot in the Caribbean"—or so the popular musical tells us.

Still, these are exceptions that prove the rule. Yes, many of the Founders were incredibly rich, but nobody should doubt their willingness to sacrifice.

Indeed, they pledged "Our lives, our fortunes, and our sacred honor" for this great republic that is now in jeopardy. The problem isn't that politicians today are rich; it's the sense that they have lost that sense of service and sacrifice—that they are out of touch and are intent on feathering their own nests (and those of their corporate overlords). The Founders risked their fortunes for America. Today, it feels like our politicians are more interested in guaranteeing their fortunes and fame in America.

As Michelle Fields wrote in her 2016 book *Barons of the Beltway*, our Founding Fathers "embraced and exuded one of America's founding virtues: humility. They were ambitious and strove for greatness for America, but were stripped of the pretentiousness of European monarchs. They disliked the ostentation of the royals and worked hard to eliminate the manners and thinking that characterized aristocratic society in Europe. But the norms and behaviors that our Founding Fathers worked so hard to eradicate have slowly found their way back into Washington's bloodstream."[4]

Over time, even these founding elites found themselves out of step with the times. Eventually, a folksy war hero named Andrew Jackson would supplant them when he ultimately defeated President John Quincy Adams (the son of our second president) in 1828. It was the first example of a populist taking down the political establishment in this new country's history. It wouldn't be the last. Despite his outsider image, Jackson was one of the richest politicians America has ever seen. He was also a self-made man who overcame humble beginnings, even if his methods were questionable.

According to NPR's Steve Inskeep, author of *Jacksonland*, Old Hickory's fortune was intricately connected to his expelling Native Americans from their homeland. "Jackson was making space for the spread of white settlers, including those who practiced slavery," writes Inskeep. "And he was enabling real estate development, in which he participated and profited."[5] *Handsomely*, I might add. The Trail of Tears apparently led to Easy Street—for Jackson, at least.

Love him or hate him, Jackson's accomplishments were significant. Heck, he has a whole *era* named after him. His immediate successors were not as significant. At least, not until our sixteenth president, Abraham Lincoln, came along. Lincoln was born into "humble surroundings, a one-room log cabin with dirt floors," Michael Burlingame noted,[6] and he struggled with finances, even into adulthood. Katharine Q. Seelye wrote in the *New York Times* that in the 1830s, "Creditors hauled Lincoln into court, and the sheriff seized his only assets—his survey equipment and his horse."[7] The debt was "so onerous that Lincoln called it 'my national debt.'" Lincoln wouldn't be out from under it until the 1840s. He finally earned some wealth (thanks in large part to his presidential salary),[8] but Honest Abe still ended up being one of our poorer presidents—financially, that is.

Despite the lionization of Lincoln, in the decades following his death, politics wasn't a glamorous pursuit that attracted elites. When "bossism" and machine politics were all the gilded rage in the Gilded Age, politics was beneath the notice of the truly (gold-plated) rich. Political careers might be okay for bartenders and the occasional bearded Great Emancipator, but that was about it. At least, that's what Theodore Roosevelt's well-heeled family believed, according to Edmund Morris's highly acclaimed book *The Rise of Theodore Roosevelt*. "We thought he was, to put it frankly, pretty fresh,"[9] wrote Emlen Roosevelt, a prominent banker, regarding his cousin Teddy's foray into Republican politics. "We felt that his own father would not have liked it, and would have been fearful of the outcome. The Roosevelt circle as a whole had a profound distrust of public life."

TR responded to this general attitude by insisting that he "intended to be one of the governing class."[10] And his status as a member of the elite didn't stop him from embracing a form of populism that would label him "A traitor to his caste."[11]

Theodore's cousin, Franklin Delano Roosevelt, would follow in TR's footsteps a couple of decades later, albeit as a Democrat. Thanks to the

Great Depression, Herbert Hoover (Roosevelt's self-made millionaire opponent) looked out of touch. This allowed FDR (whose adjusted-for-inflation net worth peaked at about $60 million, according to a report from CNBC)[12] to tool about in his pal Vincent Astor's 264-foot yacht, while touting himself as the champion of the "forgotten man."

How did FDR get rich? The old-fashioned way: he inherited it. But his life wasn't as charmed as you may think. The truth is, FDR suffered from an affliction other than polio: an overprotective mom. According to the Museum of American Finance, "When his father, James, died in 1900, he left Roosevelt a small inheritance, but most of his estate (worth about $600,000) went to his wife, Sara Ann Delano, who also inherited about $1.3 million from her side of the family."[13] As a result, FDR "remained financially quasi-dependent on his mother for decades thereafter."

Mama didn't want to cut those apron strings, and she had leverage to keep them attached. I'm not exaggerating. FDR's fabled Hyde Park residence was his mother's home, not his. The Upper East Side town-house FDR also lived in as a middle-aged man was a Christmas present from his mom. The only catch? Her townhouse was next door—and they shared a doorway, as the *New York Times* noted.[14]

FDR's reliance on his mom (and Sara's meddling in her son's life) didn't end there, however. "The added expense of [FDR's] paralysis and continued inattention to his personal finances kept Roosevelt on Sara's dole until his inauguration as President initiated a $75,000 per year salary," according to the Museum of American Finance.[15] Just imagine what this situation was like for Franklin's wife, Eleanor Roosevelt. As Jennifer J. Raab, the president of Hunter College (which later purchased the townhouse when Sara died in 1941), quipped in 2012, "Everyone out there who thought they had mother-in-law problems, this probably trumps anyone's story."[16]

FDR's successor, Harry S. Truman, could (despite his public professions of love for Bess's mom) identify with mother-in-law problems. (An unrepentant anti-Semite, she wouldn't allow Harry's Jewish former haberdashery partner into *her* house. She passed along this prejudice to Bess.) But what HST *couldn't* identify with was the Roosevelt family's wealth. After an impressive stint giving 'em hell as the most powerful man in the free world (capable of firing General Douglas MacArthur, dropping two atomic bombs on Japan, ending World War II, and making fools out of political pundits—among other notable accomplishments), Truman left the White House in January 1953 and then filed a 1954 tax return with earnings of just $13,564.74. Truman's picayune income and assets inspired Congress to eventually pass the Former Presidents Act of 1958, which provided a $25,000 annual pension for ex-presidents, as well as administrative support. It might as well have been called the Keep Harry Out of Penury Act.

As you might imagine, the pension cost continues to rise to keep pace with inflation, even if few presidents since Truman have needed it. What is more, the perks exceed what would normally comprise a pension. According to an August 2022 article for NBC News, in addition to former president Donald Trump's $230,000 pension, there is "salary for his staff at $141,000. Rental payments for his official office to [General Services Administration] at $406,000 with utilities and communications at $35,000. Printing costs at $5,000. $11,000 for supplies. $15,000 for equipment. $58,000 for 'other services.' Costs for travel and security were not listed in this budget and each former president has lifetime Secret Service protection."[17]

But Truman was an accidental president, and Dwight D. Eisenhower (his successor) was a bona fide hero. It was only a matter of time before the moneyed class would make a comeback. In 1960, Joseph P. Kennedy Sr. bankrolled his son John F. Kennedy's campaign. Joe had amassed a fortune via liquor, movie studios, and the stock market (he was smart enough to get out before the 1929 crash). During one speech, JFK read a supposed missive from his father: "Dear Jack—Don't buy a single vote more than necessary—I'll be damned if I am going to pay for a landslide."[18] The line was delivered at the Gridiron Club, which suggests it was a joke (albeit one with more than a grain of truth). Some dads get too involved in Little League, but Joe Kennedy was the ultimate helicopter parent. As *Politico* reported, Joe even helped make JFK's book *Profiles in Courage*—which Theodore C. Sorensen, not JFK, wrote—a Pulitzer Prize winner.[19] Joe also made sure his son's books sold. When he died, unopened boxes of *Why England Slept* were found in the basement of his Hyannis Port home.[20]

Money doesn't always buy campaign success (just ask Nelson Rockefeller or his successor, Michael Bloomberg), but it worked overtime for the Kennedys. Ever since Truman headed back to Independence, Missouri, a sizable nest egg has pretty much become a presidential prerequisite. (Aside from that, modern post-presidents can really cash in on memoirs, speeches, Netflix shows, and the like.)

This prerequisite is true for both the winners and the losers.

In 1980, Ronald Reagan was elected president (although a wealthy former movie star, Reagan was in the middle of the pack in terms of presidential wealth). Eight years later, the then vice president George H. W. Bush, who everyone knew was loaded, ran against Michael Dukakis, who everyone thought was not. But as the *New York Times* reported at the time, "Mr. Dukakis is indeed a direct beneficiary of $1 million out of a total of $2 million held in two trust funds set up on the death of his father, the first Greek immigrant to graduate from Harvard Medical School."[21]

Four years later, Bush would run against another regular schmo— this one's nickname was "Bubba." Arkansas governor Bill Clinton was worth only about $700,000 at the time, but Bill and Hillary's wealth had increased 84 percent in the previous three years.[22] The real problem for Bush, however, may have been running against a third-party candidate, billionaire H. Ross Perot. Perot spent $64 million on his 1992 campaign, with all but $3.9 million coming from his own bank account, according to the *Los Angeles Times*.[23] For this, he garnered about 19 percent of the vote and zero electoral votes. Still, he won the money race, outspending Bush and Clinton along the way.[24] And he also accomplished his goal of destroying Bush, whom he disliked. So maybe all that spending was worth it—if you're a billionaire.

It's entirely possible that Perot's money changed the course of history. Ask someone who knows a little about politics, and they'll tell you Perot cost Bush the election. Ask someone who knows a lot about politics, and they'll debunk the notion, citing exit polls showing that Perot took about an equal number of votes from Clinton and Bush. But ask a highly sophisticated political observer, and they'll say it's an unanswerable question. The world is dynamic, and Perot's very existence changed the contours of the race.[25]

So why did Perot run? Bush and his pal James Baker (Ronald Reagan's first chief of staff, who went on to serve as treasury secretary and secretary of state) both believed Perot was mad at "41" because, as Reagan's vice president, Bush had been tasked with the thankless job of telling Perot that he was wrong to believe there were still American POWs in Vietnam.[26] "I think he was driven by a personal dislike, a personal resentment of me, you might say," Bush said later, according to reporter Tierney Sneed.[27] If Perot really spent $64 million on a personal vendetta, that would likely be the most money *ever* spent on spite (at least up to that point).

In 2000, Bush's son, George W., would win the presidency (but not the popular vote). And in his 2004 reelection, he fared better than one-termer Poppy Bush, fending off a reelection challenge from windsurfing legend John Kerry. But it wasn't easy, thanks in part to the secondhand fortune Kerry accessed via his wife, Teresa Heinz (the Heinz ketchup heiress). Republicans portrayed Kerry as something of an effete snob and used his habit of sailboarding as a metaphor for his penchant for flip-flopping on political issues. Had Kerry won the election, he would have been (at the time) the third-richest president in history, behind Washington and

Kennedy, according to Forbes.[28] The well-coiffed Kerry came within a hair (118,457 votes in Ohio,[29] actually) of winning the presidency. The moral of this story: Never underestimate the power of money. Or ketchup. Or hair.

Four years later, it was time to paint Republicans with the out-of-touch elitism brush. Because of his reputation for "straight talk" and authenticity, we don't think of John McCain as being rich. But in 2008, McCain couldn't remember how many houses he owned. In McCain's case, the number turned out to be *eight*—but there was a catch. As *Politico* later clarified, "Sen. McCain himself does not own any of the properties. They're all owned by Cindy McCain, her dependent children and the trusts and companies they control."[30]

And here we see the convergence of two subplots in this book, the first being the number of politicians who marry into money, and the other being that some rich politicians, by virtue of their style or persona, avoid looking or acting like elites, while others look like they are about to be fitted for a monocle and top hat. John Sidney McCain III lost the election to Barack Obama (who was worth a mere $1.3 million at the time)[31] that year, but not because people confused him with C. Montgomery Burns of *The Simpsons* fame.

The same could *not* be said in 2012 for Mitt ("my wife drives a couple of Cadillacs") Romney, the son of auto executive and former Michigan governor George Romney. During the 2012 Republican primary, opponents cast Romney as a "vulture capitalist"[32] who (as Jon Stewart put it) "looks like anyone who's ever fired your dad."[33] It probably didn't help that, during the campaign, news broke that Romney was having a car elevator installed in his La Jolla, California, home, as ABC reported.[34] A man's gotta park, right?

The low point in Romney's 2012 general election campaign may have come when a recording surfaced of him saying that "there are 47% of the people who will vote for the president no matter what" because they are "dependent upon government...believe that they are victims... believe the government has a responsibility to care for them" and "pay no income tax." Denigrating people who are drawing Social Security or military pensions (or simply don't earn enough money to pay an income tax) proved an unwise strategy for the Republican hopeful. Whenever you start off by writing off 47 percent of the vote (some write-offs are bad, Mitt), you're cutting it way too close at the finish line.

Four years later, in 2016, Hillary Clinton similarly blundered by labeling some of Trump's followers as "deplorables." Meanwhile, Donald "I'm really rich and don't you forget it" Trump turned the tables by *owning* his wealth. An old political maxim says you should "hang a lantern on your problems," and Trump did just that—to an extreme. During the 2016 campaign, when Hillary Clinton accused him of paying zero income taxes in some years, Trump retorted, "That makes me smart."[35] Appearing on *Saturday Night Live* in 2022, comedian Dave Chappelle suggested this exchange was the reason Trump was beloved by so many people in Chappelle's home state of Ohio. Calling Trump an "honest liar," Chappelle explained, "No one had ever seen anything like that. No one had ever seen somebody come from inside of that house outside and tell all the commoners we are doing everything that you think we are doing inside of that house. And he just went right back in the house and started playing the game again."[36] And it didn't end there. In explaining why his cabinet consisted of so many rich people, Trump said, "I love all people—rich or poor—but in those particular positions, I just don't want a poor person,"[37] Instead of apologizing for his riches, Trump made the case that he was so rich he couldn't be bought, as *Politico* noted.[38] By being so brazen, Trump ironically inoculated himself from criticism. He looked at the culture, noticed that our culture fetishizes authenticity and conspicuous consumption, and decided to own it. Parading around one's wealth runs contrary to conventional wisdom in politics, but it worked for him.

This brings us to Joe Biden. "Middle-Class Joe" (a relative pauper) with an estimated $9 million net worth in 2022[39]—mostly thanks to real estate, book deals, and speaking gigs—was among the poorer members of the US Senate. "I entered as one of the poorest men in Congress, [and I] left [as] one of the poorest men in government in Congress and as vice president," Biden said in 2019 after urging Trump to release his tax returns. It's unclear whether that was *exactly* correct, but according to PolitiFact, "Biden ranked near the bottom in the center's data in the years before he became vice president: Biden ranked 570th of 585 officials in 2005; 614th of 636 officials in 2006; and 626th of 639 officials in 2007."[40] Indeed, during those years, Biden's estimated net worth was actually in the *red*. Biden didn't really cash in until he left the vice presidency in 2017 (more on that, later).

Could it be that Biden's somewhat modest (compared with other politicians in this book) background has caused him to carry a chip on his shoulder? Throughout his career, he has sometimes exaggerated his everyman persona (infamously in 1988, when he plagiarized a speech from British Labour Party leader Neil Kinnock about being the first person in his family to ever go to a university) while stressing his ability to overcome his background. "I think I have a much higher IQ than you do I suspect. I went to law school on a full academic scholarship, the only one in my class to have a full academic scholarship," he bragged to a New Hampshire reporter in 1987.[41]

Compared to other politicians, Biden may feel like he has something to prove. Yet compared to most average Americans, he's still loaded beyond our wildest dreams.

$ $ $

By now, we should probably be used to presidents who are much richer than the rest of us. An arguably more disturbing trend is that so many members of Congress are joining that elite group, including rank-and-file members of the lower chamber known as "the people's house." James

Madison, the father of the Constitution, believed the House should have "an immediate dependence on, and intimate sympathy with, the people," according to the US House of Representatives website. Because House elections are biennial, members are obviously dependent on the public. But do they maintain "sympathy with" average Americans? This is increasingly hard to believe.

Perhaps this trend was inevitable. Italian sociologist and economist Robert Michels's "iron law of oligarchy" suggests that, even in a democracy, a "ruling class" will eventually emerge. Michels zeroed in on organizations, bureaucracies, and political parties, but I don't see any reason why his theory wouldn't hold true in politics at the national level.

And from there, it's just a hop, skip, and a jump to conclude that this leadership caste *deserves* to rule us. And that idea is a dangerous one.

Chapter 3

Why the Rich Get Elected

We never steal cars, but we deal hard.
—*Rick Ross, "Hustlin' "*[1]

How does the Lebanese son of a Mormon mom get indicted for car theft, make a fortune selling car alarms, and get elected to Congress? Just ask California representative Darrell Issa.

Okay, okay. Let's be clear about this: despite the indictment, Issa has never actually been *convicted* of car theft. In fact, the prosecutor dropped all charges against him. But as we'll see, he certainly knew enough about the art and science of car thievery to establish a lucrative car alarm business.

Issa's origin story was anything but promising. In 1970, he dropped out of high school and joined the army. A member of Issa's army unit, First Sergeant (Ret.) Jay Bergey, told a reporter for the *San Francisco Chronicle* that Issa stole his yellow Dodge and took it to Cleveland in 1971. "I confronted Issa," he said. "I got in his face and threatened to kill him, and magically my car reappeared the next day, abandoned on the turnpike."[2] Issa, who described Bergey as an alcoholic, categorically denies ever stealing his car.[3] No charges were ever filed.

A month later (in 1971), Issa and his older brother, William, were arrested for allegedly stealing a red Maserati in Cleveland, Ohio. The case was eventually dropped.

Seven years later—in a separate incident—the Issa brothers were indicted for grand theft. The details are confusing, and the case was also later dropped. But as the *New Yorker*'s Ryan Lizza later described it, the allegation was that "the two men had conspired to fraudulently sell Darrell's car [a Mercedes sedan] and then collect the insurance money."[4] The case was also later dropped.

Next, Issa started an electronics manufacturing company called Quantum Enterprises. After one of their client's loans became delinquent, Issa orchestrated what Lizza calls a "hostile takeover" of the client's car alarm business, Steal Stopper. According to Jack Frantz, a former employee of Steal Shopper, Issa placed a box containing a gun on his desk before firing him. Issa denies "ever pull[ing] a gun on anyone in my life."[5]

Then, in 1982, Issa's manufacturing plant mysteriously burned down. According to the *Los Angeles Times*, "Circumstantial evidence aroused suspicion of arson," and the founder of Steal Stopper alleged Issa was the culprit. "Fire investigators also noted that a computer was taken off the site eight days before the fire, 'allegedly to be reprogrammed' by Issa's lawyer, and that business blueprints were put away in a safe—which was 'not previously done before,'" according to another report from the *Los Angeles Times*.[6] Investigators also noted that Issa had dramatically increased his fire insurance just weeks before the blaze occurred. As the *New Yorker* reported, "The Ohio state fire marshal never determined the cause of the fire and no one was ever charged with a crime. According to Issa, St. Paul [the insurer] paid Quantum twenty-five thousand dollars but refused to pay his claim for the Steal Stopper inventory. Issa sued St. Paul for a hundred and seventy-five thousand dollars, and the two parties eventually settled out of court for about twenty thousand dollars."[7]

Later, Issa sold Steal Stopper, moved to California, and started Directed Electronics, Inc. His new company produced aftermarket car security products, including the Viper car alarm, where Issa's own voice can be heard commanding, "Please step away from the car."

You don't get to be worth hundreds of millions of dollars without accruing real estate and other investments. But Issa's fortune was made in the car security business. He then used that accumulated fortune to kickstart his political career in 2000. When reporters started asking questions about his past brushes with the law, Issa responded by throwing brother Bill under the Maserati. "When people ask me why I got into the car alarm business, I tell them the truth," he said in a statement to the *San Francisco Chronicle.* "It was because my brother was a car thief."[8]

That's right. In a story reminiscent of Frank Abagnale (portrayed by Leonardo DiCaprio in *Catch Me If You Can*), Darrell Issa, one of the richest members of Congress, a man who formerly served as the chairman of the House Committee on Oversight and Government Reform and is worth approximately $250 million, was accused of stealing cars with his brother (all formal charges against him were dropped)—before making hundreds of millions *protecting* cars from thieves. For whatever reason, the charges against him kept being dropped.

What does it mean when you can go from such a checkered past to being a member of Congress? One view is that politics is a lateral move— that it's another type of con and another type of mark. Another view is that Issa achieved the American dream, which often entails redemption and reinvention. Maybe it's a combination of both.

Many of us have a deep-seated need to rise above humble beginnings and become successful. Could it be the case that this same instinct drives some people to illicit activities and other people to public service (where they can also acquire money and power)?

Issa isn't the only successful businessperson who wanted to trade in a corner office for the campaign plane. Following is a brief description of a few of the richest politicians in America, and how they got that way.

Greg "The Hammer" Gianforte

Governor Greg Gianforte (R-MT), with an estimated net worth of $189,334,335, according to OpenSecrets,[9] a nonprofit that tracks money in politics, had a more traditional rise than Issa—before he, too, turned to politics. The son of an aerospace engineer and landlord, Gianforte earned degrees in electrical engineering and computer science. Along with his wife, Susan (also an engineer), Gianforte founded RightNow Technologies, a company that helped pioneer cloud computing in the 1990s. In 2012, Oracle purchased RightNow for $1.8 billion.

Gianforte threw his hat into the political ring in 2016. He lost his gubernatorial bid but rebounded with a win in a 2017 special election for the House. During that campaign, he became infamous for allegedly body slamming reporter Ben Jacobs at his Bozeman, Montana, office. (Perhaps the political ring isn't the only ring he is familiar with?) Gianforte pleaded guilty to a charge of misdemeanor assault and paid a $300 fine, and he went on to win the election. With an estimated net worth of $189,334,335, he was the richest member of the House of Representatives in 2018.[10]

Then he ran for governor. In 2020 alone, Gianforte used more than $4 million of his own money to win Montana's governorship, as the AP reported.[11] That's just shy of $4 for every man, woman, and child in Montana—that's spending big bucks in the Big Sky State. This is a man who has it all.

The Telecom Tycoon

The first in his family to graduate college,[12] Mark Warner (D-VA), whose estimated net worth is $93,534,098,[13] made "his first big money by exploiting a multibillion-dollar government giveaway in the cell-phone industry."[14] In the 1980s, the FCC started awarding licenses to operate cellular franchises by lottery, a seemingly random way for the government to dole out incredibly lucrative licenses—especially because they could be awarded to people who had no interest in the business but who just wanted to turn around and sell the licenses for "in some cases over $300 for each person living in a service area."[15]

Acting on a tip from a political donor Warner met while working at the Democratic National Committee, Warner began representing a group of sellers. He then acted as a broker—in return for a piece of the action. He parlayed this into joining a venture-capital partnership that focused on the wireless industry. When a cell phone rings during one of his speeches, Warner sometimes jokes, "Most people consider them an annoyance, but I just hear 'cha-ching, cha-ching.' "[16]

The "McCongressman"

Nowadays, many so-called self-made people earn their fortune in the tech world. But there's still room for people willing to put in some elbow grease and hustle. One of my favorite examples got to Congress by flipping burgers. Sort of.

Dubbed the "McCongressman," as *Bloomberg* noted,[17] Representative Kevin Hern's (R-OK) wealth (the vast bulk of it) comes from owning a chain of McDonald's restaurants. Hern is so wealthy that he is richer than the rest of the Oklahoma congressional delegation combined, the *Oklahoman* reported.[18] Hern's rags-to-riches story began in Arkansas, where his family lived on food stamps for more than a decade.[19] He had no running water until he was in the eighth grade.[20] He also was born with spina bifida (the same condition that killed his older sister).[21] After high school, he earned a degree in engineering. He moved to Atlanta, Georgia, after being hired to work at Rockwell International, an aerospace firm that had just won a major NASA contract. But the day after he was hired, the space shuttle Challenger exploded. The industry was forever changed, and he was out of a job within a year.[22]

Hern moved back to Arkansas, got a job at McDonald's, and saved $100,000—enough to buy his first McDonald's franchise in Little Rock. Hern's wealth and restaurant connections were vital to his 2018 election. According to Oklahoma's *Frontier* news outlet, a review of donations made to Hern's campaign in 2018 "show more than half ($705,000) of Hern's $1.3 million total were loans made by Hern himself or donations by his family members. Of the remaining $656,000 in donations, $129,025 came from fellow restaurant owners, many of whom are McDonald's franchisees who do not operate in Oklahoma."[23]

Hern gained notoriety in January of 2023, when Representative Lauren Boebert (R-CO) nominated him to be Speaker of the House during the eighth, ninth, and tenth rounds of balloting.[24] Hern "went from rags to riches and, like myself [sic] and many other members, is a small-business owner," Boebert said in her nomination speech.[25] "He has lived the American dream." Hern, who cast his votes for Kevin McCarthy, garnered three votes in the ninth ballot. So far, his American dream doesn't include being Speaker.

The Winemonger

In 2016, Representative David Trone (D-MD), the son of a farmer, lost a congressional race after pumping in more than $12 million of his own money.[26] Two years later, Trone, a wine retailer who co-owns a chain of Total Wine & More stores, finally prevailed. Most recently, Trone was narrowly reelected in 2022, once again spending more than $12 million of his own money to stay in office. As the *Washington Post* reported, "Trone's huge financial advantage largely deterred any major investment from national Republicans, leaving [Maryland delegate Neil C.] Parrott to try to pull off an upset with minimal resources. Parrott had raised roughly $800,000..."[27]

Trone is a Democrat—but before running for Congress, he gave more than $150,000 to Republicans. Still, give him credit for being honest about it. "I sign my checks to buy access," he told the *Washington Post*.[28]

I grew up in Maryland's sixth district, which Trone now represents, but Democratic gerrymandering has pushed my hometown into the newer eighth district. In any event, Trone stands in stark contrast to the congressman who represented the sixth district for much of my life, Republican representative Roscoe Bartlett, who—according to a 2014 *Politico* profile—"lives in a remote cabin in the woods, prepping for doomsday."[29] He and I both ended up living in West Virginia, though he is probably better prepared for a zombie apocalypse. Still, I'd move back to Maryland for Trone's wine fortune.

The Nepo (Grand)baby

While hard work, smarts, luck, and connections still pay off, it's also fair to say that many of the richest politicians in America come from wealthy families. One such example is Representative Sara Jacobs (D-CA), who is just thirty-three years old as I write this. Jacobs is the granddaughter of Irwin Jacobs, the tech billionaire founder and former chairman of Qualcomm.

In 2018, Jacobs joined a crowded field vying to replace Darrell Issa in California's forty-ninth district. Considering Jacobs was still in her late twenties, it's no surprise that her résumé was sparse. But according to the *San Diego Union-Tribune,* Jacobs "exaggerated her work experience" by saying "she was a 'policy maker' who worked for the State Department under President Barack Obama." In reality, Jacobs "was a junior employee working for a government contractor and federal regulations prohibited her from making policies."[30] She lost that primary election, finishing third.[31]

But you can't keep the rich down for long. In 2020, Jacobs switched to California's fifty-third district in central San Diego County, where she faced off against forty-four-year-old San Diego City Council president Georgette Gómez, a fellow Democrat. The contrast was stark. Whereas Jacobs was a young woman of privilege, the *American Prospect* described Gómez as "a queer woman of color with decades of community-organizing experience."[32] Likewise, the *Times of San Diego* described

Gómez's campaign image as that of an "up-from-the-barrio fighter for social justice who found ways to move San Diego's needle even with council Republicans' support."[33] As Gómez said, "My grocery store was a liquor store, and my playground was surrounded by freeways."

Guess who won?[34]

In addition to the money Jacobs put into her own campaign, her grandparents also spent $1.5 million on a super PAC to boost her 2020 election, as *Vox* reported.[35] If you want to make it to Congress in your early thirties, it helps to have rich parents (and grandparents).

$ $ $

The pols mentioned above are just a sampling of some of America's richest politicians. We will meet more of them in future chapters. Regardless, whether they came from hardscrabble backgrounds or were born with a silver spoon in their mouth, any of them could have spent the rest of their lives on a beach drinking piña coladas. And yet, they all decided to run for political office.

The question is, *why do rich people want to go into politics?*

Some on the left allege that rich people are attracted to politics because they want to rig the system to get even richer. I may be naïve, but this theory doesn't hold Perrier. To the degree uber-rich businesspeople need to tweak the tax code or kill regulations, it seems like campaign contributions and high-powered lobbying would be more efficient. It's easier, cheaper, and less déclassé to *buy* politicians than it is to become one. Don't underestimate the importance of outsourcing in any American business model.

People who make these cynical accusations also discount the possibility that some rich people believe they are doing a public service and "giving back," as it were. Depending on your political biases, you could nominate either Herbert Hoover or Franklin Roosevelt for that "honor." One might say the same for Henry Cabot Lodge or Jack Kennedy. Consider how many rich celebrities love big, flashy examples of philanthropy, like big foundations named after themselves with elegantly furnished offices or star-studded fund-raising events for pet issues. That's not all done for tax write-offs; the rich often have a desire to give back, coupled with a desire to be in the news for something that isn't as profit-driven as whatever helped them get wealthy in the first place. It's not a big jump to get from writing grant checks for medical research to writing (or trying to write) policy that funds medical research. And politics includes public validation, too. After all, you have to get elected, right?

Along those lines, my old college professor Dr. David A. Foltz offers a deep-seated, if esoteric, psychological reason based on the Protestant work ethic embedded before America's founding. "Success is evidence of salvation, which is predestined for the elect," he says. How does this "Covenant of Works" explain the desire of rich people to run for office? Having attained financial prosperity, getting elected is further proof you are one of the elect.

Another theory: successful businesspeople become convinced that they can fix public policy because they know how to make money. Translation: they have healthy egos. In my former life as a political operative, I encountered many candidates who had been wildly successful in past careers. They all thought that they could easily apply those lessons to a political campaign. Most couldn't. I suspect that they similarly underestimate the difficulty involved in governing and legislating.

When General Dwight Eisenhower was considering running for president, the then president Harry S. Truman opined, "He'll sit here, and he'll say, 'Do this! Do that!' *And nothing will happen.* Poor Ike—it won't be a bit like the Army. He'll find it very frustrating," according to author Richard E. Neustadt.[36] As it happens, poor Ike turned out to be a pretty good president. Harry shouldn't have given him so much hell. But Truman was right—in the main. Politics is different from other businesses, including the military. Many people discover that lesson the hard way.

Others are looking for a hobby. As one Twitter follower told me, rich people go into politics "for the same reasons they buy sports franchises or rocket rides."[37] It also seems observably true that politics and entertainment have merged and that getting elected is a way to achieve some modicum of fame for people who can't sing, dance, or make a three-point shot.

Ultimately, it may be Bruce Springsteen who explained this theory best: "Poor man wanna be rich / Rich man wanna be king / And a king ain't satisfied / 'Til he rules everything."[38] Whether or not The Boss got it right, rich people *do* constitute a disproportionate share of the candidates vying for public office, especially when compared with working stiffs.

According to Duke University's Nicholas Carnes, working-class jobs (i.e., manual labor, service industry, and clerical jobs) "still make up a little more than half of our economy. But workers make up less than 3 percent of the average state legislature."[39] It's even more stark at the federal level. And while many privileged people can talk about *that summer I spent painting houses*, Carnes says, "The average member of Congress spent less than 2 percent of his or her entire pre-congressional career doing the kinds of jobs most Americans go to every day."[40]

"We need more and more normal people to run for Congress. We need more people that work in the trades," Representative Marie Gluesenkamp Perez (D-WA), an auto shop owner who won a house seat in 2022, told *Politico* in 2023.[41] "Frankly, I think there's a lot of lip service to wanting people in the trades, rural Democrats. They say it because it sounds good, but I'm not sure that there is an actual commitment to it." Gluesenkamp also gets a kick out of how some rich people pose as tradespeople in Congress. "I'm like, 'Oh, your bio says you're a small-business owner. What's your business?' They're like 'Oh, we have a family real estate brokerage firm.' Oh, okay. Sure. Yeah, technically, you have less than five hundred employees. So you are a small business."[42]

The lack of working-class Americans serving in Congress matters because everyone has a worldview, and that worldview is informed by our experience. Someone who is from a privileged background (or someone who has pulled themselves up by their bootstraps, thereby assuming that elbow grease is all it takes) may naturally support different policies than someone who is working a regular nine-to-five job. If you have figured out how to go from pauper to prince, you probably assume that if other people made decisions like you do, their lives would turn out better, too. It's not a stretch to believe that you should be making decisions on behalf of everyone else. This is a dangerous place for a representative democracy to find itself.

Of course, it's a cliché to assume that rich politicians are more likely to advance policies that help the rich. Sometimes, it goes the other way. "I'm less interested in how much money a politician has than whether they believe they earned it," Grover Norquist, the anti-tax crusader and president of Americans for Tax Reform, told me.[43] Norquist's theory is that people who work hard to earn their wealth tend to be more conservative, while people who believe they either got lucky or believe they somehow beat a corrupt system are more likely to favor progressive policies like redistribution of wealth.

The more significant point is that rich people are more likely to seek political office, while most normal, non-rich people generally don't even *try* to run for office. If you're interested in understanding why rich people tend to get elected, you must first understand why wealthy people are more likely to run for higher office.

The primary reason may surprise you. "In democratic elections, people can only be considered for office if they take time off work and out of their personal lives to campaign," Carnes writes.[44] So it's not the money, per se. It's the time.

This is not hypothetical. Consider the case of Maxwell Frost (D-FL), who won his seat in 2022 and was promptly turned down for an apartment in Washington, DC. The reason? "After a year and a half of campaigning (and winning, which, having been born in 1997, made him Congress's first elected Generation Z lawmaker), Frost had gotten himself into debt. And, as a result, he had a low credit score," reported NPR.[45] Frost will be okay, partly because he's young, but mostly because he *won.*

But imagine being a middle-class working parent and sacrificing a year and a half of your life, only to lose.

Rich people have the luxury of taking big gambles (like running for office) with little cost if they lose. The thing about making big bets is that sometimes they pay off—and then you look brilliant and daring. Working-class people don't have the luxury of such risky bets or romantic gestures. The downside is just too great. Many regular Americans simply can't sacrifice the time away from work and family to run a campaign. Even if you put aside the lack of connections to wealthy people, the amount of time that non-rich candidates have to spend fund-raising would be cost-prohibitive for many people. In 2018, the average US Senate candidate had to raise almost $16 million to win, and the average House candidate had to raise more than $2 million.[46]

It's also true that the party insiders seeking out and recruiting candidates are often looking for someone who can self-fund or at least write a big check for their own campaign. Despite self-funders having a checkered win-loss record (as they say, money can't buy me love), nominating a self-funder frees up more money to go to a party's other political candidates. These obstacles can be overcome, but make no mistake, they are obstacles.

Even a small financial cushion can make a huge difference, especially for a young aspiring pol who doesn't have a mortgage or a family to support. Sometimes all it takes is a little luck. Consider the case of Kevin McCarthy (R-CA), who was elected Speaker of the House in January of 2023. The son of an assistant fire chief and a homemaker,[47] McCarthy was a middle-class kid from Bakersfield, California, when he bought a lottery ticket that earned him $5,000. "I put the money in the stock market, made a little out of that," McCarthy told KQED in 2011. "And then, at the end of the semester, I took my money out of the market. I refinanced my car, and I went and opened a deli."[48] Opening the deli, McCarthy explains, also opened his mind to conservative concerns about taxes and regulations, which ultimately led him to his career in politics.[49]

But the interesting question is this: Where would Kevin McCarthy be if he had never bought that winning lottery ticket?

$$\$\,\$\,\$$

Now, in a populist era such as ours, you might think that being filthy rich would be a detriment—especially in a small-*d* democratic business where support from the masses is vital. And you'd be…*wrong.* Consider the case of Representative George Santos (R-NY), the serial fabulist and son of Brazilian immigrants who was elected to Congress in 2022. Soon after his election, Santos admitted to embellishing key parts of his résumé.[50] Some of his false or questionable claims bestowed on him minority or victim status. For example, Santos said he was Jewish, but later said he meant that he was "Jew-ish."[51] He claimed that his mother was working at the World Trade Center on 9/11 (in at least one of his accounts, she died there).[52] Likewise, Santos told voters he was "openly gay," while never disclosing that he had been married to a woman until just two weeks prior to launching his 2020 congressional bid.[53]

But while Santos played up identity politics, he simultaneously eschewed minority status when it came to credentials having to do with class, wealth (according to disclosure forms, his net worth increased dramatically between 2020 and 2022),[54] and refinement. In these areas, he sought to inflate his educational background, work history (he falsely said he worked for Goldman Sachs and Citigroup),[55] and social station.* According to Vanessa Friedman, the fashion director and chief fashion

---

*As I write this, the nonpartisan Campaign Legal Center has filed a complaint with the Federal Election Commission, looking into potential illegal activities having to do with Santos's sudden (and not just pretend) accumulation of wealth, as it pertains to his campaign spending. According to the *Washington Post*, Santos "reported loaning his campaign more than $700,000 in the 2021–22 cycle despite having only $55,000 in earned income during his previous run for Congress in 2020, according to a financial disclosure. Campaign Legal Center called his claims of earning millions over the previous two years from the Devolder Organization [Santos's company] 'vague, uncorroborated, and non-credible in light of his many previous lies.'" https://www.washingtonpost.com /politics/2023/01/09/george-santos-campaign-finance-complaint/.

critic for the *New York Times*, this worked partly because Santos used fashion to reinforce this con. "He went to Horace Mann, Baruch and N.Y.U. and came from money? Behold, the uniform of preppy private-school boys everywhere: the button-up white shirt, crew-neck sweater (most often in the old-school colors of periwinkle and gray), blue blazer and khaki trousers, like something straight out of 'Dead Poets Society,'" she explained.[56]

The larger question is, why did Santos run for office as an underdog member of historically marginalized groups when it came to issues of race, religion, and sexual orientation, yet simultaneously cast himself as an elite blue blood?

The things we pretend to be can tell us a lot about ourselves, and (more to the point) our *culture*. Santos posed as the kind of person who could win a congressional election in New York in 2022—and he did. As my friend Jeff Mayhugh put it in *Newsweek*, "In today's Republican Party, you can be openly gay and Hispanic. What you can't be is poor."[57]

It is rarely the case that a congressional candidate loses an election solely because he's too rich or too well connected (the opposite is more frequently true). To be sure, the growing financial divide between politicians and civilians contributes to the erosion of trust in our institutions—that is one of the central themes of this book. But while this is an important and growing problem, it's rarely top of mind in congressional elections, where the voters are understandably more focused on themselves. As a result, engaging in class warfare or otherwise trying to make hay out of an opponents' wealth is often the last refuge of a loser.

Consider a few examples from the 2022 electoral cycle.

Just before the 2022 primary victory by Daniel Goldman (an heir to the Levi Strauss fortune) in New York, one of his opponents, then representative Mondaire Jones, accused Goldman of "using his inherited wealth to distort the Democratic process."[58] As is often the case, voters were not persuaded by this sort of appeal (at least not enough to overcome the benefits of Goldman's financial advantage).

The line of attack is probably even less likely to work on incumbents running for reelection. For example, in 2022, Senator John Hoeven (R-ND) was criticized for having doubled his net worth from $22 million to over $46 million since entering the US Senate in 2011. One of his opponents sounded envious of Hoeven's haul, declaring, "He's done very well for himself. Let's let someone else in."[59] Hoeven won easily.

Around the same time, a progressive group called Opportunity Wisconsin attacked Senator Ron Johnson (R-WI)—whose assets are listed between $16.55 million and $78.3 million[60]—for having "pushed through a special tax loophole that benefited his own family's business," adding that he has "doubled his wealth since taking office."[61] The situation was more complicated than they let on. As *PolitiFact* noted, "The [tax break] change benefitted [Johnson's] business—but also applied to tens of millions of other businesses. And it was hardly a loophole, if it was widely discussed publicly. [Johnson] did sell his company for at least $5 million, but the doubling of wealth deserves more context: In that period, the S&P Index nearly quadrupled."[62] Regardless, the ploy didn't work.

Likewise, in 2022, Representative Don Beyer (D-VA) faced a progressive primary challenger named Victoria Virasingh, who sought to draw a contrast with the mega-rich Northern Virginia car dealer–turned–congressman (Beyer is one of *three* car dealers to make the "Richest Twenty-Five Members of Congress" list in this book's appendix). Beyer's opponent argued that she was closer to the "lived realities of most Americans" and said, "This is a race about passing the torch."[63] The torch, as you might imagine, was not passed.

$ $ $

As this chapter illustrates, rich people are more likely to run for political office than their working-class counterparts, primarily because they have the time away from work to devote to campaigning, but also because running and losing will not lead to a debilitating financial loss. For obvious reasons, including the fact that their personal networks allow them to raise lots of campaign dollars, they also have a leg up when it comes to winning elections.

While wealthy people usually run for office with the best of intentions, their privileged backgrounds can't help but inform their political worldviews. When a majority of a nation's politicians are disproportionately rich (again, today more than half of the members of Congress are millionaires), you can reach a tipping point where the people making the laws have dramatically different perspectives than the people they represent.

This is a problem. The big problem, though, isn't that rich people are more inclined to run and win public office. The big problem—the one that really undermines trust in representative democracy—is that people who manage to get elected (regardless of their wealth)—almost always get richer.

Chapter 4

Why the Elected Get Rich

Knowledge is power.

—Sir Francis Bacon[1]

Because they write the laws, politicians make it impossible to know precisely how rich they are.[2] But according to OpenSecrets, Nancy Pelosi's net worth in 2020 was "nearly $115 million."[3] After Democrats lost the House in 2022, Pelosi stepped down from leadership. But during her years leading her party in the House, her salary fluctuated depending on whether she was the Speaker or the minority leader (which was contingent on whether Democrats controlled the House). Between 2007 and 2022, Pelosi's salary ranged from $193,400 to $223,500. This means that if Pelosi saved her entire salary, she would have to work more than five hundred years to earn her current net worth.

Pelosi was already a multimillionaire when she won the speakership in 2006. Since then, her net worth has more than tripled,[4] largely thanks to some surprisingly fortunate investments. Pelosi's luck at picking stocks (or should I say her husband Paul Pelosi's luck) is so amazing that, as NPR's Tim Mak reported, "Among a certain community of individual investors on TikTok, House Speaker Nancy Pelosi's stock trading disclosures are a treasure trove."[5] Mak continues, "On one social investing platform, you can get a push notification every time Pelosi's stock trading disclosures are released." Moreover, Chris Josephs, cofounder of an investing app called Iris, told NPR that he was betting with the Pelosis, too. In 2021, the socialist outlet *Jacobin* noted that Pelosi and her husband "traded over $50 million in assets, with annualized returns at 69 percent as of October," concluding: "That's higher than Buffett, George Soros, Cathie Wood, and other star investors of the past."[6]

But don't start trying to fit the Pelosis' birthdays into your next Powerball ticket just yet. As you might have guessed, their stock market success is not totally blind luck; the Pelosis have had opportunities the average investor has not enjoyed.

Before TikTok noticed Pelosi's penchant for picking stocks, the media noticed the Pelosis' Midas touch. In 2011, CBS's *60 Minutes* reported that "Nancy Pelosi and her husband have participated in at least eight [initial public offerings]. One of those came in 2008, from Visa, just as a troublesome piece of legislation that would have hurt credit card companies began making its way through the House. Undisturbed by a potential conflict of interest, the Pelosis purchased 5,000 shares of 'the world's largest electronic payment network'[7] at the initial price of $44. Two days later it was trading at $64. The credit card legislation never made it to the floor of the House."[8]

Just being allowed to participate in Visa's initial public offering (IPO) was a coup. What is more, as my friend Adam Dresher, who spent twenty years on Wall Street as an institutional stockbroker covering some of the biggest and best-performing hedge funds and mutual funds, told me, "I have never seen an individual get this many shares of an IPO."

In general, only large investment corporations like BlackRock, Fidelity, or State Street are able to swing such a huge allocation. Then second-tier mutual funds get their turn. Next come hedge funds. And last, IPO shares *might* go to an individual, but this would normally be someone with *way* more money than even the Pelosis have. We're talking about someone who is a huge commission generator. We're talking about someone like Bill Gates.

That was a dozen years ago, but not much has changed in the intervening years. The Pelosis kept investing and kept getting lucky. For example, on December 22, 2020, Paul Pelosi invested between $500,000 and $1 million in twenty-five call options of Tesla stocks.

But what are call options, anyway? According to Investopedia.com, an option "gives an investor the right, but not the obligation, to buy or sell a stock at an agreed-upon price and date."[9] To the untrained ear, this sounds like a safe and noncommittal way to invest. After all, you have the "option" to buy or not buy. The catch, though, is that this option is purchased in the form of a premium. In the case of Pelosi's Tesla option, the premium was somewhere between $500,000 and a cool $1 million.

To make money, the Pelosis had to weigh multiple variables. First, they had to predict that the stock would go up and not down. Second, they had to predict how high the stock would go. (It's not enough for the stock to go up; the Pelosis would have lost everything if it did not reach the "strike price.") Finally, they had to predict the timing. The stock had to reach the strike price by the expiration date, or (again) they would have lost their entire premium. Of course, it's sometimes possible to sell out in advance of expiration. But even if they were only playing for a leveraged price gain before expiration, the odds of consistently getting that right are quite low.

Then, the December 22 bet by the Pelosis got a shot in the arm. On January 27, 2021, Joe Biden signed an executive order "directing federal officials to transition federal, state, local, and tribal government fleets to 'clean and zero-emission vehicles.'"[10] (If you're keeping score at home, these green-friendly environmental regulations were very good news for anyone betting on Tesla.)

My point is that, absent any knowledge about governmental regulations, this bet was far from safe, especially when you consider Tesla's high price and volatility. It's the kind of bet you would feel more comfortable making if you had some inside information. But the Pelosis bet correctly.

And they would keep betting correctly. On March 17, 2022, Paul Pelosi purchased 2,500 shares of Tesla at a strike price of $500 per share.[11] By March 23, it was trading at nearly $1,000 a share. I'm not great at math, but I think that's a good return on investment.

Of course, Tesla is far from being the only ambitious gamble made by Paul Pelosi. "The week before the House Judiciary Committee voted on reining in big tech, Speaker Nancy Pelosi's husband exercised a bullish bet on Google-parent Alphabet, in a timely transaction that netted him $5.3 million," according to *Fortune*.[12]

Again, optics are important. If you care about preserving the American system and worry about allegations that the game is rigged, then Pelosi's fortune (fairly obtained or not) looks suspicious. According to Pulitzer Prize–winning journalist Glenn Greenwald, "Close to 75% of the Pelosis' stock trading over the last two years [2020 and 2021] has been in Big Tech: more than $33 million worth of trading. That has happened as major legislation is pending before the House, controlled by the committees Pelosi oversees, which could radically reshape the industry and laws that govern the very companies in which she and her husband most aggressively trade."[13]

If you are like me, you barely noticed this trend. It was hidden under an avalanche of news about the election, the January 6 insurrection, the disastrous Afghanistan withdrawal, and COVID-19. But even if Pelosi isn't profiting from the power and information she is receiving, there's still this: she's profiting from things she says are bad. According to *Business Insider*, the same day Pelosi called Facebook "shameful" and "irresponsible,"[14] her husband was purchasing shares of Facebook, at a below-market rate, that he would later sell for a hefty profit.

Pelosi and her team claim that "The Speaker does not own any stocks."[15] But her husband does, making this a distinction without much of a difference.

And the number of examples is too sizable to dismiss as coincidence.

For example, on March 19, 2021, Paul Pelosi exercised options to purchase $10 million in Microsoft shares—and on March 31, the US Army announced that Microsoft had won a contract to build augmented reality headsets. "The contract for over 120,000 headsets could be worth up to $21.88 billion over 10 years," a Microsoft spokesperson told CNBC.[16] You probably won't be surprised to learn that the stock price increased immediately after the announcement.

In December 2021, in response to Representative Alexandria Ocasio-Cortez's tweet saying, "It is absolutely ludicrous that members of Congress can hold and trade individual stock while in office," Pelosi was forced to confront her opposition to this reform. In an instant, this San Francisco liberal transformed into Milton Friedman, insisting that "We are a free-market economy."[17] Eventually, Pelosi was forced to backtrack, reluctantly supporting legislation banning stock trades by members of Congress and their immediate families.

But the trades kept coming. On June 17, 2022, Paul exercised call options valued at between $1 million and $5 million in a semiconductor company called Nvidia.[18] In late July of that same year, the Senate passed a bipartisan bill that included a $52 billion subsidy for domestic chipmakers. Pelosi insisted that Paul had "absolutely not" made any trades based on inside information from her and—perhaps sensing the backlash—dumped the stock before the vote, at a loss of more than $300,000.[19]

Regardless, the Pelosis keep making trades and raking in the dough. Unfortunately, their actions are fairly common. Many members of Congress engage in such activities, and it's been going on forever.

$ $ $

According to a 2022 analysis conducted by the *New York Times* of transactions between 2019 and 2021, "At least 97…members of Congress bought or sold stock, bonds or other financial assets that intersected with their congressional work or reported similar transactions by their spouse or a dependent child."[20] That's close to 20 percent of the 535 members of the House and Senate. What is more, in many cases, members had multiple potential conflicts of interest. Representative Ro Khanna (D-CA), for example, had 149 potential conflicts.[21]

To make matters worse, the best time to turn a profit seems to be during a national crisis or when drastic changes are occurring in the US economy. For example, according to the *Washington Free Beacon*, Pelosi's "estimated net worth skyrocketed at the onset of the Great Recession, going from $31.4 million in 2008 to $101.1 million in 2010, a 220 percent increase in a window where the S&P 500 decreased by 13 percent. The Speaker also reaped a significant return during the COVID-19 pandemic, seeing her estimated net worth jump from $106 million in 2019 to $171.4 million in 2021, an increase of 60 percent."[22]

Again though, when it comes to capitalizing on a crisis, Pelosi is far from alone.

Here are a few examples:

The 2008 Financial Meltdown

On September 16, 2008, George W. Bush's treasury secretary Hank Paulson and Federal Reserve chairman Ben Bernanke held a secret meeting with members of Congress to brief them on the financial crisis. According to *Business Insider*'s reporting, the result was that "Congressmen privy to this information reacted—not by dropping everything and drawing up a plan to save the economy, but by dumping stock and avoiding the losses everyone else would take in the coming month. Others bought stocks in financial firms that would later be saved by the federal government."[23]

According to Peter Schweizer's book *Throw Them All Out*, the then representative Shelley Capito (R-WV) and her husband "dumped between $100,000 and $250,000 in Citigroup stock the day after the briefing," and "at least ten U.S. senators, including John Kerry, Sheldon Whitehouse, and Dick Durbin, traded stock or mutual funds related to the financial industry the following day."[24]

The Obamacare Battle

Schweizer's book inspired the *60 Minutes* segment we discussed earlier in this chapter, regarding Nancy Pelosi's curious stock trades. That's when many Americans learned that congressional insider trading was not only legal but common. "During the health care debate of 2009, members of Congress were trading health care stocks, including House Minority Leader John Boehner," Steve Kroft said on the show.[25] "Just days before the [public option] provision was finally killed off, Boehner bought health care stocks—all of which went up." (Boehner's spokesperson later told *60 Minutes* that the trades were made by Boehner's financial advisor "who he only consults with about once a year.")[26] The then senator John Kerry also profited millions off of what looked like insider information during the crafting of Obamacare. Kerry's office told *Business Insider* that his investments are "managed by independent trustees."[27] Regardless, to the average American, it looks utterly corrupt for the guy helping craft a bill to profit from its passage.

This *60 Minutes* report led to Congress passing the Stop Trading on Congressional Knowledge (STOCK) Act on April 4, 2012. The law prohibits any members or employees of Congress from using "any nonpublic information derived from the individual's position … or gained from performance of the individual's duties, for personal benefit." At least, that's what it is supposed to do. "The powerful shouldn't get to create one set of rules for themselves and another set of rules for everybody else," President Barack Obama said when he signed it. "If we expect that to apply to our biggest corporations and to our most successful citizens, it certainly applies to our elected officials, especially at a time when there is a deficit of trust between this city and the rest of the country."[28]

The COVID-19 Pandemic

The first test of the STOCK Act's efficacy came during the next crisis: the COVID-19 pandemic. As COVID cases increased, members of Congress who received briefings in early 2020 behaved similarly to those who received briefings during 2008's economic meltdown.

Senator Richard Burr (R-NC), one of just three senators to vote against the STOCK Act, was also one of four members of Congress—along with Senators Dianne Feinstein (D-CA), Kelly Loeffler (R-GA), and Jim Inhofe (R-OK)—who made suspicious stock trades. This occurred after they were briefed on COVID-19 and after Burr co-authored a February 7 op-ed declaring that "the United States today is better prepared than ever before to face emerging public health threats, like the coronavirus,"[29] but before the general public realized how bad the pandemic would be. (Note: Loeffler—who is married to the chairman of the New York Stock Exchange, Jeffrey Sprecher, with a combined estimated fortune of around $800 million[30]—lost her reelection in 2020. Burr and Inhofe retired at the end of 2022, and, at the time of this writing, Feinstein has announced she will not seek reelection in 2024.[31])

As chairman of the Intelligence Committee, Burr was privy to classified intel reports in January and February 2020 that contained "ominous" warnings about coronavirus, the *Washington Post* reported.[32] On February 13, 2020, he "unloaded stock shares worth $630,000 to $1.7 million, with 33 individual trades made on that single day. The shares he sold represented a significant portion of his financial portfolio," according to CNBC.[33] Coincidentally, Burr's brother-in-law, Gerald Fauth, sold off between $97,000 and $280,000 worth of stock on the very same day.[34] To make matters worse, according to FBI evidence that wasn't released until September 2022, "Burr's wife called her brother shortly after 11 a.m. ET on the 13th, and they spoke for two minutes. Twenty minutes after that, Burr also used his cellphone to call Fauth, according to records obtained by the Justice Department."[35]

A week later, the stock market plummeted. According to the *Wall Street Journal*, Burr's move saved him and his wife from "at least $250,000 in losses."[36]

On February 27, 2020, Burr spoke at a luncheon in Washington, DC, at the Capitol Hill Club. NPR described it as "a small group of well-connected constituents" whose attendees represented companies or political committees that had donated more than $100,000 to Burr's campaigns in the previous two election cycles.[37] On the same day that Donald Trump was telling the public that "It's going to disappear. One day, it's like a miracle. It will disappear," Burr's appraisal was more honest and alarming: "There's one thing that I can tell you about this," he said. "It is much more aggressive in its transmission than anything that we have seen in recent history."[38]

More than two weeks before the US banned most European travelers from entering the country, Burr told his audience that "Every company should be cognizant of the fact that you may have to alter your travel. You may have to look at your employees and judge whether the trip they're making to Europe is essential or whether it can be done on video conference. Why risk it?"[39]

Populists on the right and left were outraged. "Now maybe there's an honest explanation for what he did. If there is, then he should share it with the rest of us immediately," Tucker Carlson said on his Fox News show. "Otherwise, he must resign from the Senate and face prosecution for insider trading."[40] Likewise, Representative Alexandria Ocasio-Cortez tweeted: "Burr knew how bad it would be. He told the truth to his wealthy donors, while assuring the public that we were fine. THEN he sold off $1.6 million in stock before the fall. He needs to resign."[41]

The FBI seized Burr's phone, and he stepped down from his committee chairmanship. However, the Trump Justice Department ultimately decided not to charge him. In fact, none of the senators who made suspicious COVID-19 trades were punished. We shouldn't be surprised. Barring a smoking gun confession, it's nearly impossible to *prove* that someone acted solely on insider information. On the other hand, that certainly hasn't stopped the highly questionable prosecution of those who are not members of Congress on Wall Street, where such "proof" was also nonexistent; yet aggressive multiyear jail sentences were handed down, even in instances where the person prosecuted wasn't accused of personally benefiting.

The only member of Congress who has recently gotten in trouble for insider trading *while in office*[42] is ex-congressman Chris Collins (R-NY), who was sentenced in 2020 to twenty-six months in prison for insider trading and lying to the FBI.[43] After serving ten weeks in prison, he was pardoned by President Donald Trump.[44] But the confidential info Collins passed on (to his son) came from serving on the board of a biotech company—not from serving in Congress.[45] This kind of insider trading is easier to prove than congressional insider trading.

If I told you that some pending disaster was serious—more serious than anyone fully appreciated—you could probably find independent news reports to corroborate that warning (Burr said he was "relying on news reports coming out of Asia, where the virus first emerged, to make his investment decisions," according to the *Wall Street Journal*).[46] You could then cite this publicly available information as the impetus for your trade. In this case, news reports of COVID-19 existed as early as 2019 (hence the name), even though it took many months before the average American realized the severity of the disease or its ramifications.

The real benefit to inside information isn't that it helps you make money (which it often does), but that it prevents you from suffering massive losses. In 2021, a New Jersey high school student named George McCain spent his summer break building a website to track congressional stock trades. His research found that during 2020, the Senate's average stock return underperformed the S&P 500. But here's the thing: "when the general market plummeted 30% in late March as the COVID-19 pandemic took hold, the Senate's collective stock average dipped only 15%."[47]

According to *ProPublica*, on February 13, 2020, Burr "sold off a significant percentage of his stocks."[48] What kinds of investments might not perform well during a pandemic? Among other stocks he unloaded, Burr "dumped up to $150,000 worth of shares of Wyndham Hotels and Resorts, a chain based in the United States that lost two-thirds of its value. And he sold up to $100,000 of shares of Extended Stay America, an economy hospitality chain."[49] Instead, he bought treasury securities. According to the FBI, "As a result of Senator Burr's sales on February 13, 2020, his portfolio went from approximately 83% in equities [stocks and shares in a company] to approximately 3% in equities."[50]

Sadly, elected officials weren't the only ones to take advantage of this crisis. Prominent health officials also seem to have cashed in. According to the *Wall Street Journal*, in January 2020 (before the public was aware of the severity of COVID-19), "A deputy to top health official Anthony Fauci reported 10 sales of mutual funds and stocks totaling between $157,000 and $480,000 that month. Collectively, officials at another health agency, Health and Human Services, reported 60% more sales of stocks and funds in January than the average over the previous 12 months, driven by a handful of particularly active traders."[51]

Russia's 2022 Invasion of Ukraine

During the aforementioned Great Recession, the then Obama White House chief of staff Rahm Emanuel was criticized for saying "Never allow a good crisis to go to waste."[52] To conservative ears, it sounded like Emanuel was saying that progressives could use an emergency as a pretext for social engineering and income redistribution. But Emanuel's maxim, it turns out, has been used just as often by politicians hoping to score personal, not ideological, gains. Take, for example, Russia's 2022 invasion of Ukraine.

While Congress was debating "economic sanctions, military assistance, and billions of dollars in emergency spending, to deal with this crisis in Ukraine," reports CNBC's Ylan Q. Mui, "more than a dozen members reported trades—either their own or by their spouse or by their child—in sectors that were directly affected by the war in Ukraine."[53] CNBC estimated the total trading activity between February 1, 2022, and Mui's mid-March report to be about $7.7 million.

"It looks like Congress saw this as a gold rush," Fox News's Jesse Watters observed on his show *Jesse Watters Primetime*.[54] "They knew what sanctions could be coming down, and all they had [were] dollar signs in their eyes. Members from both sides of the political aisle poured money into the market...so as Ukraine burned to the ground, Congress got rich." Watters pointed out that Florida representative Debbie Wasserman Schultz, a Democrat, bought energy stocks in late January that "shot through the roof" after their purchase. Why was Schultz investing in planet-destroying carbon companies to begin with, much less at this specific time? "Maybe she knew something we didn't?" Watters concluded, "And unfortunately, she's not alone."

But this was a bipartisan cash grab. The day before Russian tanks crossed into Ukraine, Georgia GOP representative Marjorie Taylor Greene tweeted: "War and rumors of war is [*sic*] incredibly profitable and convenient."[55] She was right. Unfortunately, Greene later revealed that just two days before Russia's invasion, she bought stock from a major defense contractor, an oil company, and an energy company. In a statement to *Business Insider* before the invasion, Greene said that her "investment advisor...has full discretionary authority on my accounts. I do not direct any trades."[56] I guess we'll have to take her word on that. This behavior is all too common. When it comes to making money, members of Congress rarely let a major crisis go to waste.

And when it comes to making DC less swampy, the STOCK Act clearly hasn't made much of a difference. Congress severely weakened the quality of the disclosure regime in 2013, making it harder for watchdogs to monitor potential violations.[57] In 2017, the nonprofit group Public Citizen concluded that "the transaction values of stock trades, and the number of stock transactions, have significantly declined since passage of the STOCK Act," but that "many individual senators continue to be very active in the stock market and often trade stocks in businesses that they oversee in their official capacity."[58] And even if someone violates the law—and more than seventy members of Congress have[59]—the penalties are puny.

$$\$ \ \$ \ \$$

In the summer and fall of 2022, there were hints that Congress might actually pass a law banning members of Congress and their spouses from trading individual stocks. Momentum seemed to be building. But there was just one problem: although almost everybody across the political spectrum *said* they favored the law, it didn't benefit members of Congress who wanted to continue trading stocks.

Rather than embracing the existing bill introduced by Representative Abigail Spanberger (D-VA), House Speaker Nancy Pelosi tapped her close ally, Representative Zoe Lofgren (D-CA), to write a new bill. That decision wasn't well received. "The Pelosi bill would replace the government's strict blind trust requirements with a regime that would permit fake blind trusts," warned Walter Shaub, director of the Office of Government Ethics during the Obama administration. He went on to note that Pelosi's bill would allow "ethics offices for each branch of government to approve any kind of trust they want, ignoring established government-wide standards."[60]

"The Speaker has accomplished something I'd have thought impossible," Shaub continued. "She has produced a congressional stock trading ban I must oppose."[61]

Shaub wasn't the only person who opposed the ban. With just five weeks left until the 2022 midterm elections, the legislation was put on hold, a move the *New York Times* concluded may constitute a "potentially permanent setback"[62] to reform efforts. While wading through a tough reelection campaign, Spanberger complained about being "subjected to repeated delay tactics, hand-waving gestures, and blatant instances of Lucy pulling the football." Lest anyone question who Spanberger was blaming, she characterized the delay as "a failure of House leadership."

Did Nancy Pelosi and Democratic leadership conspire to introduce poison pill legislation and intentionally kill this attempt to ban individual stock trades? "There are a lot of people in the body who would rather not restrict their ability to continue to trade," said Representative Chip Roy (R-TX).[63] Roy and Spanberger reintroduced bipartisan legislation to ban congressional stock trading in January of 2023, after Republicans took control of the US House of Representatives.[64] Also in January of 2023, US senator Josh Hawley (R-MO) reintroduced his own bill aimed at this same goal, which he titled "The Preventing Elected Leaders from Owning Securities and Investments (PELOSI) Act." It's hard to imagine something derisively titled the PELOSI Act will garner much bipartisan support, but Hawley deserves credit for an epic troll.

Honest Graft

Insider trading is just one of the ways that politicians can feather their nests. Members of Congress have access to information and connections that even wealthy business leaders envy. Peter Schweizer calls it "honest graft." Legal but unethical. This term dates back to Tammany Hall, at least. Here's how *Politico*'s Jack Shafer explained it a few years ago: "To steal directly from the treasury is dishonest graft. But to get tipped off [regarding] where the city is going to build a bridge and then buy all the property at its approaches and then sell the land at a profit after the bridge is built, well that's just honest graft. 'It's just like lookin' ahead in Wall Street or in the coffee or cotton market,' [George Washington] Plunkitt said. 'It's honest graft, and I'm lookin' for it every day in the year.' "[65]

Some of the things that passed for "honest graft" a few years ago would look more like obvious corruption now. Consider the case of Al Gore's dad. "For part of his career, [former Tennessee senator] Albert Gore Sr., received two paychecks: one from the taxpayers and another from [Occidental Petroleum's Armand] Hammer," according to the Center for Public Integrity. "Hammer, who raised prize bulls, met the elder Gore at a Tennessee cattle auction in the 1940s. He put Gore, who was then a member of the House, on the payroll of his New Jersey cattle business."[66]

Basically, Hammer made Gore his partner in a cattle business, and Gore made "a substantial profit."[67] Of course, as with any friendship, Gore did many favors for Hammer.[68] But according to *Slate*, "There isn't any evidence that Albert Sr. did anything illegal, or even (within the context of the times) profoundly unethical, to benefit his wealthy patron." If nothing else, it's ironic that environmentalist Albert Gore Jr.'s political career was subsidized by a partnership rooted in cattle and petroleum.[69]

This honest graft phenomenon is not entirely relegated to some bygone era. Fairly modern Republicans (see former Speaker Dennis Hastert) and Democrats (see former Senate majority leader Harry Reid) have been embroiled in similar curious real estate deals where it appears they used their political intel and clout for personal profit.

The son of an alcoholic miner, Reid grew up in poverty in the town of Searchlight, Nevada.[70] Reid's tough background wasn't limited to financial deprivation. "I bet I'm the only senator that learned to swim at a whorehouse swimming pool," he said during an interview in 2016.[71] After he hit it big in politics, Reid's salary was impressive, yet still shy of $200,000. That's a lot of money, to be sure. But how did that beginning transition to him being worth millions?[72] "I did a very good job investing,"[73] Reid responded when a Republican opponent, Sharron Angle, asked this question in 2010. What an understatement.

The details surrounding the $1.1 million windfall Reid reaped from a Las Vegas land deal are sketchy. According to CBS News, "The complex dealings allowed Reid to transfer ownership, legal liability, and some tax consequences to a [friend and former casino lawyer's] company without public knowledge, but still collect a seven-figure payoff nearly three years later."[74] This scandal's complexity probably obscured Reid's complicity. That wasn't the case for Hastert, whose net worth skyrocketed from a few hundred thousand dollars when he was elected to Congress from Illinois in 1997 to several million when he left office two decades later.

Hastert's story is simpler to comprehend.[75] In 2005, Hastert, who was Speaker of the House of Representatives, got a $207 million federal earmark to build a project called the Prairie Parkway that would go through farmland near his home. What nobody knew at the time, however, was that Hastert and some partners (operating under a blind trust) had purchased additional land adjacent to the area designated for the highway. Four months after President George W. Bush signed the transportation bill that included Hastert's earmark (a provision that allows members of Congress to allocate spending for a special project), he sold the land, reportedly earning more than $3 million on the deal.[76] Apparently, Hastert needed the money. In 2015, Hastert pleaded guilty to a financial crime that he committed while paying off a minor that he allegedly sexually abused when he was the minor's wrestling coach.[77]

$ $ $

Public servants profiting from insider knowledge is unethical, but there are plenty of other, more pedestrian (if postmodern), forms of graft. Consider former representative Madison Cawthorn (R-NC), a shooting star elected in 2020 who quickly fell in the 2022 GOP primary. Much of Cawthorn's personal money came from a $3 million insurance settlement from a 2014 car crash that left him partially paralyzed from the waist down.[78]

During his brief congressional tenure, Cawthorn was a lightning rod for his controversial statements. But it is his apparent insider trading of cryptocurrency ("a digital, encrypted, and decentralized medium of exchange"[79]) that earns his mention here. In this case, he was trading "Let's Go, Brandon" meme cryptocurrency. If you've forgotten, "Let's Go, Brandon" is code for "F--k Joe Biden." The line gained popularity after NASCAR driver Brandon Brown won an October 2021 race; during an interview, NBC Sports reporter Kelli Stavast suggested the crowd was chanting "Let's go, Brandon." At some point, it became clear that the reporter was incorrect. The crowd was chanting something that was, shall we say, a bit edgier. The slogan took off and became 2021's "Where's the Beef?"

Sensing the zeitgeist, Cawthorn snarfed up to $250,000 of "Let's Go, Brandon" cryptocurrency on December 21, 2021. On December 29, Cawthorn made an Instagram post where he pointed to the coin logo and said, "This is going to the moon, baby! To the moon!"[80] According to the *Washington Examiner*, the very next day, "NASCAR driver Brandon Brown announced on Dec. 30 that the meme coin would be the primary sponsor of his 2022 season, causing LGB's value to spike by 75%."[81]

One day later, on December 31, Cawthorn sold a portion of his holdings, making between $100,001 and $250,000. The cryptocurrency's "market value suffered a precipitous decline beginning just one day after Cawthorn offloaded upward of $250,000 of the coin onto the market," the *Washington Examiner* continues. "The coin's troubles compounded on Jan. 4 after NAS-CAR rejected the coin's sponsorship deal with Brown. By the end of January, the market cap of the meme coin dropped all the way to $0."

In December 2022, just before Cawthorn's single congressional term ended, the House Ethics Committee found "substantial evidence" that Cawthorn had violated rules by his promotion of cryptocurrency. He was ordered to pay $14,237.49 to a charitable organization.[82]

Cawthorn might ultimately be a footnote in history. Still, this type of scandal may be a harbinger of things to come. Most congressional "insider trading" involves privileged intel that members obtain in their jobs as legislators. Conversely, the privileged opportunity Cawthorn allegedly profited from has more to do with nongovernmental information afforded by virtue of his being a political celebrity and social media influencer.

I'm not saying his situation is any better than Pelosi's. But it reflects the new breed of pols who see themselves less as legislators and more as pop culture/social media brands. So even their alleged corruption looks different.

The unfortunate lesson is simple: if you want to get rich, get elected. These days, the same goes for anyone seeking stardom. Politics is Hollywood for ugly people (as the saying goes), and getting elected is a way to leverage a platform for fame. While this trend is detrimental to democracy, it's not quite as troubling as the odd phenomenon whereby members of Congress magically have better gambling instincts than the rest of us. This truism is the worst-kept secret in America. According to a report published by Cambridge University Press, members of the House of Representatives between 1985 and 2001 outperformed the average investor by 6 percent.[83]

$$\$ \$ \$$$

Of course, insider trading isn't the only way politicians leverage their positions to enrich themselves and their families. Politicians have other insider perks at their disposal. As the old American Express commercial from the late eighties said, "Membership has its privileges."

One inventive, albeit uncommon, strategy is earning interest on money you lend to your own campaign. At first blush, this doesn't sound like a big deal. But here's how it works: rather than merely *giving* your campaign your personal money (with nary a chance of legally recouping your loot), you *lend* your campaign the money. That way, you can always retroactively raise money from donors to reimburse yourself and retire the debt. Winning your election makes this dramatically easier, while losing makes it harder (former astronaut and senator John Glenn spent twenty-two years unsuccessfully trying to pay off campaign debt from his 1984 presidential bid[84]), so it is still a gamble. But there's an interesting wrinkle that can make this move even more enticing: the ability to charge your campaign interest.

The most egregious example of this method occurred in 1998, when US representative Grace Napolitano, a California Democrat (who won reelection in 2022), loaned her campaign $150,000. As journalist Mike

Sprague documented in a 2009 *Daily Breeze* article, Napolitano "has since collected $205,922 in interest, according to a review by this newspaper of nearly 60 reports filed with the Federal Elections Commission."[85] The loan was reportedly paid off in 2010.[86]

The interest rate was initially set at 18 percent (!) in 1998 and dropped to 10 percent in 2006. In fairness to Napolitano, the money she loaned to her campaign came from a retirement account. So, she risked losing it, possibly faced penalties for early withdrawal, and certainly missed out on earning interest. Still, Napolitano's scenario shows that others could also exploit this rule. Again, she made a personal profit of over $200,000. "It makes a nice way to supplement your income," Montebello councilman Bill Molinari said. "Why should congressional members have another perk the average person doesn't have available to them?"[87]

Although it hasn't become a trend, future candidates could cash in even more from this perk. That's because section 304 of the Bipartisan Campaign Reform Act (BCRA) of 2002, which set the limit for how much debt could be retired at $250,000, was overturned in the 2022 Supreme Court ruling *FEC v. Ted Cruz for Senate*.[88] Cruz prevailed when a three-judge panel of the United States District Court for the District of Columbia determined that the limit on repayment was unconstitutional.[89]

$ $ $

A more common (and less confusing) way politicians generate personal profits involves securing lucrative book deals. Having been swindled out of his life savings, a dying Ulysses S. Grant sought to save his wife from a life of poverty.[90] The result was an autobiography that is widely considered one of the best memoirs written by a former president. Sadly, few of the books being churned out by today's politicians are of similar quality.

If you've ever wondered why writing books has become so popular with politicians, consider this: a 1991 law states that members of Congress are not allowed to get paid for speeches.[91] They are also not allowed to earn more than $29,595[92] in "outside earned income" (income from investments doesn't count, as it is considered "unearned")[93] above and beyond their salary; however, the law exempts book deals.[94]

It's no surprise that the twenty-first century has seen a spate of politicians getting into the book biz. In 2000, senator-elect Hillary Clinton got an $8 million book advance.[95] But that amount was a pittance compared with Barack Obama's future advances. Obama was already an author before being elected president in 2008. *Dreams from My Father* and *The Audacity of Hope* brought in $5 million in 2009 alone.[96] And Obama's books remain a steady source of income. In 2017, it was reported that a joint book deal with his wife, Michelle Obama (who has her own bestselling books), would bring in $65 million.[97]

But this income source isn't reserved for political celebs like Clinton and Obama. On his 2018 annual financial disclosure form, Senator Ben Sasse reported earning over $600,000 from book royalties[98] (remember, his salary that year was just $174,000). So, Sasse's work as an author in 2018 earned him three times as much money as his work as a US senator.

In 2019, six Democrats vying for the Democratic presidential nomination in 2020 made a combined $7.1 million from book advances and royalties; the top spot goes to Elizabeth Warren, who raked in $2.8 million.[99] According to *Business Insider*, in 2020 alone, 26 members of Congress wrote books and garnered $1.8 million in advances and royalties.[100]

To be sure, politicians write books to reach potential voters, tell their personal stories, and elevate their profile. But as politicians readily admit, it also can be personally lucrative. In 2022, Senator Marco Rubio (R-FL) told Fox News, "The day I got elected to the Senate I had over $100,000 still in student loans that I was able to pay off because I wrote a book. And from that money I was able to pay it, if not I'd still be paying it."[101] Rubio received an $800,000 advance in 2013 for his first book, *An American Son: A Memoir.*[102] But it was Bernie Sanders, curmudgeon and democratic socialist, who best explained how a lucrative book deal helped make him rich: "I wrote a best-selling book," Sanders declared. "If you write a best-selling book, you can be a millionaire, too."[103]

Problems arise when members of Congress use campaign or party infrastructure to promote or bulk-purchase their books, thereby boosting sales. With enough of a boost, they might land on the much-coveted *New York Times* Best Seller List (generating more buzz and subsequent book sales). For example, in 2022, one of Donald Trump's political committees bought $158,000 worth of his son-in-law Jared Kushner's then new book, *Breaking History: A White House Memoir.* Kushner isn't a politician, so the rules don't apply to him. Still, there was much speculation that the bulk purchases boosted him on the bestseller list, as *Forbes* noted.[104]

Federal Election Commission (FEC) law prohibits members of Congress from using campaign dollars to goose book royalties (which would be equivalent to laundering campaign dollars into personal funds). Still, that scenario is difficult to quantify, much less police. A 2021 complaint filed with the FEC by a government watchdog organization, the Campaign Legal Center,[105] alleges that Ted Cruz's campaign committee spent as much as $18,000 on Facebook ads promoting his 2020 book, *One Vote Away: How a Single Supreme Court Seat Can Change History.* Why might it be unethical for a politician to advertise his book on Facebook? "According to Cruz's financial disclosure report," the complaint reads, Cruz "receives 15% royalties on every hardcover copy sold, and received a $400,000 advance from the publisher. Therefore, by using campaign funds to promote purchases of his book, there is reason to believe that Ted Cruz for Senate violated the ban on the personal use of campaign funds."

Cruz's fellow Texan, Representative Dan Crenshaw (R-TX), has also drawn attention to bulk book orders. In 2020, the National Republican Congressional Committee (NRCC) spent about $400,000 to buy 25,500 copies of Crenshaw's book *Fortitude: American Resilience in the Era of Outrage.*[106] The NRCC's solicitation told prospective donors, "Not only will you be getting this great book, but you'll also be supporting efforts to take back President Trump's Conservative House majority in November."

Of course, Trump and conservative candidates for the House of Representatives weren't the only beneficiaries: book buyers would be helping Dan Crenshaw, too. Crenshaw's book was already a bestseller when the NRCC boosted it. But when you consider that a normal author can make a bestseller list by selling as few as five thousand copies in a single week, you'll get the sense of how helpful it was that the NRCC purchased 25,500 copies.

To be fair, Crenshaw *is* a former Navy SEAL with a life story that might be *worth* reading. Still, normal authors (let alone normal people) can't count on such favors from deep-pocketed institutions.

Crenshaw received a $250,000 advance for the book,[107] which isn't exactly chump change. What is more, the large number of books sold likely increases the odds that his next book advance will be even larger—assuming he's still a prominent congressman or in another position that would garner more bulk sales. But what about the additional royalties that authors can sometimes make on the back end of book sales?

FEC law prohibits members of Congress from keeping the royalties from books purchased by the author's political campaign. This law was established in 1995, when the reelection committee of the then senator Al D'Amato (R-NY) was granted permission to purchase bulk copies of his book *Power, Pasta, and Politics* to give to donors, as long as he didn't keep the royalties.[108] But it's not clear that this provision applies to party committees.[109] Former representative Beto O'Rourke (D-TX) alleged that Crenshaw was "getting rich selling his own book to the GOP."[110] But that accusation might be a bit too strong. According to the *Dallas Morning News*, "It's unclear to what extent Crenshaw may have benefited personally from the bulk purchase."[111] His staff only said that Crenshaw "fully complied with election and ethics rules with his bestselling book."[112]

Another potential lucrative loophole exists when the book publisher uses the campaign's resources to promote a politician's book. In 2021, the FEC said Representative Adam Schiff (D-CA) could rent his campaign email list to his own publisher. Talk about a scam. "It would be illegal for the campaign to use its list to promote the candidate's book, but the FEC says it is legal for the campaign to take money from the publisher so that the publisher may use the list to promote that same book," Brendan Fischer, director of federal programs at the Campaign Legal Center, told the *Daily Beast.*[113] "In other words, a publisher may lawfully pour money into a candidate's campaign so that more royalty money will go into the candidate's pocket."[114]

It *does* seem like the deck is stacked in favor of public servants who want to write a book and turn a profit, while possibly blurring ethical lines. Still, it's not unheard of for a book scandal to take down a politician.

In 1989, one such scandal took down then Speaker of the House Jim Wright (D-TX). As the *New Yorker* explains it, "Wright had been using the book as a way to bypass caps on speaking fees [as of 1991, members of Congress have been prohibited from accepting any amount of money for speeches[115]]: an organization would invite him to speak, and instead of paying him for a speech, they would agree to buy copies of the book in bulk, for which he received an outsized fifty-five per cent of the royalties."[116] There were also examples of Wright's personal friends making bulk purchases of the book, which was titled *Reflections of a Public Man*, as a way to "make a contribution to Jim's income" while bypassing FEC laws.[117] There were also allegations that a staff member (using taxpayer time) was involved in writing the book.[118]

Ironically, the man largely responsible for taking down Wright, Representative Newt Gingrich (R-GA), would later face his own book scandal. In 1994, the then incoming Speaker of the House was forced to relinquish a $4.5 million book advance when the scandal threatened to derail the Republican Revolution's agenda. But he kept the royalties (and his agent told the *New York Times*, "It may make far more than $4.5 million in the end").[119]

Still, a word of caution for those who may see writing a book as a sure win-win: not every politician's book deal makes money . . . *for the publisher.*

Consider the case of former governor Andrew Cuomo (D-NY), who was accused of using state resources to write his memoir, *American Crisis:*

Leadership Lessons from the COVID-19 Pandemic.[120] Cuomo made $5.1 million on the book (which sold when his popularity was riding high during the COVID-19 crisis). But Cuomo's fortunes fell, and he infamously sold just 71 copies in the last week of July 2021.[121] Cuomo still got paid.

$ $ $

Between the lucrative book deals, the insider intel they pick up on the job, and various other perks that normal people don't have access to, politicians have plenty of ways to increase their wealth far beyond what they earn from their taxpayer-funded salaries.

When it comes to things like insider trading, members of Congress set their own rules. The same can't be said for almost any other job. Consider, for example, Major League Baseball (MLB) managers. Pete Rose, who got more hits (4,256) than anyone ever has or likely ever will, was unceremoniously kicked out of baseball and kept out of the Baseball Hall of Fame. His crime? Betting on baseball. Now, as far as we know, Rose never bet *against* his team, the Cincinnati Reds. While Rose was obviously an obsessive gambler, there's no evidence that he ever threw a game. So Rose was banned for life for betting on his own team, while members of Congress get reelected for betting on a game where they know the score before anyone else (and can sometimes even manipulate the game).

Rather than litigating the details on a case-by-case basis, MLB has a hard-and-fast rule against betting; it seems to me that this rule is both wise and easier to police.

This principle isn't limited to sports gambling. Once you've made the decision to enter the betting market, it goes against human nature to not leverage all of your knowledge to make your best bets. Let's say, for example, you own a bunch of stock in a biopharmaceutical company. One day, you get a call from the CEO, who tells you that the Food and Drug Administration (FDA) will come out with some negative news about the company's cancer drug—information that is sure to make the stock's price plummet.

Do you (a) dump your stock ASAP or (b) pretend you didn't know anything and take a bath on it? Frankly, I'd rather not know the inside information. But once you *do* know, you'd be an idiot to sit on your hands and watch your life's savings swirl down the toilet. If you're billionaire "domestic lifestyle innovator" Martha Stewart, you pick up the phone within ten minutes of getting that call, and you sell like a broke crack dealer hearing sirens. That's what happened on December 27, 2001, when Stewart unloaded stock in a biotech company that was about to implode. Stewart's subsequent incarceration may raise questions of prosecutorial priorities but likely did wonders for the craft prison decor industry.

The rules are different for our public servants. Nancy Pelosi went to the speakership; Martha Stewart went to jail.

The truth is that politicians have been able to legally (for the most part) leverage their public office to feather their own nests (and those of their friends and families) since the dawn of time. The good news is that things have gotten better over the years. In the old days, politics was the Wild West (see the aforementioned story about Albert Gore Sr.). But in the wake of the Watergate scandal, Congress passed the Ethics in Government Act of 1978, which, among other things, "mandated annual financial disclosure by all senior federal personnel, including all Members and some employees of the House."[122] That act provided some transparency.

Still, we've got a long way to go. For many politicians, the question isn't really whether they'll take advantage of the situation, but rather how obvious they are about cashing in. For some public officials, these perks are simply a way to make more money than they could in the real world. For the truly ambitious and shameless, it can involve building generational wealth and using the spoils of office to reward friends and family.

For a select few, it can even start a dynasty.

Chapter 5

All in the Family: How Politicians Spread the Wealth

I seen my opportunities and I took 'em.
—*Tammany Hall's George Washington Plunkitt*

"No Title of Nobility shall be granted by the United States." So says the Constitution. But don't let that fool you. For a minute there in 2016, it looked as though America was destined for a Bush-Clinton rematch, with former Florida governor Jeb Bush going up against Hillary Clinton. At least one person sounded the alarm early on: "There are other people out there that are very qualified and we've had enough Bushes," declared Jeb's mom, Barbara Bush, on NBC's *Today Show* in 2013.[1] Um... thanks, Mom? The voters agreed with Babs about seeing other people, and Jeb flamed out (albeit to a candidate who was not necessarily "very qualified").

So far, the voting public seems to feel that two presidencies are enough for any family. But don't expect political dynasties to end anytime soon. I used to joke that a future presidential race would feature Mitt Romney's son challenging Dick Cheney's daughter for a shot at taking on Barack Obama's wife. The debate would be moderated by Tim Russert's son. Of course, that was before Ivanka Trump and Don Jr. came along. The children of political elites have a leg up.

Dynasties are a natural condition, and though we may say we don't like them, our preferences tell a different story. Consider the proliferation of "nepo babies" in the entertainment world.[2] Actor Martin Sheen may be more highly esteemed than his sons, actors Charlie Sheen and Emilio Estevez, but both have carved out long, successful Hollywood careers. Tom Hanks's son Colin seems to be on the same trajectory (though hopefully without the Charlie Sheen penchant for public meltdowns). Actors Billie Lourd and Emma Roberts are following in the footsteps of Carrie Fisher and Debbie Reynolds (Lourd's mother and grandmother) and Julia Roberts (Emma's aunt). If you rooted for 1990s or early 2000s baseball stars like Craig Biggio, Dante Bichette, or Vladimir Guerrero, you might root for their sons as teammates on the Toronto Blue Jays.

And these are pop culture dynasties; these are the people we follow in our free time. We vote with our fandom, our money for a movie ticket, or our time to stream their television shows. (I have no judgment here, as I grew up rooting for Cal Ripken Jr., whose father and brother were both career baseball men.)

If we choose this in our culture, you can bet we are going to choose it in our politics, even if we swear that we don't believe in power or fame being passed down like an heirloom. The proof is in our choices.

Rich and powerful people often marry rich and powerful people, and their children enjoy the residual benefits. And those politicians who start off as working stiffs before getting elected can start their own dynasty by marrying up. Those possessing political power have a way of finding and marrying into families with financial power; in this way, both traits help ensure their survival.

According to Stephen Hess's book *America's Political Dynasties*, "the correspondence of Presidents John [Adams] and John Quincy Adams is filled with tales of money miseries; then the latter's son married the daughter of Peter Chardon Brooks, Boston's first millionaire." Before the marriage, the Adams clan already had a *political* dynasty. The older

Adams appointed the younger as the United States minister to Prussia. Less well known is that he also "appointed his brother-in-law as a postmaster and named John Quincy's father-in-law as superintendent of stamps."[3]

The marriage of political power and wealth has a long history. "The powerful Livingston family of New York in one generation had five girls marry U.S. congressmen, creating a powerful commercial-political alliance," writes author Peter Schweizer. "The great industrialists of the nineteenth century often married their daughters off to politicians so they could literally be 'wedded' to power in Washington."[4]

The trend of politicians marrying rich followed us into the twentieth century, too. Take, for example, the case of our thirty-sixth president, Lyndon Baines Johnson, "who was virtually penniless when he wooed Claudia (Lady Bird) Taylor in 1937," yet was "one of the largest land owners in the central Texas hill country when he died."[5] LBJ once said of his wife that she "has the first nickel she ever had tucked in her bra."[6] It was good for him that she did. After he spent "$10,000 of her inheritance to win a seat in Congress in 1937,"[7] Johnson's lifestyle and career was funded by the fortune derived from Lady Bird paying $17,500 for an Austin, Texas, radio station: KTBC.

His wife's dowry might have served as the seed money, but LBJ's political connections also helped avoid FCC red tape that otherwise might have interfered with the station's purchase; more importantly, it allowed the station to broadcast twenty-four hours a day.[8] It also helped him get a CBS affiliation, increase the station's wattage, expand his media empire into TV, and keep out the competition—thereby driving up profits. When it was founded in 1952, KTBC was Austin's only VHF TV channel and remained so until 1965.[9] And Lady Bird's money started it all. As *Texas Monthly* put it, "He had the influence, but she had the cash."[10] Kinda sounds like a country song, if you ask me.

Wealthy spouses (or wealthy in-laws) are often a prerequisite for a meteoric political career. This remains true today. Consider Representative Michael McCaul (R-TX), whose Texas district stretches from Houston to Austin. *Business Insider* estimates his wealth at $125,880,292, with the bulk of it coming from his wife, Linda McCaul. Linda's father, Lowry Mays, is CEO of Clear Channel Communications. McCaul's "dramatic rise in net worth appears to be the product of generational wealth transfer," reports *New York* magazine.[11] "Due to this influx of spousal wealth, McCaul unseated [the previous] richest member of Congress, John Kerry—the John Kerry married to Teresa Heinz Kerry of the ketchup fortune."

The outlet went on to say, "We're beginning to see a pattern here."[12] Indeed.

Take Senator Richard Blumenthal (D-CT), one of the richest politicians in America. Most of his wealth is derived from his 1982 marriage to Cynthia A. Malkin, who is the daughter of Peter L. Malkin. To give you a sense of his wealth, Malkin controlled a real estate partnership whose portfolio included the Empire State Building. Around 2000, Malkin famously fended off Donald Trump's attempts to acquire the building and rebrand it the "Trump Empire State Building Tower Apartments."[13]

Much of Senator Dianne Feinstein's (D-CA) wealth can be attributed to her 1980 marriage to Richard Blum. The two met when she was president of the San Francisco Board of Supervisors.[14] One of Blum's best stories was about the time he helped arrange the 1967 purchase of the company that ran Ringling Bros. and Barnum & Bailey circuses. Their "biggest assets have four legs, and they walk around and poop," he recalled telling his business partners.[15] Blum, who died in 2022, ran Blum Capital Partners and had a net worth estimated at $1 billion.[16]

The wealthy in-law trend continues in the lower house. Representative Ro Khanna (D-CA) represents parts of the San Francisco Bay Area. His father-in-law is chairman of Mura Holdings and chief executive of Transmaxx, a supplier of car transmission parts. Same song, different verse.

Sometimes, wealthy in-laws arrive later in life. Such was the case for Senator Mitch McConnell (R-KY), who is the Senate minority leader. Critics noticed that McConnell's reported net wealth skyrocketed around 2008, raising questions that linger to this day. In December 2022, for example, former Fox News host Tucker Carlson asked, "How did Mitch McConnell get so rich?"[17] The answer? McConnell's boost in wealth was the result of a $9 million inheritance that his wife, former Labor and Treasury Secretary Elaine Chao, received in 2007 when her mother died.[18] (Her dad founded a shipping company that traded with Taiwan and shipped rice during the Vietnam War.)[19]

Sometimes marrying into money is a double-edged sword. In 2017, Senator Sheldon Whitehouse (D-RI) was plagued by his membership in what was described by local press as an "exclusive all-white private club."[20] The club and Whitehouse later disputed the "all-white" premise but provided no corroborating evidence. Whitehouse refused to resign, and according to WPRI, "obliquely suggested that his wife, Sandra, is the one who has decided to remain a part of Bailey's."[21] Sandra also happens to be one of the largest shareholders of the club.

Your Brother's Banker

This yin and yang relationship isn't limited to just spouses. For every rich and generous family member, there are a dozen delinquent brothers and uncles and children. Even well-meaning relatives can cause financial headaches. Anyone who has seen *It's a Wonderful Life* knows that George Bailey's trouble wasn't caused by Mr. Potter; it was caused by the hapless Uncle Billy, who loses George's money. The same is true in political circles, where Uncle Billy often appears in sibling form.

Billy Carter (the marketer of Billy Beer and younger brother of former president Jimmy Carter) and Roger Clinton (brother of former president Bill Clinton) are often thought of today as punchlines, diminishing some of their more troubling actions. In 1980, Billy got sideways with the Justice Department for failing to register as a lobbyist...for Libya. "Billy had taken two all-expenses-paid trips to Tripoli pursuing business deals there," *Mother Jones*'s David Corn explains, "and he had accepted $220,000 from the Libyans to develop what he called a 'propaganda campaign' to promote the foreign policy objectives of dictator Moammar Qaddafi."[22]

Likewise, Roger Clinton had serious problems. While brother Bill was governor of Arkansas, Roger was arrested for selling cocaine to an undercover officer. One of Bill Clinton's final acts as president included pardoning his ne'er-do-well brother. To make matters worse, as the *Washington Post* reported, "It was [later] revealed that Roger gave Bill a list of people he thought should be pardoned, but that he had not been paid to make those recommendations (none of which were granted)."[23]

Lest I be accused of focusing solely on Democratic siblings, here's one from the "Where are they now" vault. Back in the early aughts, Neil Bush (brother to former President George W. Bush and former Florida governor Jeb Bush, and son of former President George H. W. Bush) was accused of violating conflict of interest laws in connection with his involvement in a failed savings and loan. As Peter Carlson wrote in the *Washington Post*, "[Neil] Bush has done something that no other American has ever accomplished: He has become the embarrassing relative of not one but two presidents."[24] Congrats or something!

And the Republican sibling embarrassment goes back even further than that. Richard Nixon was plagued by a $205,000 loan that his brother, F. Donald Nixon, received from a company owned by Howard Hughes Sr. (the father of the famous and eccentric billionaire business tycoon). As the *New York Times* reported, "The disclosure of the transaction was widely believed to have contributed heavily to Richard Nixon's narrow loss to John F. Kennedy in 1960."[25] Donald subsequently filed for bankruptcy. But when brother Dick was finally elected president in 1968,

Donald's fortunes increased. "As a newly hired vice president of Marriott Corp., Donald Nixon traveled the world, often getting VIP treatment.... Some airlines regulated by the Nixon Administration switched their food catering contracts to Marriott."

Well, if Dick Nixon was going to be taken down, it wasn't going to be for something his kid brother did. According to the *Los Angeles Times*,[26] "Watergate investigators said they concluded that Nixon and his White House aides feared that the brother was involved in questionable financial deals and wanted to keep tabs on them."[27] That's right. President Richard Nixon was so worried about a potential scandal involving his brother that he did what any loving brother would do: he had him bugged!

Other People's Money (OPM)

The benefit of talking about presidents is that everyone is familiar with them. The problem with focusing on presidents is that it creates the impression that all the fun and dysfunction is relegated to the top of the political ladder. In actuality, the merriment continues at the congressional and local level. The problem is that politicians have access to a lot of money that isn't their own. Their campaigns have access to donor money earmarked for elections, and their official offices have access to taxpayer money earmarked to serve the public good. This creates a sense of entitlement and an environment rife with temptation.

While outright stealing of campaign or taxpayer dollars is obviously bad and illegal, what about the gray areas? This problem is not unique to politicians. Anyone who has ever had to fill out an expense report or filed a tax return has probably, at some point, asked themself, *Was this really a business lunch?* How about the airline points you personally accrue from booking official business on your company credit card? What if you use those points to take your family on a nice vacation? When it comes to using campaign or official resources to help family members, such rationalizations can be compounded by our familial bonds. *If helping my family is wrong, I don't wanna be right.*

Of course, one man's family values are another man's corruption. This problem is pervasive. Back in 2012, the Citizens for Responsibility and Ethics (CREW) put together an exhaustive report on how members of Congress spread the wealth around (from congressional and campaign accounts) to themselves and their families. As *Roll Call* described the report, "More than half of the Members of the House of Representatives have used their position to financially enrich themselves or their families."[28]

There are many ways to use your office to enrich your family. One way is to help them get a job they aren't qualified for. "When I was governor, you'd think you were meeting somebody on a policy issue," former governor Mark Sanford (R-SC) told me, but "The number of folks who came on behalf of relatives was endless."[29] This happens at all levels of politics. For example, near Sanford's stomping grounds, the *Charleston Post and Courier* editorialized in 2020 against giving a $290,000-a-year job to county council chairman Elliott Summey. "Mr. Summey has at best minimal job qualifications," the editorial read. "The main 'qualification' he has are [*sic*] political connections: his own position and his family's deep political connections, which include his mayor father and several close friends and family in assorted public jobs or roles."[30]

A similar incident happened in 2011, when the then Senate majority leader Harry Reid (D-NV) intervened to help his son, Josh Reid, score a $199,000 salary and become city attorney of Henderson, Nevada— a move described by a resident who attended the city council meeting where he was approved for the position as "disgusting" and "nepotism," as the *Las Vegas Sun* reported.[31] At least Josh Reid was an attorney.

A less-direct way to spread the money around to family is for them to garner business based on the assumption that their proximity to you will influence your decisions. "We find that one really effective way for a corporation to do influence peddling without actually bribing a member of Congress is hire the spouse," Craig Holman, government affairs lobbyist for the consumer advocacy organization Public Citizen, told CBS News in 2012.[32] "They'll hire these spouses at exorbitant salaries, and that money really goes directly into the pocket of the member."

This method delves into a gray area, and (I suspect) it has gotten more difficult to detect in the modern era; both spouses often work, and it's not uncommon for people at the top of the same industry to be married.

Here's an example that hits close to home. My wife is a political fundraiser. She was a professional political fund-raiser before we got married, and she's very good at what she does. The idea that her client list might influence my political commentary is insulting to both of us as professionals. The idea that she should quit her job for the sake of my career is likewise offensive. (This might be a good time to disclose that some of her past clients are named in this book, including Ted Cruz and Josh Hawley.)

Now, it's a little different for politicians who, after all, are public servants paid by taxpayers. It's perfectly understandable that people with successful careers in similar fields might fall in love and get married. But doing so can create (at least the appearance of) a conflict of interest. When your paycheck comes from taxpayers, every effort should be made to avoid the mere appearance of impropriety.

Take, for example, Senator Roy Blunt (R-MO), who retired at the end of 2022 and joined a DC lobbying firm himself in 2023. Blunt is married to a lobbyist and has *three* kids who are also lobbyists.[33] This looks, at best, nepotistic and swampy and, at worst, corrupt. On the other hand, one of his sons, Matt, was governor of Missouri. Should an ex-governor be barred from lobbying because his dad is a senator? That limitation seems extreme.

Likewise, when they married, Blunt's wife, née Abigail Perlman, was already the head of government affairs for Altria Corp., the parent company of Philip Morris.[34] This courtship was not without (warranted) controversy. In June 2003, the *Washington Post* alerted its readers that "Blunt tried to slip language aiding Philip Morris into a homeland security bill last year."[35]

Democrats tried to make an issue of the Blunt family business during the 2016 elections. The effort to unseat him included ads noting that his net worth had increased "by up to $7 million" since taking office[36] and highlighted "how Blunt puts his lobbyist family members ahead of hard-working Missourians." Another ad, run by an outside PAC, mentioned that Blunt's house in Washington cost $1.6 million.[37] Regardless, having four lobbyists in the family wasn't enough to help Democrat Jason Kander, then Missouri's secretary of state, oust him. Blunt survived politically, but our institutions may have been weakened in the process.

Another example is Senator Joe Manchin (D-WV), who has interests in a coal company that progressives see as a conflict of interest when it comes to his votes on energy and climate.[38] As is so often the case, though, Manchin's family has also been accused of having at least the appearance of financial conflicts of interest, going back to his days as the state's governor. According to the *Times West Virginian*, "During his one term as governor, Manchin has appointed his wife to the West Virginia Board of Education; their son, Joseph Manchin IV, to the West Virginia Tourism Commission; and his cousin, Mark Anthony Manchin, as executive director of the West Virginia School Building Authority in November."[39]

But let's focus on his immediate family. In 2007, Manchin appointed his wife Gayle Manchin, a teacher, to the West Virginia Board of Education. In 2012, she became president of the National State Boards of Education (NASBE), where, according to *USA Today*, "she spearheaded an unprecedented effort that encouraged states to require schools to purchase medical devices that fight life-threatening allergic reactions."[40] As a result, Mylan (the maker of EpiPens) assumed "a near monopoly in school nurses' offices."

The only problem? The CEO of Mylan was Joe and Gayle Manchin's daughter, Heather Bresch.

Bresch is interesting, in part, because of a résumé scandal that dates back to roughly the same time Manchin's wife was appointed to the state's board of education. The unvarnished version seems to be that West Virginia University gave her an MBA degree, even though she failed to complete the required credits, and then rescinded it after allegations of cronyism.[41] More concerning, however, is that under Bresch's leadership, Mylan jacked up the price for the life-saving EpiPen device by 400 percent, as CNN reported[42] ("because of the patent on the EpiPen delivery device, a true generic doesn't exist," explained NBC News[43]). During this time, Bresch's own salary increased from $2,453,456 to $18,931,068.[44] It might not surprise you to learn that Mylan gave large amounts of money to the campaign of (you guessed it!) Joe Manchin, according to OpenSecrets.[45]

Spreading the Wealth Around

Another way to enrich your family is to add them to the campaign and/ or office payroll. There's theoretically nothing wrong with this if (a) they are qualified for the job, unlike, say, Hunter Biden's lucrative career as a painter[46] (at least the taxpayers aren't footing that bill), and (b) they are performing a legitimate service (as opposed to accepting a sinecure). There is a long history of this type of conduct. According to the *Atlantic*, "Approximately 40 of President Ulysses S. Grant's family members and family connections benefited from his presidency. Both Franklin D. Roosevelt and Dwight Eisenhower had sons working in their White House."[47] Would someone other than Robert F. Kennedy have made a better campaign manager for John F. Kennedy in 1960? Probably not. But should JFK have made RFK his attorney general? Definitely not.

Family values are universally important, but when it comes to spreading *campaign* cash (money donated to elect or reelect a politician) around to family members, some politicians are more generous than others.

Take Representative Maxine Waters (D-CA), for example. In 2020, Waters paid her daughter more than $80,000 out of her campaign coffers for various mailing and get-out-the-vote services.[48] This behavior has been raising eyebrows for years, and it's not limited to just her daughter. In 2004, the *Los Angeles Times* reported that Waters's family members "have made more than $1 million in the last eight years by doing business with companies, candidates and causes that the influential congresswoman has helped."[49]

Waters isn't the only one bankrolling family members with campaign funds. Representative Bobby Rush (D-IL), a former Black Panther leader, has paid his family—including his son, who was found guilty of having sex with female inmates while he was a prison official[50]—tens of thousands of dollars in campaign funds for "field services."[51] Representative Jahana Hayes (D-CT) has spread campaign money around to family members,[52] and, in recent years, Representative James Clyburn (D-SC) has (indirectly) paid relatives $200,000 for campaign-related services and office rent.[53]

According to the *New York Times*, a 2012 report showed that former congressman and presidential candidate Ron Paul (R-TX) "paid salaries or fees to his daughter, brother, grandson, daughter's mother-in-law, granddaughter and grandson-in-law, totaling more than $300,000."[54]

But is this wrong? "Nepotism has long been recognized to be a feature of dysfunctional government," Pete McGinnis, a spokesman for the Functional Government Initiative, a federal watchdog group that probes ethics in government, told the Daily Caller News Foundation.[55] "While this practice of hiring family members as campaign workers is not necessarily illegal, it can raise ethics concerns. To pay your spouse with campaign contributions can appear as a self-payment."

It's arguably worse when the money comes from taxpayers, not political donors. Progressive icon Bernie Sanders knows something about this. "Jane and [Bernie] Sanders were living together while he was approving her paychecks," according to *The Atlantic*.[56] "After paying her $4,900 in 1982 (about $13,000 today), the mayor put her on what became a $21,000 annual salary (about $54,000 today) as part of a formal seven-person expansion of the city's staff." Her position "was not advertised and no applicants were considered aside from [her], according to Sanders," the *Burlington Free Press* reported in 1985.[57]

After Bernie was elected to Congress in Vermont, Jane "took home at least $30,000 in fees as a media buyer for his campaigns, paid for with money he'd raised, though she had no prior experience in media buying. Two companies she'd registered, Progressive Media Strategies and Leadership Strategies, received more than $91,000 from Sanders's 2002 and 2004 congressional campaigns."[58] At various times, Jane's son and daughter have also been paid by Sanders or Sanders-adjacent organizations.[59]

Some young members of the new left, also known as "the Squad," are already taking a page from their elders. Alexandria Ocasio-Cortez has been criticized because a PAC she was aligned with paid her live-in boyfriend $6,000 for marketing services.[60] But that's nothing compared with Ilhan Omar, who has already directed *millions* of campaign dollars to her husband's consulting firm.[61]

Progressive Stacey Abrams isn't part of the Squad, per se, but that's probably just because she can't manage to get elected. Still, her activism and her losing campaigns for Georgia governor have made her famous and rich. What is more, she has spread the wealth around. In 2019 and 2020, alone, her nonprofit Fair Fight Action has steered $9.4 million to the law firm of her close friend.[62] Craig Holman, a campaign finance and ethics expert at the nonprofit group Public Citizen, told *Politico* that "It is a very clear conflict of interest because with that kind of close link to the litigation and her friend that provides an opportunity where the friend gets particularly enriched from this litigation."[63]

Of course, Abrams's situation was perfectly legal. The same cannot be said for our next example. You might remember the 2009 case of

Representative William Jefferson (D-LA), who was found with $90,000 in his freezer (cold hard cash, as the joke goes). Prosecutors said it was money he planned to use to pay a bribe to secure an even more lucrative business deal.[64] But maybe his motives were somewhat noble.

According to reports from the *Times-Picayune* during his trial, "The prosecution's contention [was] that Jefferson solicited bribes to help pay his daughters' tuition or other expenses at Harvard, Brown, and Boston universities and to help provide for them would seem to provide a motive and a measure of poignancy to the proceedings at the Virginia courthouse."[65]

As a humble writer with two kids who will (sooner than I can imagine) head off to college, I can sympathize. Maybe he should have considered a state school.

Trust Fund Babies

Most of this chapter has focused on how politicians use the trappings of their office to help family members make money, but it works in reverse. Rich families also use their wealth to help their children break into politics. As Representative Marie Gluesenkamp Perez (D-WA) told *Politico* in 2023: "A lot of candidates are self-funded people with trust funds."[66]

One of the most prominent (and annoying) wealthy lawmakers is Florida Republican Representative Matt Gaetz, aka "Baby Gaetz," a Republican who "earned" his position by virtue of daddy's money. "Matt would be an assistant manager at Walmart if it weren't for his father,"[67] according to Steven Specht, a Democrat who lost to Gaetz in a run for Congress in 2016. So how did he end up on third base, thinking he hit a triple? In the 1970s, Don Gaetz cofounded a nonprofit hospice company[68] that eventually sold for $400 million to the parent company of Roto-Rooter, the plumbing company.[69] Don then won a seat in Florida's state senate. Eventually, Matt parlayed his dad's political connections and money into his seat in the US Congress.

For now, Matt Gaetz is moderately wealthy (with assets of $235,000 to $625,000[70]), but not uber-rich. That distinction belongs to his parents, Don and Victoria Gaetz, who, according to *Forbes*, "are among the nation's top 1% of ultra-high net worth individuals. Don, who sits on the board of Florida nonprofit Triumph Gulf Coast, reported that the couple's net worth was $29.6 million as of June 2020, according to a document he submitted to the state's ethics commission. They own a portfolio of publicly-traded stocks, 13 pieces of real estate, seven-figure stakes in three private companies, as well as $375,000 worth of 'antiques, imported rugs, furniture, books' and a 2013 Mercedes-Benz S550."[71]

Of course, many of the benefits of having a rich family are not directly related to money, per se; equally important are the contacts that can be made. California governor Gavin Newsom, a Democrat, demonstrated that the perks of being in the upper class transcend mere dollar signs. "Gavin Newsom wasn't born rich, but he was born connected," the *Los Angeles Times* noted.[72] Newsom's father, Bill, "was a lifelong friend of Gordon Getty, the son of oil magnate J. Paul Getty—they attended high school together. Bill Newsom later managed the Getty family trust on behalf of Gordon, estimated by Forbes to be worth more than $2 billion in 2018. Bill Newsom was so close with the family that he helped deliver the ransom money after the 1973 kidnapping of J. Paul Getty's grandson, John Paul Getty III."

According to my political fund-raiser wife, a politician has to raise a minimum of $300,000 the first quarter they run—from their *personal network*—before anyone else will invest in their campaign. And that's for a lowly House seat. You can see the importance of rich friends and colleagues.

But while having a network of rich friends can get you far, the richest politician in America, according to *Forbes*,[73] got there the old-fashioned way. I'm talking about Democratic Illinois governor J. B. Pritzker, the Hyatt Hotels heir, who is worth an estimated $3.6 billion. He's only one of eleven billionaires[74] in a family that also includes former Obama commerce secretary Penny Pritzker.[75] In a 2022 battle that included three billionaires, Pritzker and the Democratic Governors Association poured tens of millions into the Illinois Republican primary to boost the weaker Republican candidate, thus making it easier for him to win that November's general election.

Pritzker dominates in the wealth department, but the honorable mention goes to Republican Bill Haslam, who served as governor of Tennessee until 2019. According to *Forbes*, Haslam's father "bought a gas station in Virginia in 1958 and founded [the truck stop company] Pilot Flying J, which now operates in more than 900 locations in North America. Berkshire Hathaway paid a reported $2.8 billion for 39% of Pilot in 2017 and will acquire another 41% by 2023."[76]

And who could forget Mark Dayton, a Democrat, who was governor of Minnesota until 2019. Dayton's father, Bruce, founded Target Corp.[77] But it was his real estate developer grandfather, George Draper Dayton, who founded the family empire when he bought a store in 1903.[78]

A more recent example is Daniel Goldman, a former assistant US attorney who prosecuted Donald Trump's first impeachment case for the Democrats (perhaps seeking to sink his chances, Trump endorsed Goldman in his Democratic primary). His family wealth helped him overcome a crowded Democratic primary field in 2022, which paved his way to a congressional seat. "Mr. Goldman, an heir to the Levi Strauss fortune, has a net worth of up to $253 million and pumped nearly $5 million of his own money into the race," the *New York Times* explained.[79] Money, it turns out, is a great equalizer, making up for other deficiencies that would sink a "normal" candidate. "Mr. Goldman lacked the political connections of many of his opponents. He had never held elective office before, nor had he been particularly involved with local Democratic political clubs or neighborhood community boards. But his wealth enabled him to carpet bomb the district with television ads."[80] Having won election, his money also allows him to live in comfort…in a $27 million Tribeca condo.[81]

As you can see, many politicians are the product of generational wealth and privilege that accumulates over time. Perhaps having triumphed in the business world, their descendants instead turn to politics. In a 1780 letter to his wife, Abigail, John Adams wrote, "I must study politics and war [so] that my sons may have liberty to study mathematics and philosophy."[82] In modern America, this concept has been turned on its head to be "I must make money so my sons can be politicians."

Joe Biden's Family

It would be journalistic malpractice in this day and age to write a chapter about political families and money and *not* mention Donald Trump or Joe Biden. But because numerous books and articles have been (and will be) written about the Trumps and Bidens, I will avoid the temptation to get too bogged down in that discussion here.

I'll start with the Biden family. Partly because Trump set the standard for nepotism and shady business deals, the Bidens generally received kid glove treatment from the media. This was especially true during the 2020 campaign. However, the Biden family has engaged in behavior that is, to say the least, unethical. This has been going on for decades and persisted after Biden was elected president.

For example, according to CNN, "A year after Biden was elected... his youngest brother, Frank, boasted in a speech in Boston for a medical group called BioSig of the 'bully pulpit' he was afforded due to 'my brother Joey,' and vowed to help attendees 'get federal dollars.'"[83] He also gave a speech for that same firm in Italy, and then gave conflicting reports as to who paid for the trip. If you want to fully appreciate how sketchy this is, Frank Biden told CNN he had consulted for BioSig for about a year. He then reversed himself, saying he had never worked as a consultant for the company. He later clarified in a text message that he had provided BioSig with informal sales assistance. As for his Italian travel, Frank Biden said in another text message 'someone' paid for it, though he did not say who."[84]

Meanwhile, James Biden, the president's other kid brother, has raised eyebrows over loans he has received and other business dealings, including partnering with Joe Biden's ne'er-do-well son, Hunter. But the family affair runs deeper than that. Joe Biden has a long history of family members being entangled in the family business, including his sister Valerie, who managed his first local race back in 1970. According to *The Atlantic*, "about a fifth of the $11.1 million raised by Biden's [1988] presidential campaign went to his family members or companies that employed them."[85] It certainly seems like James was trading on brother Joe's name and position. As the *Washington Post* reported, "Shortly after Joe Biden became a senator, James Biden opened a nightclub in Wilmington, Del., with bank loans from lenders who may have been eager to please the new young senator on the Banking Committee."[86]

On another occasion, a Joe Biden donor made a substantial loan to James, hired James's wife, Sara, and paid the couple close to $250,000 to travel internationally (to try to gin up business for his firm). According to a lawsuit filed by the donor, Leonard Barrack, James Biden, "through his family name and his resemblance to his brother, United States senator Joseph Biden of Delaware," had promised to land clients. James apparently didn't live up to those expectations.[87]

It's impossible to say if something untoward or illegal happened, but those circumstances certainly smell swampy. So why didn't brother Joe, who has wanted to be president since at least 1988, put his brother in line? One theory suggests that to make it to the top of the dirty world of politics, Joe Biden needed loyalists with lower ethical standards. As the old saying goes, "Don't keep a dog and bark yourself." Another theory (not that they're mutually exclusive) is simply that blood is thicker than water and that Joe Biden prizes family loyalty above all else. This theory, while romantic, isn't crazy.

Consider what family means to the Bidens. When Biden's first wife, Neilia Hunter Biden, and their daughter, Naomi, died in a horrific car crash in 1972, brother James was the one who identified the bodies, as the *Washington Post* reported.[88] Then, like the setup to the eighties TV show *Full House,* James moved in to help Joe (then in the US Senate) raise his two boys. According to Hunter Biden's memoir, years later, Uncle James flew to LA, checked a drug-addled Hunter out of the hotel where he was staying, and checked him into a rehab facility.[89] Uncle James's business dealings over the years have been questionable, but he handled his uncle role like a real mensch.

Then again, enabling Hunter hasn't helped anybody—including Hunter. Putting aside Hunter's affair with his dead brother's widow and his other personal indiscretions, there is no doubt that Hunter traded on his dad's name and influence. A 2022 NBC News analysis of Hunter Biden's laptop hard drive showed that "From 2013 through 2018 Hunter Biden and his company brought in about $11 million via his roles as an attorney and a board member with a Ukrainian firm accused of bribery and his work with a Chinese businessman now accused of fraud."[90] Ask yourself: would Hunter *Smith*, with expertise similar to Hunter Biden's, have been so well compensated by a Ukrainian gas company? It's highly unlikely. In his memoir, Hunter Biden acknowledges that his last name was a "coveted credential" and that the Ukrainian firm Burisma "considered my last name like gold."[91] Simply put, this situation stinks to high heaven.

The Hunter Biden scandal barely made a dent in the 2020 presidential campaign (for various reasons, both understandable and not). One reason it didn't was that no definitive proof existed that Joe Biden was "the big guy" that Hunter Biden's former business partner said (in an email) would get a 10 percent cut of a sketchy proposed deal. But I suspect there was another reason. Biden's predecessor, Donald Trump, who was constantly mired in scandals and controversies (including those involving his own family business), raised the bar for what kind of behavior was newsworthy, much less scandalous.

The Trump Family

Donald Trump's financial scandals and nepotistic familial conflicts of interest are too numerous to thoroughly delve into here (consider China fast-tracking sixteen trademarks for Ivanka Trump's companies while her dad was president—just one of many curious events that could fill an entire book[92]). After Nordstrom announced it would stop selling Ivanka Trump's clothing line and accessories in 2017, Donald Trump took to Twitter to criticize her treatment,[93] and presidential aide Kellyanne Conway publicly urged Americans to "Go buy Ivanka's stuff." According to the *Washington Post*, sales of Ivanka's products then exploded.[94]

The Trump scandals are qualitatively different from other scandals, partly because Trump's children were intimately involved in his business and partly because Trump named his daughter Ivanka and her husband, Jared Kushner, to be *official* White House advisors. According to the *Boston Globe*, "While serving in the Trump White House, Ivanka and Kushner did indeed leverage their positions to bolster their profits. Like Trump, neither of them had fully divested from their businesses, and Kushner sold his stake in one of his businesses only after it directly benefited from the tax bill that his father-in-law signed into law."[95]

And the conflicts of interest didn't end when Trump reluctantly left office. "Six months after leaving the White House, Trump's son-in-law Jared Kushner (Ivanka's husband) secured a $2 billion investment from a fund led by the Saudi crown prince, a close ally during the Trump administration, despite objections from the fund's advisors about the merits of the deal," reported the *New York Times*.[96] This resembled a payback, since "Mr. Kushner played a leading role inside the Trump administration defending Crown Prince Mohammed after U.S. intelligence agencies concluded that he had approved the 2018 killing and dismemberment of Jamal Khashoggi, a Saudi columnist for the *Washington Post* and resident of Virginia who had criticized the kingdom's rulers."[97]

Another example among many: in 2020, a group called the Campaign Legal Center filed a complaint alleging that the Trump campaign laundered hundreds of millions of campaign dollars through shell companies started by Kushner and other close Trump allies, "making it virtually impossible for the public to know how the money was spent."[98] In 2022, the FEC once again deadlocked along party lines, which meant they decided against taking action on it.

Again, the allegations leveled at Trump and his family are too numerous to litigate here. To paraphrase a line from former Trump aide Steve Bannon, by flooding the zone with shit, Trump has made it hard to zero in on any one of his many scandals.

Through it all, Trump has lived a life of privilege and conspicuous consumption. I mean, if you own a gold toilet, I think that says it all. Even when he was bankrupt, he acted like the king of the world (and his family acted like royalty). Nobody is better at faking it till he makes it or finding ways to fully leverage every opportunity to live a glamorous life, often on somebody else's dime. As the next chapter will demonstrate, the Donald isn't alone in excelling at this particular skill (even if he is at the top of the list).

$ $ $

So far, we have discussed why rich people tend to run for office (and get elected), as well as why elected people tend to almost always get richer. We also talked about how politicians use their perch to help enrich their families and—in some cases—build dynasties. Our next chapter looks at one of the main reasons that politicians are desperate to hold on to power, and why they are so reluctant to relinquish it: the lifestyle.

Chapter 6

The Lifestyle: Living Large

It's very expensive to be me.

—Anna Nicole Smith[1]

So you want to be rich and cable news famous? Even for the winners, political campaigns can be a very unglamorous experience that involves eating corndogs at public fairs and attending pancake breakfasts at the local Ruritan club. Then, upon winning, they are greeted by a public and a press who are more critical than adoring. It's easy to see how a politician who grew up on a steady diet of images of John F. Kennedy and the Camelot myth might suppose that he has earned the chance to revel in the glamour. These politicians are especially susceptible to the temptation of living above their means. For some people, being wealthy isn't primarily about having a big bank account; it's about the bling.

Whether you blame family pressure or lust for a better lifestyle, former Virginia governor Bob McDonnell (R-VA) fell prey to both. Once considered a political rising star, McDonnell's career crashed and burned when his wife asked a political donor (the chief executive of a dietary supplement manufacturer) to purchase an expensive Rolex watch so she could then give it to her husband. The donor also spent $15,000 to pay for catering at McDonnell's daughter's wedding.[2]

What always interested me about the story was the sense that this happened because the McDonnells aspired to live a lavish lifestyle that exceeded their financial grasp (something non-politicians also often struggle with). "We are broke," Maureen McDonnell lamented to a staffer via email after her husband told her she couldn't buy an Oscar de la Renta dress for his December 2009 inauguration ball. We "have an unconscionable amount in credit card debt already, and this Inaugural is killing us!!"[3] she wrote. At what should have been one of the happiest times of their lives, McDonnell's wife was worried about not being able to afford a designer dress.

In 2014, McDonnell was indicted and found guilty of eleven corruption-related charges. He was looking at a prison sentence when, in 2016, the US Supreme Court unanimously overturned the conviction—not that they exonorated him, exactly. "There is no doubt that this case is distasteful; it may be worse than that," Chief Justice John Roberts wrote. "But our concern is not with tawdry tales of Ferraris, Rolexes, and ball gowns. It is instead with the broader legal implications of the government's boundless interpretation of the federal bribery statute."[4]

Regardless, McDonnell's once-promising political career was over, and so was his marriage. The irony is that all they had to do was bide their time. "A former governor can make a lot of money,"[5] wrote the *Washington Examiner*'s Byron York at the time. "He can cash in on the influence he still has after leaving the statehouse. But if the indictment is correct, the McDonnells, in debt and wanting to drive Ferraris and wear Rolexes and play golf at swanky courses, couldn't wait, even four years, for the payoff."

We assume that *all* elected officials are rich. They're not. Despite half of the members of Congress being millionaires, almost a quarter have a negative net worth, as *Roll Call* reported.[6] And it's not just backbenchers who are members of this "fake it till you make it" caucus. As recently as 2016, Representative Debbie Wasserman Schultz (D-FL)—a member of Congress since 2004 who served as chair of the Democratic National Committee—had an estimated net worth of zero.[7] And as recently as 2017—the same year he was critically wounded after being shot on a baseball field—House Majority Leader Steve Scalise (R-LA) had a net worth of -*$232,501.*[8] According to *Business Insider*, the poorest member of Congress currently is Representative August Pfluger, a Republican from Texas whose net worth is -$2,000,002 (now there's a man who knows about deficits). But not to worry: If he carries his lunch to work and saves all of his $174,000 salary, he will have that debt paid off in no time!

And even though most members of Congress and governors are well off, they are rubbing shoulders with people much richer than they are. It's natural to want to have what your friends have—and (if you don't keep it in check) to want to live above your means. "In my view, there is an expectation by the public that our senior public leaders (governors, senators, especially presidents) 'look the part,'" one former political operative with ties to McDonnell told me. "We have this weird and paradoxical desire to see dignified and almost regal politicians, who of course also need to possess a personal touch. So wouldn't there be almost an expectation that the governor of the Commonwealth...be appropriately dressed, feted, and enhanced by some sort of demi-regal aura?"

I'm not trying to make excuses for McDonnell, but I do think it's helpful to explore explanations for this type of behavior. It's entirely possible for someone to seek public office for the right reasons but then become seduced by the lifestyle. On one hand, you have tremendous power and lots of yes-men to inflate your ego and create a sense of entitlement. On the other hand, you are now rubbing elbows with political donors and other elites who are wealthier and more cultured than you are. Not everyone is susceptible to the temptations, but you can see how one ethical compromise leads to another. You can begin to rationalize that you (or your family) deserve the best. That you've earned it.

This rationalization is perfectly understandable. It's also morally bankrupt and corrupt. And it's also one of the reasons that many normal Americans rightly believe politicians are using their perch to benefit themselves. Decades of this sort of behavior have created a low-grade sense that the game of politics is rigged. Rarely do any of these examples capture the public's imagination the way that a sex scandal might. Instead, what we see is a slow accretion of evidence that gradually erodes trust in our elected leaders.

$$$

A more recent, if less dramatic, example involves Governor Kristi Noem (R-SD). Noem took flak in 2022 for allegedly influencing the approval of her daughter's application for a real estate appraiser license, as the AP reported.[9] Then she used an official state airplane on separate occasions to attend her son's prom and help her daughter make wedding preparations.[10] It takes around five hours to drive across South Dakota (assuming you never stop), so the use of an airplane is incredibly helpful. Although the state ethics board ultimately dismissed a complaint lodged against Noem for questionable air travel, the question remains: Should taxpayers pay for trips that are largely personal in nature?

One of my old bosses might know the answer. At the beginning of this book, I discussed how I got involved in politics. But I skipped past how I went from managing a Roy Rogers restaurant in Frederick, Maryland, to working at a conservative nonprofit in Arlington, Virginia. I omitted the link between the two. In 1998, a young and exciting Republican named Alex Mooney was running for Maryland State Senate in the Frederick area. I volunteered to help with his campaign, and he immediately hired me to be his campaign manager (which involved everything from writing speeches to driving him around the district).

Four years later, my now wife managed his 2002 reelection campaign. Mooney won that race, too, but he lost a subsequent election. After he was elected chairman of the Maryland Republican Party, he moved to neighboring West Virginia and ran for Congress. Indeed, he is my congressman as I write this. That, in and of itself, is an interesting feat, but here's the tie-in to this book's theme: Mooney might not be rich, but (according to reports) he rolls like he is.

In 2021, the Office of Congressional Ethics (OCE) presented evidence that Mooney used campaign funds for food and family vacations. What is more, in his interview with the OCE, Mooney "stated that he feels justified in charging meals to the campaign any time there are constituents at the location he happens to choose to eat at that day."[11] In May 2022, the OCE found that Mooney took his family to the Ritz-Carlton in Aruba in March 2021 and that this trip was paid for by a direct mail fundraising firm to which Mooney had "significant personal ties."[12] There was also the sense that his family treated congressional staff like personal servants. "When the Mooneys were unable to watch their dog Skipper, for instance, they asked a former aide to drive Skipper from their home in Charles Town, W.Va., to a relative's home in Bethesda, Md.," reported the *New York Times*.[13] "I think the understanding is: If you work on the campaign, you also work for the Mooney family," one former staffer told the OCE.[14] "You were at their beck and call for anything, even though you got [an] official salary as well."[15] (In a statement, Mooney's campaign said there was "no improper connection between any gift and any official action by the Congressman" and that Mooney "flatly rejects the OCE's allegations of evidence tampering and false statements.")

Regardless of the merits of this specific case, it's possible for politicians to use the perks of office to live a luxurious lifestyle that is otherwise beyond their means, regardless of whether they personally are getting rich. There are numerous perks that come with the job, including access to both taxpayer dollars and campaign cash.

Perhaps my personal experience will give you a sense of how pervasive this phenomenon is. Fifteen years after working for Mooney, my wife consulted for Scott Pruitt, then the attorney general of Oklahoma (a job for which he reimbursed himself nearly $65,000 from his two campaigns).[16]

As you may recall, Donald Trump tapped Pruitt in late 2016 to head the Environmental Protection Agency (EPA). During his tenure, he was embroiled in numerous scandals (including the use of private and military planes). One offense involved having EPA staffers reach out to Chick-fil-A's CEO about letting Pruitt's wife become a franchise owner. While living in DC, Pruitt also lived essentially rent-free at an apartment owned by a lobbyist. According to CNN, he was charged just $50 a night—only on the nights he stayed—and the landlord still had a hard time collecting![17] (For what it's worth, Pruitt also had such a weird obsession with Ritz-Carlton hand lotion that he sent his staff out to track it down,[18] and he was a frequent diner at the French restaurant Le Diplomate in Washington, DC, as *Vox* reported. Remember, this is a conservative from Oklahoma who worked for "Mr. Populist" Donald Trump.)

$$$

Once upon a time, the legal standard for alimony was "the lifestyle to which one has become accustomed." For many politicians, losing an election or an appointment must feel worse than going through a divorce because of losing the lifestyle to which *they* have grown accustomed. The good news for them (as we will learn later) is that they can usually continue to enjoy many of the perks of elected office. One of those fringe benefits involves getting to take (in some cases, family) vacations that are paid for or subsidized by campaign coffers because these vacations double as work trips. Whether you're a politician who is hosting the event or an ex-pol turned lobbyist who is attending the event, you'll be treated to a great time—on someone else's dime.

Below are some examples of fund-raising events advertised in 2022 by the National Republican Senatorial Committee. Rest assured, the Democrats roll just as lavishly—probably more so. Please note that I have omitted the names and contact information of staffers. Additionally, I have added some quotes and commentary about these exclusive destinations.

Senator Marsha Blackburn (TN)

September 18–19, 2022

Sea Island Overnight Retreat at the Cloister at Sea Island

The Cloister at Sea Island's Pinterest account describes it thusly: "Tucked away on a private island, it's spacious, inside & out, with expansive rooms & suites. Forbes Five-Star accommodations, but you'll feel right at home, like family."

Senator John Boozman (AR)

Sunday, October 9, 2022

Family Supper in Kiawah benefiting ARK PAC with Special
    Guests TBA

Kiawah Island, SC

The Town of Kiawah's website describes it as "An oasis of untouched natural beauty and renowned hospitality for those seeking a retreat into adventure and luxury. Enjoy our perfectly preserved maritime forests, sand dunes, and marshes where turtles, whitetail deer, and seabirds abound."[19]

Senator John Boozman

March 11–13, 2022

Palm Beach Weekend benefiting ARKPAC

Palm Beach, FL

Senator John Boozman

Friday, September 9–Sunday, September 11, 2022

Weekend at Walt Disney World to Benefit Wild &
    Wonderful PAC

The Grand Floridian Resort and Spa, 4401 Floridian Way, Lake
    Buena Vista, FL 32830

Suggested Contribution: $5,000 PAC/$2,000 Personal

Senator Tom Cotton (AR)

Friday, November 11–Sunday, November 13, 2022

Fall Retreat with Senator Cotton

Salamander Resort and Spa

Middleburg, VA

Host: $10,000

PAC Sponsor: $5,000

PAC Attend (Up to Two People): $3,000

Individual: $1,500 or $2,500 for Couple/Family

According to its website: "Salamander Resort & Spa is a timeless destination, located in historic Middleburg, Virginia. This quintessential town is steeped in equestrian traditions, and easily accessible to Washington, D.C. The Forbes Five-Star resort is the ultimate place of discovery and the epitome of luxury, combining artfully designed facilities with unparalleled experiences, all resting on 340-acres framed by the Blue Ridge Mountains, lush vineyards, and horse farms."[20]

Senator Ted Cruz (TX)

Monday, September 19, 2022

An Evening of Pinot & Cigars with Sen. Ted Cruz hosted by
    John Kingston: 6:30 pm

Location: Home of Hon. Jack Kingston & Alexandra Kendrick
    address upon RSVP

Cost: $2,500 Host or $500 Attend Personal, Trade Assoc. or
    Partnership PAC

(Pinot?)

Senator Deb Fischer (NE)

October 14–15, 2022

Fall Retreat at the Camelback Resort, Scottsdale, AZ

Friday, 7:00 pm dinner at the Lincoln Steakhouse

Saturday, 7:00 pm dinner at El Chorro

$3,000 PAC or $1,500 personal

"Located at the base of Camelback Mountain in Scottsdale, Arizona, Scottsdale Camelback Resort provides a wide range of onsite activities and amenities—and you won't find a more perfect home base hotel for shopping and dining in nearby Old Town Scottsdale, world-class golf, and exploring the beauty and natural wonders of the Sonoran Desert."[21]

Senator Cynthia Lummis (WY)

Sat. Aug. 6–Sun. Aug. 7, 2022

Weekend in the Tetons, Jackson Hole, Wyoming

"Grand Teton National Park is one of the most spectacular, awe-inspiring places in America. Occupying a majority of the Jackson Hole valley, the park is home to massive mountains, pristine lakes and rivers and abundant wildlife."[22]

$ $ $

Keep in mind that this is just a small sampling of events that were advertised by one political party during one year.

If you're a politician who wants to travel to one of these destinations, you simply make that your fund-raiser. Sure, there's some business involved, but this business largely involves attending a party with lobbyist pals where you are the guest of honor. Okay, sometimes before the party you also play a round of golf with the top-tier donors (some of whom may be lobbyists who are former members of Congress). If you like golf, you build that into the event.

But say you don't want to go on a posh or ritzy vacation. Maybe you represent a rural area and are more of a simple guy or gal. That's okay. I didn't even mention all the events that were built around pheasant shoots, an Idaho potato fest, or something called "Rodeo Weekend" in Las Vegas.

Or say you don't want to leave Washington, DC. Again, no problem. There are events centered around local sports teams (the Baltimore

Orioles vs. the Washington Nationals), wine-tasting receptions, and happy hours. Want to go see your favorite rock band perform live? Have your campaign host an event in a box at a rock concert (which, of course, includes free parking and catering). There's really something for everyone.

$$\$\ \$\ \$$

Keep in mind that these "vacations" only account for political fund-raisers here in the United States. If you'd prefer your free five-star accommodations be international, you can do that, too, and call it part of the job.

According to OpenTheBooks.com, "Between 2017 and 2021, more than 500 congressmembers and their staff reported taking almost 8,200 trips paid for by about 700 third-party organizations."[23] This is a significant savings for would-be tourists. In 2013 alone, members of Congress received around $3.7 million worth of trips.[24]

As *USA Today* reported, Representative John Garamendi (D-CA) "had the most expensive itinerary of any lawmaker, taking nearly $70,000 worth of trips in 2013. His wife, Patricia, accompanied him on a $40,000 trip in February 2013 to South Sudan and Tanzania, organized by the aid group CARE and underwritten by the Bill and Melinda Gates Foundation."[25]

It's all legal, of course. In fact, according to the House Committee on Ethics, "House Members and employees may accept travel paid for by a foreign government under MECEA [Mutual Educational and Cultural Exchange Act] without Committee review."[26]

Free trips to exotic locations and opulent hotels aren't the only perks that come with one of those congressional lapel pins. You also get access to an exclusive gym (with a swimming pool) and (in the Senate) a hair salon. They also have private elevators and a subway underneath the Capitol. Each member also receives a Member's Representational Allowance (MRA), which includes each member's annual operating budget for their office (for example: staff salaries, supplies, mail, other expenses, and travel). In 2022, the average (mean) MRA for a House member was $1,509,219.[27] In addition to the ability to tap their MRA and fly free (for official business, of course), they also get free prime parking spots at DC airports—and an exclusive phone line to book air travel.

This book is about how the rich get elected and how the elected get rich. But the truth is that you don't have to have a huge bank account to live like a king. For many politicians, their normal lives consist of being treated like big shots, getting referred to as "The Honorable So-and-So," having a taxpayer-funded staff do their bidding, and getting to take free lavish vacations. It's easy to see why many working stiffs see this as nothing more than a racket. At the same time, it's also easy to understand why so many politicians become addicted to the perks of public office.

Is it any wonder that people elected to Congress never want to leave?

Chapter 7

Latte Liberals: Rich and Privileged with Influence

Was it a millionaire who said, "Imagine no possessions"?

—Elvis Costello[1]

You don't have to be megarich to be removed from the average person's experience and seek to impose self-serving rules on others that you don't live up to yourself. Today's American Left includes one group that is richer, in the sense of being more famous, powerful, and influential, than almost anyone, including the Democratic Party's establishment. They're known as "the Squad."

That's the nickname embraced by four members of Congress—Representatives Alexandra Ocasio-Cortez (D-NY), Ilhan Omar (D-MN), Ayanna Pressley (D-MA), and Rashida Tlaib (D-MI)—who were elected in the 2018 "blue wave" that course-corrected Donald Trump's 2016 win. And in adopting the millennial-era moniker for a young women's circle of supportive friends, they signaled their position as up-and-comers in Congress. The nickname also provided convenient shorthand for white-bread talking heads on right-leaning outlets to more easily rail against their politics, unwittingly providing grist for the foursome's social media and fund-raising machines.

The Squad had fresh electoral wins and the critical ability to back one another up. But most significantly, this quartet of young women of color has given a new voice to the progressive avant-garde of the Democratic Party. Sometimes, this activism feels more like opportunism. Such was the case in 2021 when Ocasio-Cortez (aka AOC) attended the Met Gala, a posh New York City event where the price of a seat starts at $35,000.[2] An event that included "plant-based dishes from 10 rising New York chefs and featured a performance by Justin Bieber," as the *Washington Post* reported.[3] Ocasio-Cortez also sat at the same table as *Vogue's* editor-in-chief, Anna Wintour, the *New York Times* noted.[4] But that wasn't what turned heads and raised eyebrows; it was her white dress with the words "Tax the rich" written in red on the back. AOC "wore a white gown by Brother Vellies, splashed with the political slogan across the back (the bottom curve of the *C* in 'rich' nicely mirrored the tulle hem)," as *Vogue* described it.[5] "The outfit was finished by a pair of red shoes from Brother Vellies, with long laces and bright flowers along the heel."[6]

She certainly sent a message, but perhaps not exactly the one she intended. Indeed, this symbolic moment underscores how far removed today's Democrats are from being the party of the working class. As conservative writer Andrew Ferguson put it, "It's hard to imagine Eleanor Roosevelt posing in a backless number at the Met Gala."[7] And while it might be easy to dismiss Ocasio-Cortez 's actions as a young, progressive star indulging in harmless showmanship, such stunts feed the sense that our public servants are indulging in hypocrisy and taking advantage of the system.

The Squad (with Ocasio-Cortez as its titular head) constitutes an influential, if small, wing of the Democratic Party. They now carry the philosophical mantle that was advanced by Senator Bernie Sanders (I-VT) in his 2016 and 2020 bids for the Democratic nomination for president. Sanders's campaigns were electorally quixotic but impactful in igniting interest in some of the elements of democratic socialism that

Democrats had been flirting with—things like single-payer health care, student debt cancellation, and a universal basic income.

But despite the apparent energy from his campaign (mainly from the younger and more ideological supporters), Sanders had been little more than a voice during his time in Congress—first in the House and then in the Senate. If democratic socialism ever reaches its promised land, Sanders may be remembered as a John the Baptist figure: a curmudgeonly forerunner who survived on locusts and wild honey while ushering in a different, younger savior.

$ $ $

In many ways, the Squad's moment arrived in 2020 when the COVID-19 pandemic upended an economy humming along steadily under President Donald Trump's policies (if not his rhetoric). As white-collar workers shifted to setting up home offices, rocking Zoom meetings in shirtsleeves and pajama pants, and puzzling over what to do with two dozen Amazon boxes, hourly workers wondered when they'd see their next paycheck. Retail workers, restaurant workers, and other clock punchers found that their "nonessential" jobs were reduced or that they were furloughed.

This squeeze wasn't temporary, either. As the pandemic raged through March and April 2020, no one knew how long businesses would remain shuttered or what reopening would look like. People across the political spectrum called for government infusions of cash into the economy through direct assistance, expanded unemployment benefits, and business payroll loans.

Some Democrats, led by the Squad, called for more than simple assistance programs, insisting on regulations to protect workers who were living paycheck to paycheck. These policies included an eviction moratorium, which prevented landlords from evicting tenants whose rent payments were in arrears.

It wasn't a bad idea as a short-term policy proposal. But it also echoes a pet issue for the Left: the natural conflict between landlords and tenants. The history of organizing tenants is about as old as the history of landlords. But since the 1970s, there has been a proliferation of organizers in America forming official "tenant unions" to consolidate renters' power, both within local government and against landowners. They unabashedly use the same playbook and rhetoric as organized labor, too. The Tenants Union of Washington State's website includes a manifesto that pooh-poohs property rights, declaring that "when conflict arises between tenants' needs and owners' profits, the basic need for affordable decent housing must take priority over the economic interests of the landowners."[8]

The Richmond, Virginia, tenant union website manages to channel both the Industrial Workers of the World and Mr. Spock from *Star Trek*: "We believe that our city's housing system should serve the needs of the many, rather than to increase profits for a few."[9] And one of the oldest organizations, the San Francisco Tenants Union (SFTU—although the acronym STFU might better describe how they feel about landlords), minces no words in defining tenant advocacy as part of a broader movement: "The fight for tenants' rights is inseparable from the broader fight against structural oppression based on race, national origin, immigration status, family composition, gender, sexual orientation, age, disability or economic status."[10]

It makes sense that organizing tenants would have similar beats as organizing workers, doesn't it? If you've worked in enough places, chances are you've had at least one jerk for a boss. And if you have lived in enough places, you've undoubtedly had at least one jerk for a landlord. Anyone who tells you what to do can come off as a jerk (whether at home or work, and whether you pay *them* or they pay *you*). No wonder the Left has willing participants when they seek to organize against these people.

After the onset of COVID-19, tenant unions organized rent strikes and other actions to force landlords and policymakers into leniency with those who had trouble making rent payments. And they found willing, natural allies in the Squad. In April 2020, Omar announced a bill to cancel rent and home mortgage payments during the pandemic,[11] with her fellow progressives eagerly jumping on as co-sponsors. The bill did not pass, but the resolute Squad reintroduced the idea in March 2021, pushing the rent/mortgage cancellation to April 2022.

Squad members were adamant about the need for relief, and Pressley was especially vocal. "It's absolutely time to #CancelRent,"[12] she declared in a tweet in early May 2020. A few weeks later, she doubled down: "11 days until rent is due again. It's past time to cancel rent & mortgage payments."[13] The tweets calling for rent cancellation continued through the bill's reintroduction in March 2021.

Notably, the bill also sought to create a fund to repay landlords for missed rent. For a couple of Squad members, this meant more than just a dose of pragmatism to help win over more moderate colleagues. According to financial disclosures, both Pressley and Tlaib took in rental income in 2020 and 2021. Tlaib reported between $15,000 and $50,000 in rental income in each of those years;[14] Pressley reported $5,000 to $15,000 in rental income in both 2019 and 2020,[15] followed by an increase of up to $117,500 in 2021.[16] That increase came after purchasing a second rental property in May 2021—a transaction consummated two months after she and her fellow Squad members reintroduced their "cancel rent" legislation with its protection for landlords.

Pressley and Tlaib are certainly not the only members of Congress who make some side money on rental properties. They are also not the only left-leaning politicians who spew sanctimonious calls for policies on behalf of the "common man," the "working man," "working people," "working families," or any other buzzword meant to conjure up images of the poor and lower middle class—all while sitting in a position of relative privilege. Or, to use a more descriptive label, one might call them "latte liberals."

Latte, Anyone?

The name has nothing to do with caffeine or steamed milk. The term evolved from the pejorative "limousine liberal"—ironically, a term popularized by Democratic candidate Mario Procaccino against Republican John Lindsay in a New York City mayoral primary, according to the *Wall Street Journal.*[17] (The incumbent Lindsay lost the GOP nomination but ran—and won—as a candidate for the Liberal Party.) The term has evolved to "latte liberal" to reflect changing attitudes about privilege and (maybe) the increase in gourmet coffee consumption (thanks, Starbucks)—not to mention our changing transportation options, thanks to the increasing prevalence of services like Uber and Lyft.

Despite its origins, the "limousine liberal" epithet came to label Democrats over the past fifty years. Plenty of wealthy Democrats existed before that time, but none who reasonably fit the label. President Franklin Delano Roosevelt came from old money. Still, his early domestic policies primarily focused on combating the poverty and economic challenges brought on by the Great Depression (with debatable efficacy). His creation of the Tennessee Valley Authority and emphasis on rural electrification projects ensured that he could not be accused of letting his New York roots obscure his vision for the entire country.

President John F. Kennedy and his brother Robert saw their political careers cut short by assassins' bullets (the actual number of assassins is in doubt) before they could push progressive legislation along the lines of the Great Society, so neither was tarnished with the "limousine liberal" label. (Senator Ted Kennedy was the only Kennedy brother who lived to see a backlash against rich liberals living in ivory towers. It reached its peak as irate white Boston parents protested and threw tomatoes at him in 1978 when he spoke in favor of Boston's school busing program to promote racial integration in public education.)[18]

However, Roosevelt and the Kennedys did represent an idea that has driven much of the party's messaging for almost a century: noblesse oblige. Noblesse oblige is the concept that the most fortunate have a societal obligation to care for the less fortunate. Taken in the best possible light, it's a reminder that everyone should share a little bit of their success with those around them. It can also be a patronizing statement of arrogance: a Rudyard Kipling–esque call for society's betters to care for incapable lower classes, as a parent might care for a toddler. (Given the choice, I'd prefer a world where the rich see it as their duty to be nice to us little people.) Ironically, this noblesse oblige ethos sometimes results in the uber-rich being friendlier to us little people than their counterparts who had to claw their way to the top. Representative Sheila Jackson Lee (D-TX), for example, is one of the poorer members of Congress, according to OpenSecrets,[19] yet consistently ranks number one in the category of "meanest"[20] Congress member, according to a ranking in the *Washingtonian*. You never hear that about Mitt Romney.

After the days of the Roosevelts and Kennedys, Democrats retained their populist appeal with the working class. Their success in this endeavor came not from patrician families from New York and Massachusetts, but rather in the form of sons of the South. Between JFK's election in 1960 and Barack Obama's in 2008, Democrats' rare White House victories came with a Southerner leading the ticket: Lyndon Johnson (Texas), Jimmy Carter (Georgia), and Bill Clinton (Arkansas). Such candidates would speak with authority about the plight of rural, working-class whites, while still positioned as the most progressive and compassionate candidates for working-class minority voters. It was such a tried-and-true strategy that in 1992, the then candidate and Arkansas governor Bill Clinton doubled down by selecting another Southerner, Tennessee senator Al Gore, as his vice president.

Since Clinton left office (and Gore barely lost his bid in 2000), Democrats have moved away from Southern candidates. (Meanwhile, the South has gotten steadily more Republican, with a few exceptions.) As

Democrats nominated (and found success) with candidates (and messages) who appealed to college-educated, white-collar, urban, and suburban voters, their distance from rural voters created a natural disconnect between their rhetoric and reality. Democrats still claimed to be the party of the working class, but they couldn't be the party of the *whole* working class.

As Democratic power has calcified in the urban and suburban districts, and Republicans have gained footholds with some working-class voters, the latte liberal label remains potent today. This phenomenon poses a serious electoral problem for a Democratic Party trying to cobble together a majority coalition. For generations, the Republican Party was perceived as being the party of the rich. In recent years, however, a reordering has taken place; this perception has started to reverse itself. The Democratic Party has become a party of highly educated and privileged "woke" young progressives. This transformation has led to an avalanche of working-class whites *and* minorities moving to the GOP. The Democratic Party had long banked on the triumph of identity politics, but they assumed that race, not class status, would be the litmus test. This trend toward joining the GOP is devastating for Democrats who assumed that demographics are destiny and that Hispanics ("the coalition of the ascendant," as some put it) would inexorably lead to electoral triumph. Instead, progressivism seems most attractive to wealthy and highly educated whites. You know, the kinds of people who never stop talking about the damage your gas-guzzling SUV is doing to mother earth. The dirty little secret is that they don't always practice what they preach. Want to see this hypocrisy on full display? Attend a climate summit.

Climate Change Hypocrisy

In late 2021, the United Nations convened a climate change summit in Glasgow, Scotland. President Biden was one of several world leaders who spoke out on the need for impactful change to halt humanity's devastating effects on the global environment. Beyond political leaders, the summit welcomed VIPs, including the CEOs of some of the world's biggest companies. Jeff Bezos, Bill Gates, and Arnold Schwarzenegger (speaking of rich politicians) flew in for the event.

But they didn't exactly fly coach. The climate change conference welcomed more than one hundred private jets, as *Forbes* noted.[21]

Environmental activists will admonish us to drive less, recycle more, reduce waste, and eat less meat to whittle down our carbon footprint. That's all good advice, of course. But it's laughable when the preaching comes from those not heeding their own advice. When asked about how his private jet and penchant for hamburgers affect his carbon footprint, Gates pointed to his large monetary investments in green tech. A fair, but unconvincing, point.

Maybe business titans get a pass, since we expect them to be a little shady. But it rings especially hollow when government officials spew that trash. John Kerry—the former senator from Massachusetts, former secretary of state, and the Democrats' 2004 nominee for president—now fills his days as the "special presidential envoy for climate." It's a new position: a Biden administration creation intended to highlight the current president's firm stance on the threat of climate change. As part of his role, Kerry flies on commercial or military aircraft for official trips to avoid rolling up to a climate event in the lap of luxury. Bad optics.

His family's jet is a different story.

If you followed the 2004 election, you'd recall how Kerry apparently found it difficult to forge a connection with common voters between his enjoyment of windsurfing and his choice of Swiss cheese on Philly cheesesteaks. Kerry had also married into wealth when he tied the knot with Teresa Heinz, the widow of his former Senate colleague John Heinz. To no one's surprise, the family owns a private jet operated by an aviation company that Teresa Heinz Kerry owns.

Also unsurprising: that plane is a big polluter. According to a Fox News report using data from a flight tracking service, Kerry's plane belched three hundred metric tons of carbon into the air in the first eighteen months after he took the job as special presidential envoy for climate.[22]

It's one thing for a celebrity or business leader to tut-tut about the need to do more for the climate. Kerry is a government official, and though his role is more symbolic (like an ambassador), he is still part of an administration that has sought to curtail domestic fossil fuel production. Can the Biden administration enjoy any credibility on climate policy when their special presidential envoy for climate has a private plane with a carbon footprint that would give Sasquatch a complex?

Credibility becomes a real problem when environmental policies carry real-world costs. For example, suppose a lack of domestic energy production makes the price of gas tick upward. The working class is directly affected when they fill up their family cars or indirectly affected when they purchase groceries shipped by truck. If the cost of heating oil rises, so too do the winter heating bills of northern homes. Merry Christmas, Bedford Falls!

Are these sacrifices necessary to halt catastrophic climate change? Maybe. But you simply can't fly to a climate conference in a private jet one day, tell someone that running their cars and heating their homes will get more expensive the next day, and then expect your message to be received with a straight face.

Housing Hypocrisy

Environmental activists often overlap with urbanites who call for greater population density and fewer suburbs, typically when calling for "affordable housing." More density means more available housing, which drives down costs and makes it more affordable. The environmental overlap makes some sense, too. The closer people live to their jobs in urban centers, as the thought goes, the less they will drive. Public transportation would be easier to build and maintain, too.

Opponents of this new urbanism vision run the ideological gamut: from Republicans worried about who would move into their lily-white neighborhoods to moderate Democrats with a sense of community who enjoy the comfort of the suburban setting and fear change. Speaking at a conference of architects, former president Barack Obama called out both ends of the spectrum: "The most liberal communities in the country aren't that liberal when it comes to affordable housing," he admonished.[23]

The data backs him up. An October 2020 survey commissioned by the real estate company Redfin showed a majority of Americans (56 percent) supported policies that encouraged more housing construction, but only 27 percent supported policies that would increase population density in their own neighborhoods.[24] You may recognize this phenomenon as "NIMBY" or "not in my backyard"—the idea that a community may support a policy as long as its effects don't hit too close to home. Even the liberal bastion of Manhattan is not immune; in 2020 a group of Upper West Siders banded together to form an organization to preserve their community and "advance safer and more compassionate policies regarding New Yorkers who are struggling with homelessness, mental illness, and drug addiction."[25] The city then promptly kicked out thousands of homeless people from hotel shelters on the Upper West Side.[26]

In Congress, Representative Maxine Waters (D-CA) has been a vocal advocate for many policies designed to address low-income housing, including a since-nixed provision in Biden's behemoth Build Back Better bill that would have encouraged local municipalities to quash zoning requirements and promote apartment buildings over single-family houses, according to *Bloomberg*.[27] In 2020, Waters's election opponent, Joe

Collins, criticized her for her own housing choice—a $6 million mansion that sits outside the district she represents in Congress.[28]

Student Debt Hypocrisy

But if the debate over housing policy remains focused on urban and suburban enclaves, another issue that excites the progressive wing of the Democratic party has squarely hit the mainstream: student debt.

The issue got fresh ink in August 2022 when President Biden announced that the federal government would forgive up to $10,000 in debt for each borrower making less than $125,000 per year.[29] But that decision was the consummation of years of discussion on the issue, which had gained traction in Bernie Sanders's campaigns and continued as a pet cause for the Squad and other progressives.

And why wouldn't it? After all, the campaigns of Sanders (and many progressive candidates) were largely fueled by younger, more ideologically driven supporters. Some were still in college. Some were recent grads trying to make it in society and struggling through their first difficult years of professional life. Either way, the college debt issue was deeply personal to the people providing the critical human energy that drove the campaigns.

The issue is also deeply personal to some members of Congress, who are either still paying off their loans or taking out loans for their children to attend school. According to financial disclosures reported by TheCollegeInvestor.com, that category includes three of the four original members of the Squad: Ocasio-Cortez, Omar, and Tlaib.[30] (The landlord gig must work well for Pressley.)

And let's be clear: a problem *does* exist. Amid skyrocketing tuition and other fees, costs to attend college have been climbing steadily for decades. *Forbes* reports that the average annual cost of a four-year college has risen from $10,231 in 1980 to $28,775 in 2019.[31] Meanwhile, bachelor's degrees have become highly valued culturally and viewed in many lines of work as a critical first step to securing a career (the way a high school diploma might have been viewed a few generations back). The Census Bureau found that the percentage of Americans over twenty-five years old with a bachelor's degree had increased from 30.4 percent to 37.9 percent from 2011 to 2021.[32] In 2000, that number was only 25.6 percent, and that was up from 17 percent in 1980.

And college has not been sold solely as a career development exercise. It is also sold as a continuation of personal development. College, many high school students are told, is as much a place to "find yourself" as it is a place to learn skills for your intended career.

If you combine drastically increasing costs with more people attending college, it's clear that our aggregate spending on higher education has exploded. Like many other acquisitions in America, we go into debt to pay for it. According to Federal Reserve data reported by NerdWallet, through the second quarter of 2022, America (as a country) owed $1.75 trillion in student loans.[33] (Note to the editors: Yes, that's trillion with a "t.") The average bachelor's degree recipient graduates with $28,950 in debt.[34] Thanks to ridiculously high interest rates, many loan recipients spend years paying down interest without ever touching the principal.

This stark reality has forced many to make tough choices about their higher education, choosing less-expensive schools, pursuing nontraditional education options (like starting in a community college or a certificate program), or opting for a lucrative career in a trade like carpentry or plumbing.

Opponents of debt cancellation point to these folks, or those who have already repaid their loans, as examples of the policy's inherent unfairness. And it's hard to argue with their logic. If some people realized that going into massive debt was a bad idea, should their tax dollars then be used to bail out other people without their same foresight?

Someone posed that question to Ocasio-Cortez during one of her

Instagram Stories updates just after the Biden administration announced their relief program: "How does canceling student debt help us who paid their loans?"

Ocasio-Cortez urged the commenter to "reject the scarcity mind-set that says doing something good for someone else comes at the cost of something for ourselves."[35]

Ocasio-Cortez has argued that the Biden program didn't push hard enough, telling the *Washington Post* she thought the $125,000 income cutoff should be abandoned ("especially for so many of the front-line workers") and that the amount of debt canceled should be up to $50,000 ("Canceling $50,000 in debt is where you make the real dent in inequality and the racial wealth gap").[36] For those scoring at home, AOC's financial disclosures reported up to $50,000 in student debt,[37] and her congressional salary is about $174,000.

Maybe student loan forgiveness didn't affect that Instagram commenter, but it sure may affect Ocasio-Cortez.

Student debt cancellation doesn't seem poised to affect colleges, either. Neither the Biden program nor the more-progressive calls to cancel more student debt (most of which is held by the federal government) include measures to address the ever escalating cost of college. Progressives like Ocasio-Cortez have called for reversals of Trump-era tax cuts to pay off student debt with higher taxes on businesses and high-income earners,[38] but none have called for taxes on the endowments that institutions like Harvard ($53 billion[39]) or Yale ($42 billion[40]) have tucked away. One might imagine that taxes or restrictions on the institutions driving student loans into the stratosphere would be an important issue for Democrats serious about handling the student debt crisis. Alas, 70 percent of political donations from the higher education industry have gone to Democrats over the past twenty years.[41] You don't have to be a heavily indebted PhD to know you don't bite the hand that feeds you.

Higher education isn't the only place where left-leaning politicians blur the lines between public and self-interest; it happens in lower education, too.

School Lockdown Hypocrisy

While many progressives are financially wealthy, progressive elites also enjoy tremendous power and privilege over the commanding heights of our society. This includes, but is not limited to, power over cultural institutions like academia, Hollywood and entertainment, and the news media. This creates a situation where many average Americans feel powerless. And while this asymmetric imbalance has generated much resentment, loss of control when it comes to our children generates even more. For many Americans, the COVID-19 pandemic was a wake-up call, as debates about K–12 education became especially contentious as parents sought to reopen schools after COVID-19-induced lockdowns.

As schools shut down and instituted remote learning in March and April 2020, it became glaringly apparent that virtual classrooms would not (and could not) replace in-person school on a large scale. Many parents, concerned about the quality of education their kids would receive, began pushing for their kids to return; however, teachers' unions and school administrators were understandably cautious.

The backlash against COVID-19 lockdowns and masking cannot be overestimated. Busy parents experiencing stress adjusting to a pandemic were pressed into service as homeschool teachers, while other parents were exposed to liberal indoctrination for the first time via Zoom classes. There was a strong sense in many parts of the nation that teachers' unions, an incredibly strong force within the Democratic Party, were using their political clout to keep schools closed much longer than was prudent or healthy. Too often, anyone who dared bring up the obvious consequences of sequestering students was accused of "wanting their babysitters back" or "not caring about teachers' lives."

But the problem didn't go away when schools finally reopened. Indeed, the anger is unlikely to abate any time soon, since the aftereffects will likely continue for decades. You can't blame everything on a stubborn refusal to reopen schools, but the pandemic did erase decades of progress in reading and math; as the *New York Times* reported, minority students were disproportionately harmed in the process, thus increasing inequality.[42]

But lower test scores weren't the only negative externality. According to a March 2022 report from the Centers for Disease Control and Prevention (CDC) on COVID-19, more than a third of high school students "reported they experienced poor mental health during the COVID-19 pandemic," with 44 percent saying they "persistently felt sad or hopeless during the past year."[43]

Managing a global pandemic is an all-hands-on-deck phenomenon that demands a bipartisan response. But over time, progressives became the COVID "hawks" and bore the brunt of the anti-lockdown backlash. As the pandemic wore on, parents grew increasingly angry about the shutdowns. Then, as students returned to school, some parents pushed to end mask mandates; once again, teachers and administrators fought back.

To complicate matters, behavior by liberals often conflicted with their own mandates. Usually, this hypocrisy was a twofer. Not only were progressives guilty of flouting their COVID policies, but their actions also demonstrated conspicuous consumption. For example, in November 2020, California governor Gavin Newsom, a Democrat, was photographed maskless and eating indoors at Napa Valley's French Laundry (a three-star Michelin restaurant). The hypocrisy was stunning. Newsom was breaking his own mandated COVID protocol to celebrate the birthday of a Sacramento lobbyist.[44] He was doing so at one of the nation's most luxurious, opulent, and exclusive restaurants. A typical meal there starts at $350. In 2019, a *New York Times* food critic described their dining experience: "The servers brought the gold-rimmed dish sets out and placed them down in unison. After lifting the egg tops and revealing the macaroni, they rained down a messy shower of black truffles, half on the food and half on the table, filling the air with perfume."[45]

Newsom was also in attendance at an even more over-the-top affair: the lavish November 2021 wedding of heiress and model Ivy Getty and photographer Tobias Alexander Engel in San Francisco. Amazingly, the wedding was officiated by then Speaker of the House Nancy Pelosi. Keep in mind that this wedding happened during the COVID-19 pandemic (when California mandated all teachers and students wear masks). According to *Vogue*, "Guests were asked to mask up before Speaker of the House Nancy Pelosi entered the room and took her position at the microphone,"[46] but photos from the event showed Pelosi hobnobbing maskless.[47]

Former president Barack Obama's sixtieth birthday party in August 2021 on Martha's Vineyard evoked a similar backlash. The event was supposedly "scaled back" due to the outbreak of COVID-19's Delta variant, but the star-studded list of attendees—including John Legend, Chrissy Teigen, Dwyane Wade, Gabrielle Union, Jay-Z, Beyoncé, Stephen Colbert, and Oprah Winfrey,[48] just to name a few of the most-prominent guests—drew attention and controversy. "The party crystallized the caricature of the Democratic Party that Joe Biden had to fight against in order to get elected," scolded Maureen Dowd. "It was as far from Flint and Scranton as you can imagine: an orgy of the 1 percent—private jets, Martha's Vineyard, limousine liberals and Hollywood whoring—complete with a meat-free menu."[49]

"We all love Beyoncé," former *Vogue* editor André Leon Talley said. "But people have so many things to worry about with Covid, voting rights, climate warming. People are afraid of being evicted from their homes. And the Obamas are in Marie Antoinette, tacky, let-them-eat-cake mode. They need to remember their humble roots."[50]

School Choice Hypocrisy

Examples of rank hypocrisy certainly didn't help as anger over the lockdowns resulted in closer scrutiny of curriculum. Now taking on a larger role in their children's education, moms and dads began questioning what students were being taught. National media discussion focused on the debate over critical race theory (CRT). Depending on whom you speak with, CRT is either an unvarnished, warts-and-all view of American history or a deeply race-oriented educational philosophy that directly blames white students for all crimes ever committed in history. The disparate definitions made the CRT debate perfect fodder for Fox News *and* MSNBC. In Virginia, the off-year 2021 gubernatorial race was probably over when Democratic candidate Terry McAuliffe—the former governor who won in a landslide in 2013—said, "I don't think parents should be telling schools what they should teach."[51] He lost to a very wealthy first-time Republican candidate named Glenn Youngkin.

Underlying all of this was tension between the completely legitimate interest parents have (and arguably, always should have had) in their child's education, and the legitimate concerns teachers had about the integrity of their classrooms (concerning both health and academics). Things got chippy during school board meetings, resulting in shouting matches and occasional fisticuffs.

When a discussion bumps up against irreconcilable differences, sometimes you just shake hands, agree to disagree, and walk away. But what happens when one side can't simply say "good day" and leave the chat? That's the conundrum in which many parents found themselves. Parents certainly have leeway to opt for religious, private, or homeschooling, but often only if they can afford the great personal expense of tuition and time.

For years, school choice advocates have called for policies that free up more options for parents through tax rebates or vouchers. If you're going to pay taxes for education, their reasoning goes, those taxes should help pay for your kid's education.

Democrats need organized labor (in general), and they need well-organized teachers' unions (specifically) to win elections. So you can imagine that they aren't thrilled with tax money going to non-unionized private schools over unionized public schools: parental choice and education quality be damned.

But Democrats' opposition to school choice, private schools, and charter schools only extends to *other* people's children.[52]

During the 2020 primary, Democratic candidates fell all over themselves opposing school choice. The Cato Institute documented some of the more egregious and hypocritical examples. For example, then South Bend mayor Pete Buttigieg (a product of private schools) claimed that voucher programs hurt public schools;[53] his husband taught at a private Montessori school that accepts vouchers.[54] Senator Elizabeth Warren (D-MA) released an education plan that promised more funding for public schools, while cracking down on "efforts to divert"[55] public funding to private and charter schools. Warren sent her son to private schools after fifth grade—a fact she conveniently forgot when questioned by a parent advocate who wanted the same opportunity. The senator replied, "No, my children went to public schools."[58] But Warren is far from the only member of the upper chamber to send her kids to private schools. According to the Heritage Foundation, "49 percent of members of the Senate send or have sent at least one of their children to a private school."[57] It's just not something they want to admit.

During his Pennsylvania Senate race against Republican nominee/TV personality Mehmet Oz, the tatted-up and dressed-down then lieutenant governor John Fetterman managed to look more like the "outsider" candidate than his political neophyte opponent. Typically clad in shorts and hoodies, with a shaved head and a chin goatee, Fetterman looks less like the Keystone State's freshly minted US senator than a talking head from a reboot of VH1's *Behind the Music*. His offbeat looks made him a social media darling and belied his privileged upbringing. Fetterman took money from his parents and housing from his sister well into his forties.[58] Fetterman, who claims that the family's assistance allowed him to forego a more lucrative career in favor of public service, also collected graduate degrees from Harvard and the University of Connecticut (incidentally, without incurring any student debt).

The good news for Fetterman was that his 2022 opponent, Dr. Oz, looked like an even bigger phony. It's hard to win in a working-class state like Pennsylvania when you own a six-bedroom, eight-bathroom mansion in New Jersey,[59] refer to veggie trays as "crudités," and have no idea when the Pittsburgh Steelers play.[60] Compared to Oz, Fetterman looks like William Jennings Bryan. This is probably why, despite suffering a stroke that curtailed his ability to campaign aggressively, Fetterman ultimately prevailed.

Still, Fetterman's everyman image is something of a contrivance. And Fetterman's children enjoy some of the same privileges he did: they attend the exclusive (and private) Winchester Thurston School in Pittsburgh. Otherwise, they would be stuck in the below-average Woodland Hills School District, according to the *Washington Free Beacon*.[61]

Surely Fetterman would want his neighbors to have the same choices his family has, right? Wrong. Fetterman campaigned against school choice and voucher programs. Fetterman may have dressed and presented himself as a different kind of candidate, but his fealty to the teachers' unions stayed in lockstep with his new national Democratic colleagues.

Tax Hypocrisy

Jared Polis, a Democrat, is the first openly gay male governor of any state and Colorado's first Jewish governor. While this makes him something of a progressive pioneer, his moderate (by today's standard) political stances (including his handling of the COVID-19 pandemic)[62] and style have earned him respect from some conservatives. "Although his parents were, [Polis] says, 1960s hippies, he chose to make a mint from capitalism rather than overthrowing it," explained conservative columnist George Will in a 2022 column.[63] "After sailing through high school in three years, at 17 he arrived at Princeton, where, as a sophomore, he and two friends founded an internet-access company. He founded two other internet-related companies, sold all three for more than $1 billion, and used some of this to found—heresy alert—two charter schools. This sin against progressivism was perhaps forgivable because the schools' primary purpose was to help children of immigrants."[64]

For the entrepreneurial among us, Polis's story is impressive. After taking his parents' greeting card company online, he founded (and later sold) ProFlowers.com. His entrepreneurial accomplishments paid off politically when he poured over $20 million into his first run for governor, according to ProPublica.[65]

But Polis's wealth has not gone without criticism. "When Jared Polis was first elected, his net worth was $160 million. And after serving a decade in Congress, his net worth is now estimated to be $312 million. It's up to Jared Polis and Jared Polis alone to explain why he didn't pay taxes for years," said a spokesman for Polis's 2018 Republican opponent, Walker Stapleton.[66] Both charges were valid.

According to OpenSecrets, Polis's wealth grew from about $143 million in 2010 to more than $306 million in 2017.[67] During that time, he served in Congress, where he was the third-richest member of the House.[68] Yet, according to a 2021 ProPublica report, "Despite a net worth estimated to be in the hundreds of millions, Polis paid nothing in federal income taxes in 2013, 2014, and 2015. From 2010 to 2018, his overall rate was just 8.2%—less than half of the 19% shelled out by a worker making $45,000 in 2018."[69] What makes this finding incredibly hypocritical is that Polis "led the charge for President Trump to turn over his tax returns" before refusing to release his own.[70]

How does this happen? Rich people (like Polis and Trump) profit from investments, but the taxes can be deferred indefinitely until those investments are officially sold. What is more, vehicles can be created that allow them to claim deductions and reduce their amount of taxable income. One of the vehicles Polis used employed an expert at "maximizing cost savings both operationally and with all taxing authorities." As ProPublica noted, "Ironically, the investment apparatus that helped Polis avoid taxable income became a tax break."[71]

$ $ $

In the interest of fairness, it is worth noting that the phenomenon of hypocrisy is not limited to latte liberals. As Republicans have increased their appeal to working-class voters (including rural and/or churchgoing folks), their opportunities for hypocrisy have increased proportionally.

Perhaps no one in Congress represents the current Republican zeitgeist quite like Representative Marjorie Taylor Greene (R-GA). Greene first rose to prominence with a Facebook Live performance that showed her grilling local library officials about a "drag queen story hour."

You can probably guess what she thought about the CDC recommendations during the COVID-19 pandemic: Greene was a vocal opponent of mask mandates and other CDC guidelines. In fact, when Speaker Nancy Pelosi instituted a mask mandate in the House of Representatives, Greene likened it to the gold stars of David that Nazis forced Jews to wear during the Holocaust. She bragged that she incurred $25,000 in fines for refusing to wear masks in the chamber.[72] Incidentally, that's just less than half the median income of the typical household in her district.

So you can understand why a fellow airline passenger had fun at her expense, snapping and tweeting a surreptitious photo of Greene obediently wearing a mask while reclining in her first-class seat. It was retweeted by original Squad member Representative Ilhan Omar, who called out Greene's hypocrisy for wearing a mask and for flying first class.

Omar—the leading proponent of the legislation to cancel rent and send money to the landlords co-sponsoring her bill—apparently saw no irony in calling out Greene's hypocrisy. "I love how she walks around railing against mask mandates but time and time again complies when no one is paying attention. Typical hypocrite cult leader," Omar tweeted.[73]

That's so funny it might make latte come out of your nose.

Or beer (if you're Elizabeth Warren cracking open a cold one). More on Warren's penchant for pilsners in our next chapter.

Chapter 8

Ivy League Populists: Rich and Privileged Networks

I'd feel a whole lot better about [the experts guiding the Vietnam War] if just one of them had run for sheriff once.

—Sam Rayburn to Lyndon Johnson[1]

Elizabeth Warren's background made her a formidable candidate for Democrats...in 2012.

Warren, a Harvard Law professor, was one of the intellectual architects of what would become the Consumer Financial Protection Bureau (CFPB). Warren had championed the agency's creation as far back as 2007 in a *Democracy Journal* article.[2] After the 2008 financial crisis, the CFPB emerged to propose a regulatory cudgel with which to smack down financial institutions. Warren would go on to help President Barack Obama's new administration steer the proposal through Congress.

With her policy bona fides proven—financial regulation and legislation are not realms for intellectual lightweights—Warren offered Democrats a formidable candidate to take on the then senator Scott Brown in 2012. Brown, a Republican, was the incumbent thanks to a 2010 special election to fill the Senate seat vacated upon Senator Ted Kennedy's death. (Convention dictates that I'm supposed to add "D-MA" after his name, but come on. It's Ted Kennedy.) Brown had won with a populist message, but Massachusetts is a liberal state. Brown was no match for the policy powerhouse, and Warren roared back from early polling deficits to thump Brown by eight points. Thanks in part to her background in academia, Warren filled the role of progressive policy wonk in the Senate and became an intellectual guiding light for Democrats.

But six years later, on the eve of a White House run, Warren decided that her nerdy yet competent and educated persona wouldn't do.

On December 31, 2018, Warren announced that she was forming an exploratory committee as the precursor to a presidential campaign—a sort of announcement-before-the-announcement that operates as part of the silly performance art White House wannabes engage in every four years. If it wasn't a campaign kickoff by the letter of the campaign finance reports, it was undoubtedly Warren's way of throwing her headdress in the ring (one of the campaign's many low points came in 2019, when Warren was forced to apologize for calling herself a Native American in the past).

Now, about that image...

Warren was pursuing a Democratic nomination in a crowded field. The big dog in the race was former vice president Joe Biden, the avuncular everyman who papered over gaffes with a toothy, aw-shucks grin. Other competitors included Senator Bernie Sanders (I-the People's Republic of Vermont) and former congressman Beto O'Rourke (D-TX), who shed his formerly centrist appeal in favor of increasingly progressive campaign rhetoric. If Warren overtook them, she would face President Donald Trump in a general election. Trump, who had ridden a wave of massive, boisterous rallies and Rodney Dangerfield–style anti-establishment vitriol, upset fifteen accomplished Republican contenders and the Woman Who Would Be Queen, Hillary Clinton, in 2016.

Uber-academic Warren, however, was in danger of losing the so-called beer primary—that old political axiom predicting the winner as the one with whom you'd most enjoy grabbing a cold beer.

She fought back by inviting America in for a beer. Literally.

After kicking off her campaign (that wasn't yet a campaign) with a press conference outside her home (featuring her golden retriever, Bailey—who doesn't love dogs?) and an online video announcing her not-quite-yet-but-soon candidacy, Warren took to Instagram live to answer questions and connect with "the kids." Warren started the stream by welcoming her audience, and then she added, "Hold on a sec. I'm going to get me a beer." She moves off camera for a few seconds. After clinking around (channeling Betty Ford instead of Eleanor Roosevelt), she reappears with a brown bottle. She then cracks it open and takes a swig before interacting with the audience.

Between the folksy choice of words and the hearty swig, the video comes across like a ham-fisted attempt to highlight Warren's down-home Midwestern roots. She tried to deemphasize her professor role at *two* Ivy League law schools (she was the highest-paid professor at Harvard) and mask her position in the upper echelon of American government.

But in 2020, Democratic primary voters didn't buy it. She subsequently dropped out of the race after a Super Tuesday shellacking, but it hasn't stopped her from further refining and redefining her populist image.

As recently as May 2022, Warren showed up on the steps of the Supreme Court after a Supreme Court opinion was leaked in *Dobbs v. Jackson Women's Health Organization* indicating the imminent negation of *Roe v. Wade*. Warren particularly decried the decision's effects on working-class women. "I am angry because of who will pay the price for this,"[3] Warren shouted in front of an embankment of cameras with a crowd of protesters cheering her on. "It will not be wealthy women...they can get the protection they need," she warned, shaking with fury. "This will fall on the poorest women.... This will fall on mothers who are already struggling to work three jobs to...support the children they have." She punctuated the impromptu speech by leading the crowd in a few chants.

Her transformation from intellectual to beer-swigging, speechifying, rabble-rousing, left-wing populist may be stark. But it isn't unique. It resembles the personality of the man she hoped to face in 2020.

After building her career in an ivory tower, Warren now sounded more like Trump Tower's most (in)famous resident.

$ $ $

President Donald Trump is a graduate of the Wharton School of the University of Pennsylvania—one of the world's most prestigious business schools. And as the *Atlantic* noted, "His inner circle was every bit as much a part of the American elite as its opponents—Steven Mnuchin (Yale '85), Ben Carson (Yale '73), Wilbur Ross (Yale '59), Stephen Schwarzman (Yale '69), Jared Kushner (Harvard '03), Steve Bannon (Harvard '85), Mike Pompeo (Harvard Law '94), and, of course, Trump himself (University of Pennsylvania, '68). Trump's inaugural cabinet had more Harvard alumni than Obama's. In the aftermath of the January 6 insurrection, many of the strongest supporters of the stolen-election theory have been Ivy League graduates. Ted Cruz (Princeton '92) was one of the first to challenge the election's certification, and Kayleigh McEnany (Harvard Law '16) actively spread fraud claims as the president's press secretary. Elise Stefanik, who graduated from Harvard in 2006 and is the youngest Republican woman elected to Congress, has described Donald Trump as the 'strongest supporter of any president when it comes to standing up for the Constitution.'"[4]

Still, no one would ever accuse Trump of emphasizing his own Ivy League education. From the time he descended the Trump Tower escalator in 2015 to kick off his presidential campaign, Trump set himself apart from other contenders in a crowded Republican field. His competitors for the 2016 GOP nomination included multiterm governors and senators, some with accomplished records boasting policy victories. Trump charged past them with empty (but bombastic) promises, like the now-infamous, mind-bogglingly stupid claim that Mexico would pay for a wall on our southern border.

During the 2016 campaign (and pretty much ever since then), Trump has marched from coast to coast, thundering anti-elitist talking points that completely ignore his privileged education and upper-crust upbringing. Like many populists, Trump frequently plays fast and loose with reality, but he never scrimps on volume. He fueled his 2016 campaign with raucous rallies, dutifully covered by a national news media looking on with macabre fascination usually reserved for covering train wrecks, high-speed police chases, and the Kardashians. From the podium, Trump riled massive crowds with exhortations about illegal immigration, the demise of American manufacturing, corporate control of the mechanisms of government, overeducated elitists, political correctness, and any other topic being debated by bar patrons in a struggling twenty-first-century Rust Belt town.

All of his rants held a common thread: Trump reminding his supporters that they were being ignored, disregarded, and cast aside by America's elites. He promised that he would be the one to "drain the swamp," cast out the influences of special interests in Washington, and return power to the hands of "the people," where it belonged.

For those feeling abandoned by a changing economy and a rapidly evolving country, Trump's promise to "drain the swamp" must have sounded refreshing. But it wasn't authentic. After winning his election by banging the drum of anti-elitism, Trump's cabinet appointments—though off the beaten political path—had a decidedly upper-crust feel. He tapped ExxonMobil CEO Rex Tillerson for secretary of state, despite his close ties with Vladimir Putin's Russian government. In his role with ExxonMobil, Tillerson had also lobbied Congress.

Betsy DeVos, chairwoman of a private investment group and failed Broadway producer (a bomb called *Scandalous!*), got Trump's nod for secretary of education. She is married to former Amway CEO Dick DeVos. Despite decades spent championing school choice, DeVos had little to no experience in education, but (surprise) she did have extensive history in Republican politics.

When she wasn't dabbling in Republican politics, Linda McMahon (along with her husband Vince McMahon) cofounded one of the world's largest sports and entertainment companies: the billion-dollar World Wrestling Entertainment. Trump put her in charge of the "thousand-dollar" Small Business Administration.

For all his promises to drain the swamp, Trump instead appointed a slate of wealthy businesspeople instead of political insiders. And as it turns out, Ivy League alumni claiming to be men (or women) of the people still frequent the swamps of Washington, DC.

"Middle-Class Joe" Biden's team members aren't exactly paupers, either. Domestic Policy Council director Susan Rice is worth between $36 and $149 million.[5] Biden's former chief of staff Ron Klain has a net worth of between $4.4 and $12.2 million.[6] Klain's 2023 replacement Jeff Zients, who had previously served as Biden's COVID-19 czar, reportedly owns somewhere between $89.3 and $442.8 million in assets.[7] As Market-Watch put it, Zients "has just about enough assets to swap it for the entire White House, were it ever for sale."[8] Then again, Zients might get a run for his money from other past and future Biden administration members. Biden's top science advisor, Eric Lander, had over $45 million in assets when he was nominated[9] (Lander resigned in early 2022 on the heels of bullying accusations.) He also managed to profit from vaccine stocks while promoting COVID-19 vaccinations.[10] And we've already discussed US special presidential climate envoy John Kerry in the "Latte Liberals" chapter.

The Ivies

An ambitious young person hoping to succeed in politics needs more than just personal wealth to succeed. While graduates of prestigious academic institutions certainly have a head start when it comes to earning potential, that is merely the tip of the iceberg in terms of their privileged status. Arguably the most important commodities imparted while attending an elite institution are the familiarity with upper-crust culture and an extensive network of wealthy, connected friends and contacts. Remember that, according to my political fund-raiser wife, a politician has to raise a minimum of $300,000 in the first quarter they launch their campaign—from their personal network—before anyone else will invest. And that's merely for a seat in the lower chamber. The cost is significantly higher if you want to run for the US Senate.

The Ivy League universities—Harvard, Yale, Columbia, Brown, Cornell, Penn, Princeton, and Dartmouth—have symbolized academic prestige for centuries. Their collective reputation precedes that of the nation itself. Harvard was the first college founded in North America, back in 1636. Movies, television, books, and other media use Ivy League acceptance and attendance to illustrate a character's high academic achievement. Even the Harvard dropout list (including the likes of William Randolph Hearst, Bill Gates, and Mark Zuckerberg) puts other schools' lists of proper alums to shame.

Speaking of pop culture, Ivy League alumni aren't solely destined to be upper-echelon lawyers and business moguls. Many have become staples in television writer's rooms, shaping touchstones like *The Simpsons* and *Saturday Night Live*. And they have increasingly infiltrated Hollywood (lookin' at you, Natalie Portman).

Despite their reputation for excellence and cultural significance (or perhaps because of it), many assume that Ivy League schools cater to, and preserve the existence of, America's upper class. Exclusivity is a feature, not a bug. Keep in mind that just 0.4 percent have graduated from an Ivy League institution.[11]

The price tag for a Harvard education (not counting financial assistance) is an estimated $75,000 per year (this includes tuition, fees, and other costs, such as room and board).[12] Yale and Columbia cost even more: closer to $80,000 per annum. That puts the list price of a four-year Ivy League education somewhere north of $300,000.

We imagine that upon graduation, Ivy Leaguers must have a willing network of alums ready to help them secure cushy, white-collar jobs. America may not have nobility like the European nations that sent over our earliest colonists, but we do have wealthy elites who play tennis at country clubs, vacation in the Hamptons, own boats, and find jobs for their unqualified nephews. (Check out the dynamics outlined in 1961's *How to Succeed in Business Without Really Trying*. They haven't changed much.)

Ivy League institutions have become symbols of the American elite—in both good ways and bad. We see them as institutions that demand excellence from an exclusive few, while only being available to an exclusive few. That makes graduating from an Ivy League school a conflicting bragging right for an elected official. Politicians need to win elections, and voters get to decide those elections. If a candidate can't make a credible connection with voters, they won't win.

Consider the 1992 presidential election. Incumbent George H. W. Bush, scion of a blue-blooded family of Connecticut, was the son of a senator and—Boolah! Boolah!—a Yale Skull and Bones man. A news crew famously caught Bush asking a grocery checkout worker how the infrared scanner worked. This was unfair—"it was a special scanner with advanced features."[13] Still, his affable curiosity and interest was presented as an aloof disconnectedness from the realities the rest of us face daily. Given that his reelection was coming in the middle of a recession, it was a bad look. His opponent, the then Arkansas governor Bill Clinton, was a study in contrast. While Bush relied on legacy media to communicate his message, Clinton fearlessly appeared on MTV and played his saxophone on *The Arsenio Hall Show*. He famously drawled that he felt voters' pain and discussed his rural upbringing in a broken home. He didn't mention his Yale Law degree as much... or his days at Oxford... or undergraduate drudgery at Georgetown (the unofficial Beltway branch office for the Ivy League).

When Clinton's term ended, he was succeeded by his predecessor's son, George W. Bush. Bush combined a public affability with a habit of misspeaking. On *Saturday Night Live*, Will Ferrell legendarily mocked Bush by making up words ("strategery") with a mix of idiocy and confidence. Dubya didn't seem to mind being portrayed as an affable but effective dunce—he certainly didn't feel the need to make a big deal out of the fact that he was a two-time Ivy Leaguer with an undergrad degree from Yale and an MBA from Harvard. He still managed to eke out victories over the wonkish and robotic vice president Al Gore (Harvard) in 2000 and the snooty Boston Brahmin–esque senator John Kerry (Yale) in 2004.

When Barack Obama won in 2008 to become America's first Black president, he did so on the back of a campaign that famously emphasized the concept of change. As part of that theme, he crafted an image of his backstory in politics, which highlighted his door-to-door and block-to-block community organizing efforts in Chicago. The idea of a political door-knocker fighting for parochial issues fosters a connection with voters much more readily than announcing that he (the grandson of a bank vice president[14] and the son of a Harvard grad) had attended Columbia and Harvard Law. However, he broke a twenty-year chain of Yalies in the White House. When compared with most of his recent predecessors, President Joe Biden's transcript looks like a CV for a trucking school that would have been advertised during daytime reruns of *All in the Family* circa 1988. Although, an undergraduate degree at the University of Delaware followed by a law degree from Syracuse is certainly nothing to sneeze at—if you're in the *state* legislature.

Incidentally, the pool of recent Ivy League presidential victors isn't that much deeper than the pool of recent Ivy League presidential losers. For a candidate, seriously competing for a party's nomination is like making the majors in baseball—it's the upper echelon of the upper echelon. The best of the best. To be a serious contender on that level, you need connections: people who can help you, do favors, and, yes, write checks. Lots of checks. You need a network of people to help—the type of personal/professional network many Ivy League alumni seem to enjoy. (As a Yale Law alum who lost her presidential race might say, it takes a village—but said village is in the Hamptons.) The secret to political success isn't skipping the Ivy League education; it's enjoying its benefits without flaunting your membership in upper-crust society.

$$\$ \ \$ \ \$$$

An Ivy League education doesn't *always* correlate with net worth, but it usually does. Regardless, grads of such institutions are bestowed with credentials and connections that are worth more than gold. There's nothing wrong with being rich, of course. What makes them hypocritical is that, despite checking both boxes, they credulously cast themselves as populist outsiders. The amazing thing is how well the ruse works.

Perhaps you find all of this as absurd as I do. The very elites who seek to rule us also rile up the public to hate their fellow elites. Consider, for example, Steve Bannon: the erstwhile advisor to President Donald Trump. Although he claims to be a "Leninist,"[15] Bannon is also "an alumnus of Harvard Business School, Georgetown School of Foreign Service, Goldman Sachs, Hollywood."[16] This form of populist demagoguery is dangerous. Aristotle warned of what happens when oligarchs woo the mob, writing that "tyrants have mostly begun as popular leaders, being trusted by the people because they disliked the upper class."[17] Not much has changed since then.

Speaking of demagogues, current Senator John Kennedy is a Republican from Louisiana (not a Democrat from Massachusetts), but he is still known for his strong accent. In fact, it's a little too strong, according to some former colleagues and friends. "Kennedy and I were fellows in the same class for the 1990–91 Loyola University New Orleans Institute of Politics," wrote journalist Quin Hillyer[18] in 2019. "Kennedy had a mild Southern accent but still sounded rather patrician, befitting his record both at Oxford and as former executive editor of the University of Virginia's *Law Review*. His folksy, exaggerated Southern-cornpone accent now was affectation, mere political theater to stand out among the Senate's bevy of stuffed shirts. It's about as authentic as a cow in a camel costume."[19] Once upon a time, it was Democrats like Hillary Clinton who were guilty of affecting a long drawl. Today's phony everyman is more often a Republican politician. And the more ambitious they are, the more country they sound.

In the current populist-tinged political zeitgeist, the would-be heirs to the Oval Office are eager to form connections with voters based on visceral emotion. Senator Ted Cruz, one of the final contenders against Trump during the 2016 primaries, likely has his sights set on another run at the White House. In 2012, Cruz—whose office wall boasts sheepskins from Harvard Law and Princeton (and whose wife, Heidi, has been a managing director at Goldman Sachs since 2012)—launched an outsider bid for the Senate against the then lieutenant governor David Dewhurst. (Note: my wife was Cruz's national fund-raising consultant.) Cruz beat the odds to win the nomination and a seat in the Senate by brandishing endorsements from former vice presidential nominee Sarah Palin and center-right grassroots groups like the Club for Growth. Once there, Cruz presented himself as a highly principled conservative with a keen ear for grassroots concerns—a sort of latter-day Jesse Helms (without the problematic racial history).

And then he turned into the cloying populist demagogue that so many love to hate. He cemented his position as a conservative firebrand by quixotically attempting to defund the Affordable Care Act in 2013 (in a marathon speech that saw him, at one point, reading from Dr. Seuss's *Green Eggs and Ham*).

Cruz railed against Republicans who capitulated to President Obama's legislative proposals, calling them the "surrender caucus," and he drew the ire of more traditional Republicans like former Speaker of the House John Boehner, Senator Lindsey Graham, the late Senator John McCain—and, most spectacularly, the then GOP Senate majority leader Mitch McConnell.

Since losing the 2016 Republican nomination to Donald Trump, Cruz has taken a page from Trump's playbook, using social media to comment on current affairs even if the issue isn't up for debate in the Senate. Cruz has been fairly consistent in his beliefs and brand, despite all of the criticism he has weathered from other senators over the past decade. Unfortunately, his brand is that of an elitist posing as a populist, who, according to his law school roommate, "said he didn't want [to study] anybody from 'minor Ivies' like Penn or Brown."[20] "What the Ivy League produces, in spades, on both the left and the right," wrote Stephen Marche at the *Atlantic*, "is unwarranted confidence. Its institutions are hubris factories."[21] That sounds about right to me. But then again, what do I know? I went to Shepherd College. Talk about a lesser Ivy.

$ $ $

Cruz may believe he can outlast Trump, but if he wants to dominate the populist lane in a future Republican Party, he may have some competition from one of his current Senate colleagues, Senator Josh Hawley (R-MO). (Note: my wife also worked as a fund-raising consultant on

Hawley's race for Missouri attorney general.) Like Cruz, Hawley has an Ivy League law degree (another Yale man); his undergraduate degree is from Stanford, which is the closest thing to an Ivy League school west of Rochester, New York. (If Stanford were in, say, Vermont, it would be the ninth Ivy.) Hawley put that wonderful education to good use on January 6, 2021: just hours after greeting "Stop the Steal" protesters with fist pumps of encouragement, Hawley had the good sense to flee willy-nilly once they stormed and breached the Capitol. (Enterprising internet users have set a few seconds of slow-motion security camera footage featuring Hawley's flight to all sorts of music—from *Benny Hill*'s "Yakety Sax" theme to the Kate Bush revival hit "Running up That Hill.")

When he wasn't cheering on—or running from—the Capitol mob, Hawley railed against big tech. In 2021, he proposed heavy-handed regulations for social media companies to answer the perceived censorship of right-wing voices. In 2021, Hawley released a book likening modern-day technology companies to the monopolies enjoyed by early twentieth-century industry giants like U.S. Steel and Standard Oil. Hawley has criticized other big businesses, too: he railed against Walmart's employment practices during a Twitter fight, calling the retail giant out for "the pathetic wages you pay your workers as you drive mom and pop stores out of business."[22]

Hawley also bangs the people's drum on other issues, having railed against multiculturalism, left-wing bias in academia and media, and critical race theory. In 2023, Hawley delved into one of the weirder corners of right-wing populism by releasing a book titled *Manhood: The Masculine Virtues America Needs*. It echoed themes he has touched on in speeches and public comments, such as the November 2021 speech he gave weaving male unemployment, depression, declining marriage rates, and vaccine mandates into a narrative about how the federal government systematically devalues men's role in society.

Hawley now has a pal—and fellow author—in the Senate to commiserate with on these topics. Senator J. D. Vance (R-OH), author of the

Rust Belt anthem *Hillbilly Elegy* and Yale Law School grad, has decried the "childless left" and recommended policies that would pay young couples to procreate, essentially cribbing from a child tax credit policy President Biden already enacted. But Hawley's too green to run for president in 2024, leaving the door open for other young populists to try to own that lane.

Hawley's wading into populist waters has him frequently listed as a Republican rising star. But like fellow Ivy League populist senator Tom Cotton (R-AK), a graduate of Harvard and Harvard Law School, Hawley has announced he will not run for president in 2024.[23]

Fortune favors the bold. That leaves one important populist to discuss.

Florida Man

Assuming Donald Trump isn't the Republican nominee in 2024 (admittedly, a big assumption), the leading Republican in most polls is Florida governor Ron DeSantis. And DeSantis has earned his pole position.

In less than one term in the governor's mansion, DeSantis (a fundraising juggernaut whose net wealth as of December 31, 2021, was surprisingly just $319,000[24]—a dramatic improvement over his 2018 net wealth, which was -$357,000[25]) has created a blueprint for conservative populist governance and arguably implemented it better than Donald Trump's presidential administration.

DeSantis first ascended to quasi–folk hero status among many conservative Republicans by flouting federal COVID-19 guidelines. He refused to enact the shutdowns that many other states enacted and bristled against vaccine mandates. In doing so, he took on a defiant, even pugilistic, tone that echoed Trump's bravado—the practical side being that Florida's economy is built on the foundation of tourism. Restrictions that would be damaging elsewhere could have proved catastrophic in Florida; vaccine mandates could prevent hotels, theme parks, and other tourism-oriented businesses from maintaining adequate staff.

DeSantis is more widely known—and, in some circles, celebrated—for taking a stance against the state's biggest corporate presence: the Walt Disney Company.

The war between Disney and DeSantis started with another populist policy, Florida's Parental Rights in Education Act. Riding a national wave of skepticism over the quality of public education, the Florida legislature passed what became known as the "Don't Say Gay" bill: a measure that restricted sex education discussions in public schools. After it passed, the bill began to draw heat from progressive activists. Florida's biggest employer, the Walt Disney Company, got put on the spot too, as activists and employees—ahem, "cast members"—wondered why the Mouse hadn't spoken out against the bill. After the not-so-gentle push, Disney CEO Bob Chapek apologized and promised the company would work to repeal the law.

DeSantis, apparently upset that Disney employees (sorry, cast members) would dare exercise their right to free speech, sought to punish the business by moving to dissolve the municipal districts that had allowed Walt Disney World to experience unprecedented growth and become a cash cow for the state.

Previous generations of Republicans might have blanched at such a move. From the protective tariffs and internal improvement subsidies of the late 1800s to the pro-growth supply-side economics of the 1980s, the GOP had a long tradition of being the party more favorable to the business community. Even Donald Trump sought to stoke economic growth by cutting taxes and regulations on businesses.

But in recent years, the party's more populist wing has come to look at big business as a villainous power center similar to big government—and holds skepticism for both. Put another way: Big Government, Big Business, Big Tech, or Big *Anything* always finds a way to screw over the little guy. And who else are populists supposed to defend if not the little guy?

This sentiment was clear in the criticism of corporate bailouts initiated by President George W. Bush and President Barack Obama during the economic downturn of 2007–2009. As the government moved to relieve debt for banks, auto manufacturers, and other giant industries, many taxpayers faced personal debt of their own in the form of mortgages, student loans, or credit card debt. Yet no one seriously proposed bailing out such debts. It became easy to view big business and government as a symbiotic pair.

Donald Trump's 2016 campaign further moved the GOP away from their traditional Chamber of Commerce loyalties, as Republicans became increasingly critical of "woke" corporations. But it was DeSantis who actually took this rhetoric to a whole new level in Florida.

The Reedy Creek Improvement District (RCID) had been incorporated in 1967, as Walt Disney himself sought to build the East Coast version of the then twelve-year-old Disneyland. When constructing his first park, Disney had been frustrated by the building limits in Anaheim, California, and he sought the freedom to develop and expand his new park in Florida. The RCID was born as a quasi-municipality to prevent battles with county commissioners and other local authorities every time Disney sought to develop some new attraction or resort. It was also to help govern the Experimental Prototype City of Tomorrow (EPCOT), originally conceived as a futuristic city that instead became a second theme park and a giant golf ball after Disney's death in 1966. The Walt Disney Company has provided its utilities, services, and infrastructure for its parks—all thanks to the RCID.

Flustered by Disney's reaction to the "Don't Say Gay" bill, DeSantis and his minions in the state legislature moved quickly to dissolve the RCID just weeks after Disney's opposition statement. The RCID's ultimate fate may be decided by the courts or by a follow-up bill; dissolution is a messy process.

But the ultimate fate of the RCID is moot now. Ron DeSantis has the result that will eventually matter most to him: he can now claim to be a governor who defends the "little guy." He started with a bill that asserted parents' rights in education and ended up in a fight with one of the country's largest virtue-signaling corporate entities. That's a key notch to have in your belt when you saunter onto the debate stage for a Republican presidential primary, isn't it?

Regardless of the rhetoric and posturing, Ron DeSantis scored a big win in his showdown with Disney. He is probably smart enough to know it, too—he's no dummy.

After all, he went to Yale.

And Harvard Law.

Chapter 9

You *Can* Take It with You: The Revolving Door

[I]t is not the most intellectual of the species that survives; it is not the strongest that survives; but the species that survives is the one that is able best to adapt and adjust to the changing environment in which it finds itself.

—*Attributed to Charles Darwin*

For most families from Arkansas (or anywhere, for that matter), getting kicked out of public housing after one parent loses his job would present a daunting challenge—even if the other parent had managed to find a new job out of state.

That's the situation that Bill and Hillary Clinton found themselves in on January 21, 2001. President Bill Clinton was leaving the White House term-limited and tarnished by scandal; Hillary Clinton had just taken office as the junior senator from New York.

At fifty-four years old, Bill was actually a few weeks younger than his successor, George W. Bush. Yet he had spent most of the previous twenty-four years as an elected official—first as Arkansas attorney general, then as governor, and ultimately as president of the United States for two terms. Hillary also had forged a high-profile career in politics and advocacy.

Yet, as prominent as the first couple of the 1990s was, Bill and Hillary weren't exactly raking in paychecks at the same level. Questions existed about Hillary's success in the cattle futures market in the late 1970s and the infamous Whitewater investigations regarding the Clintons' involvement in a failed land deal. But it added up to supplemental income—what passed for a side hustle for pre–App Store–era politicians in a time before Uber. It was certainly nothing that led to an extravagant, jet-setting lifestyle. In a 2001 financial disclosure,[1] the then senator Hillary Clinton reported the family faced up to $10.6 million in debt.[2]

Of course, the Clintons didn't exactly run up this debt by maxing out credit cards at Walmart or the Piggly Wiggly. This debt included mortgages on two multimillion-dollar homes and legal fees (including those spent defending Bill from accusations of perjury and obstruction of justice).

Unlike actors, athletes, and other hallmarks of pop culture who see their earnings potential diminish once their time in the spotlight ends, many politicians see their paychecks go up once they leave office. It turns out that former first families can make bank on the speaking circuit. CNN reported that the Clintons made $153 million (not a misprint!) in speaking fees from the time they left the White House until Hillary officially launched her own bid for the presidency in 2015.[3] (To give you a sense of inflation, I am reminded that the media was scandalized when former president Ronald Reagan made $2 million for a speaking tour in Japan.) Early on, many of those speeches were Bill's (remember that Hillary served in the Senate until being appointed secretary of state by President Barack Obama in 2009). Yet, after leaving Foggy Bottom at the end of Obama's first term, Hillary found herself in high demand in 2013.

And why not? By 2013, Hillary Clinton had built an impressive résumé of accomplishments. More importantly, she started claiming the inside track for the 2016 presidential election. The Democratic nomination was hers to lose. She even loomed large in the Republican primary:

in covering early GOP debates, a *Politico* headline wondered, "Who Can Beat Hillary Clinton?"[4] (Spoiler: "You'd be surprised!" was the correct answer.)

It gave voice to the major question voters and activists on the right had been asking themselves as they considered which candidate to support. Three years before a single vote was cast, Clinton was the proverbial eight-hundred-pound gorilla in the 2016 race.

Clinton's opponent in the 2016 Democratic primary, Senator Bernie Sanders, called her out for speeches to large financial institutions—specifically the $675,000 she received from Goldman Sachs for a series of three speeches, as *Politico* reported[5]—in an attempt to lump her in with the out-of-touch, corporatist wing of the Democratic party. (Sanders was curiously mum on her book advances.) And Sanders was not entirely wrong: corporate America saw the perfect intersection of accomplishment and potential. She had held the reins of power and was poised to grasp them even tighter and shriek "giddyup!" It didn't work out that way, but it felt like a safe bet at the time.

Her star was never brighter, so it's hard to blame Clinton for cashing in when she did. And while her perceived status as a once and future White House resident was unique, her post-office (not the USPS kind of post office) focus on pocketing some coin was certainly not. We heard plenty about the ongoing activities of the Clintons just as we had for a quarter of a century on cable news. But unless you're plugged into inside-the-Beltway news (and, let's be honest, *gossip*) you might not hear about the dozens of outgoing members of Congress who, like swallows who instinctively know the way to Capistrano, flock from Capitol Hill to K Street.

One might argue that, in the grand scheme of things, Hillary Clinton didn't sell out nearly as blatantly as some fellow former pols. After all, giving speeches and advising big banks seems pretty on-brand for someone who spent the 1990s and 2000s in the most exclusive corridors of power.

It was also on-brand for someone who had a prominent (if officially unde-fined) role in the administration that oversaw a booming mid-to-late-1990s economy fueled in part by Wall Street's dot-com bubble. And paid speeches are a common avenue for former officeholders to make some extra scratch after leaving office.

On the other hand, Clinton did sometimes come off as a bit of a prima donna. According to the *Washington Post*, her 2014 appearance at UCLA included lots of persnickety demands. For example, as UCLA adminis-trator Patricia Lippert told her colleagues, group photos with Clinton have to be "prestaged" because "She doesn't like to stand around wait-ing for people."[6] Her rider didn't exactly demand a bowl of just brown M&Ms, but it did demand "a spread of hummus and crudité in the green room backstage."[7]

Nowadays, getting paid handsomely for a speech is common for a famous former (and maybe future) politician. The Clinton Foundation, however, is a bit unique. Plenty of politicians start organizations when they leave office, but few (if any) have matched the profile and reach of the Clinton Foundation. Set up as an evolution of Bill's presidential foun-dation (the type of group that sets up libraries and mini museums for for-mer presidents), the Clinton Foundation evolved into a network of groups funding and executing philanthropic initiatives around the world.

Between 2001 and 2015—predating Hillary Clinton's presidential campaign but overlapping her stint as secretary of state—the founda-tion raised an estimated $2 billion. Most of that (an estimated 97 percent) stayed with the foundation—which is another way of saying they did their own work rather than acting as a pass-through to other smaller charities. And as a charitable organization, the foundation could take donations from anyone, with no limits attached.

That fact became an issue at the dawn of the 2016 campaign cycle. The *Washington Post* noted that half the donors from her proto-campaign group, Ready for Hillary, had contributed $10,000 or more to the foundation.[8] Furthermore, one-third of the foundation's donors who contributed $1 million or more were foreign governments or entities.[9] Financial institutions (foreign and domestic) were big backers, too. As with her lucrative speeches to big banks, it appeared that plenty of monied interests wanted to be Hillary Clinton's friend. The Clinton Foundation certainly reaped the benefits. The Clintons only lifted their "long-standing cloak of secrecy" surrounding the foundation's donors in December of 2008 in order to avoid conflict of interest allegations during Hillary Clinton's secretary of state confirmation.[10]

For other politicians, the caginess and lack of explanations might suggest something nefarious. Yet with the Clintons, the lack of transparency—and impatience with skepticism—are features, not bugs. Remember that in the 1990s, investigations into the Clintons spawned the infamous charge "vast, right-wing conspiracy" from Hillary Clinton, delivered with a shrug and a laugh (and adopted with glee by the galaxy of right-wing groups that independently discovered that bashing the Clintons was good for business).

If Hillary Clinton ever "sold out," it was in the early 1980s when, after spending a term as Arkansas first lady under her maiden name, "Hillary Rodham," she accepted her husband's surname in advance of his second campaign for governor. Plenty of people on the left and right might bristle at Clinton's politics, but nothing she has done to enrich or advance her interests could be called out of character.

The same could be said for her former boss, President Barack Obama. After bursting onto the national scene with a keynote address at the 2004 Democratic National Convention, Obama's star rapidly shot skyward. In 2008, his primary bid for the presidency against the front-runner Clinton got a big boost from his appeal to celebrities and pop culture; will.i.am of the Black Eyed Peas famously turned his New Hampshire primary concession speech into a viral video echoing the slogan "Yes We Can," with a galaxy of stars repeating the candidate's words.

It comes as little surprise, then, that after his two terms ended, Barack and Michelle Obama took a course that differed from the Clintons'. In May 2018, they created a production company, Higher Ground Productions, and signed a deal with Netflix. The terms of the deal were not disclosed, but it came at a time when Netflix was inking deals in the tens of millions with content creators. It probably didn't hurt that Netflix's chief content officer at the time, Ted Sarandos, was the husband of Nicole Avant, Obama's onetime ambassador to the Bahamas.[11]

It may be a different type of racket, but, as with Clinton, Obama's deal keeps him doing what he does best—in his case, rubbing elbows with celebrities and pop-culture icons. As post-official moneymaking plans go, it's decidedly on-brand.

The Biden Interregnum

Joe Biden is our current president, so it may seem weird to include him in this section. But what he did in the intervening four years, between serving as Barack Obama's vice president and being elected president, was similar to what we see from most former presidents. Simply put, he cashed in.

It's hard to blame him. As I have previously noted, Biden, by his own description, was "one of the poorest men in Congress." According to *Forbes*, until leaving the US Senate, Biden made money from essentially three sources: "First, Biden brought in about $155,000 a year as a U.S. senator. Second, he had a teaching gig at Widener University on the side, which generated roughly $20,000 annually. Third, Jill earned about $60,000 a year from the State of Delaware. She worked as an English professor at Delaware Technical Community College."[12]

Upon becoming vice president, Biden got a raise ($225,000 a year), and Jill got a pay boost when she moved to Northern Virginia Community College. Around that time, they also started collecting Social

Security and receiving a total of $171,600 in rent from the Secret Service for a property they owned in Wilmington, Delaware[13] (as you might imagine, the rent President Trump charged the Secret Service made Biden's look like peanuts).

But Biden finally struck it rich after leaving the vice presidency, earning more than $16.7 million in the three years, according to *Forbes*,[14] and amassing a net worth of $9 million.[15] How'd he do it? About $900,000 came from being a "professor" for three years at the University of Pennsylvania. Though he did make a few public appearances at the college during those years, there's no evidence he actually taught a class.[16] But according to the *Washington Post*, Biden's bucks came "largely from book deals and speaking fees for as much as $200,000 per speech."[17]

Compared with most politicians in this book, Biden is a regular guy—for a *politician*, that is. But he wasn't exactly born in a log cabin, either. Biden's grandfather, Joseph, was an American Oil Co. executive. Biden's father fell on some hard times, but Joe Biden still attended private schools, got a degree from Syracuse University, got a job as an attorney, and was elected to the US Senate.

Nevertheless, Biden retains his "Middle-Class Joe" image. And when you consider that he's still far from being one of the richest politicians in America, his brand is relatively authentic. Although Biden has shifted some of his positions leftward over the years (his position on abortion, for example), there is no indication that personal money has played a role in shifting his policy positions. On the other hand, there's John Boehner.

From Wine to Weed

From 2011 to 2015, John Boehner served as the Speaker of the United States House of Representatives, swept into that office on the crest of the

Tea Party wave of the midterm elections of 2010 that handed congressional control to the GOP for the first time in four years. Thrust into the limelight, Boehner became the paragon of traditional Republicanism. His bio reads like the two-dimensional backstory of a "relatively good Republican" character in a Hollywood movie: working-class background, worked his way through college to pay for his degree, and first member of his family to graduate from college. Before being elected to Congress, the newly graduated Boehner started as a plastics salesman (apparently, he followed the unsolicited career advice given to Dustin Hoffman's character in *The Graduate*) before becoming president of the company. It was a traditional retelling of the American dream.

And even if he occasionally let his emotional side slip out publicly (remember how he teared up occasionally during interviews?), Boehner was traditional, too. His love of red wine and cigars underscored his stuffy, nouveau riche country club bona fides. Like any good Republican of his era, he stood up for pro-growth economics. He took stances against policies that he thought would damage the country's moral fiber—policies like legalizing marijuana.

Boehner only voted on the issue once but had taken public stances against pot legalization over the years. It was hardly a controversial stance for a member of either party during the years he sat in Congress. Yet as more states started to loosen marijuana laws in the 2000s, the cannabis industry started to make more money. And as with any industry making a lot of money, they began hiring lobbyists. After Boehner resigned from Congress in 2015, he (a non-lawyer) latched on with the prominent law firm Squire Patton Boggs as a "senior strategic advisor." He eventually joined the board of Acreage Holdings, a cannabis company, and by 2018 was giving speeches advocating for legalization at venues like the annual South by Southwest conference and festival in Austin, Texas. *Tune in, turn on, get rich, man!*

The Revolving Door

Let's talk a bit more about K Street. In contrast to the smooth, history-steeped marble of the Capitol's corridors, K Street is pockmarked by potholes and scourged by endless construction. Its buildings reflect a mix of 1970s brutalism, 1980s glass-covered modernity, and (later) ham-fisted revival attempts at both styles. The stench of illegally idling, carbon-belching delivery trucks hangs over the lunchtime eateries, where junior staffers trade ten spots for mediocre sandwiches to eat at their desks. Starbucks and CVS locations are so plentiful that you can measure the rate of a walk by counting them, as sailors once measured speed by knots in a rope slipping through their hands.

High above all that, in windowed offices and cubicled bullpens, the real business of Washington, DC, happens.

Boehner is not the first former member of Congress to make the transition. (And, in the interest of transparency, honesty, and geography, Squire Patton Boggs's Washington, DC, office is on M Street. There are slightly fewer potholes and Starbucks locations, but otherwise, the description is equally apt.)

A 2016 study showed that between 1976 and 2012, about one out of every four members of Congress registered as a lobbyist upon leaving the Capitol.[18]

According to OpenSecrets, 460 former members of Congress work in corporate governmental affairs, either directly lobbying or offering "strategic advice and counsel" to companies and organizations.[19] The distinction between being a registered lobbyist and a "senior advisor" is often a designation without a meaningful difference. No matter what type of official paperwork they have to file about their activity, the name of the game is influence: those who become familiar with the halls of power are willing to navigate for others—for a price.

The migration from public servant to lobbyist knows no party preference, either. Consider former New York Democratic representative Joe Crowley. Heading into the 2018 election season, Crowley looked like a slam dunk to be reelected, facing only pitiably token Republican opposition and a far-left primary challenge from some twenty-nine-year-old bartender. Neither seemed much of a match for Crowley, the House's fourth highest-ranking Democrat and a possible successor to Representative Nancy Pelosi for the speakership.

But something happened on the way to the gavel: Crowley lost his primary to the bartender: Alexandria Ocasio-Cortez. Ocasio-Cortez was part of a grassroots trend in both parties fueled by suspicion of longtime officeholders. She was able to make hay by painting Crowley as the secret puppet of corporate interests.

Crowley landed at Squire Patton Boggs, where he could be a more overt puppet of corporate interests. Yes, that's the same "high"-flying firm that snapped up Republican Boehner. What's more, Crowley shared his hiring announcement with former Pennsylvania Republican congressman Bill Shuster, who had retired after eighteen years in Congress. (During his time on Capitol Hill, Shuster had earned a reputation for being in bed with a lobbyist—literally. He admitted to an affair with an airline lobbyist just before his retirement.[20]) Crowley and Shuster were welcomed by another bipartisan tandem of ex–elected officials, Mississippi Republican senator Trent Lott and former Louisiana Democratic senator John Breaux.

It's not just Squire Patton Boggs that does this, by the way. Another power lobbyist firm, Akin Gump Strauss Hauer & Feld LLP, boasts former senator Joe Donnelly (D-IN), former senator John Sununu (R-NH), former representative Ileana Ros-Lehtinen (R-FL), and former representative Filemon Vela (D-TX). Any major lobbying firm worth its salt will try to build a bipartisan team of big names. They want to promise influence for their clients, no matter which party is in power.

One might reasonably observe this phenomenon with a noncommittal shrug. If you want to be that dog in the internet meme (sipping coffee and telling everyone "This is fine" as the house burns around you), you could argue that old politicians heading to K Street are the industry's equivalent of being put out to pasture. Just as aging star athletes find jobs as coaches and broadcasters after their playing careers end, politicians might find comfort in being adjacent to their former profession without being "in the game." Taking it a step further, you might argue that as pols get further away from their time in office, their effectiveness becomes moot. Does anyone on the Hill care what John Boehner has to say now, eight years after his speakership ended?

That's a fair point and might be a mitigating factor if the migration between Capitol Hill and K Street was only one way. Yet, like many DC streets, that path is circuitous and often brings you back to where you started (thanks, L'Enfant). The relationship between politicians and lobbyists is known as the "revolving door" for a reason.

Former Arizona senator Jon Kyl (R-AZ) had an excellent twenty-year career as a public interest attorney and lobbyist when he was elected to Congress in 1986. He served three terms in the House and another three in the Senate before retiring in 2013, rising to the rank of Senate minority whip. After his long career, he signed on as a lobbyist with Covington & Burling. And then things got interesting. When Kyl's former colleague Senator John McCain died in 2018, Arizona's Republican governor Doug Ducey (former CEO of the ice cream parlor company Cold Stone Creamery) appointed Kyl to the seat until a special election could decide who would fill out the remainder of McCain's term. Kyl spent a few months in the halls of Congress before yielding to a former senator (and serial loser), Martha McSally. He then hurried right back to the friendly skies of Covington & Burling.

Kyl was prohibited from being a registered lobbyist immediately; congressional rules include "cooling off" periods that prohibit direct lobbying from former members and staff for at least a year. Yet the fact that his lobbying firm allowed him to take what was essentially a leave of absence illustrates how little the official title of "lobbyist" actually matters.

$$\$ \ \$ \ \$$$

Lobbying, by definition, is a direct attempt to alter a policymaker's decision. For the legislative branch, that means meeting directly with elected representatives and their staff to convince the representative to vote a certain way. (For the executive branch, the decision point may be a rule-making or enforcement action; we'll have some fun a little later when we discuss lobbying the executive branch.)

Former Louisiana representative Billy Tauzin (a Republican originally elected as a Democrat) showed he knew just how the system worked. Tauzin gave a different meaning to the term "revolving door." After winning election to the House in a 1980 special election, Tauzin represented his district as one of the most conservative Democrats in the caucus for fourteen years. When the Republicans claimed the majority in 1995, so did Tauzin (who promptly switched parties to continue as a Republican).

By 2003, Tauzin's experience and partisan affiliation resulted in his election as chair of the House Energy and Commerce Committee—which made him a crucial congressional ally for President George W. Bush's efforts to create a prescription drug benefit for Medicare recipients. As with any bill involving government subsidies, business communities took a not-so-passive interest, seeking a piece of the government largesse while trying to ensure their opponents didn't enjoy an outsized piece of the pie.

In this case, insurance companies and the pharmaceutical industry were key players. The latter wanted to ensure the largest possible subsidy amount; the former wanted to drive drug prices down to maximize profits for insurance companies. Tauzin, one of the bill's writers, was careful to include several provisions favorable to the prescription drug industry (such as prohibitions on price controls or measures that would artificially decrease drug costs), as NBC reported.[21]

In 2004, a year after Medicare Part D passed, Tauzin called it a congressional career. As soon as his term ended in January 2005—as in, *the very next day* after his term ended—he signed on as the chief lobbyist for PhRMA, the pharmaceutical industry's trade group. His estimated annual salary? A cool $2 million. Tauzin spent the next five years working for—and being well compensated by—the industry he had dutifully helped during the legislative debate around Medicare Part D. He hadn't lost his touch, as he proved instrumental in helping shape the Affordable Care Act in 2009 to allow for critical pharmaceutical support. He later started a pair of companies and served a stint with the lobbying firm Alston & Bird. It turns out, there *are* second acts in American lives. At least, when it comes to our political elites.

$ $ $

Congress has occasionally given lip service to the problem of influence peddling, with reforms drawing positive attention from both sides of the aisle. But politicians are predictably reluctant to poke holes in their own golden parachutes. And regulating lobbying can be tricky because no one quite knows how to define it.

When most of us think of lobbyists, we might imagine slick players in pinstriped three-piece suits and gold pinky rings using their relationships to glad-hand officials. "John, we go all the way to the state legislature," this imaginary lobbyist might drawl to a harried congressman. "Can't you do your old pal a favor and vote for this here chicken subsidy bill?" (A briefcase full of money is usually thrown in, for good measure.)

The reality is more banal and involves excessive haggling over Outlook calendars. Informal conversations and a good relationship here or there can grease the skids to make meetings happen; knowledge of the process is essential. Further, an "off-the-record" conversation between friends can provide insight into what it takes to win an official's support or vote. Former members of Congress who bring their contact lists and understanding can provide value for lobbying firms, even if they never set foot in a Capitol Hill office. The associations and personal relationships they retain after years of service also provide cover for any conversations they may have. After all, if no one is taking notes, who can tell the difference between a lobbyist meeting and a couple of friends catching up over drinks?

Consider former Senate majority leader Tom Daschle (D-SD). After losing his South Dakota seat in 2004, Daschle joined Alston & Bird (the same lobby shop that would eventually hire Tauzin). There, Daschle served as a "special policy advisor." He later signed on with DLA Piper for a while before moving to Baker Donelson—serving as a non-lobbyist for both firms. He wouldn't officially register as a lobbyist until 2016 (for health insurance giant Aetna), *Politico* reported.[22] Daschle still had illusions of returning to elected office one day and thought the title "lobbyist" would make him sound dirty to voters.

Ironically, not registering as a lobbyist includes other perks that could be advantageous for someone looking to influence his former colleagues, such as access to the Senate gym.[23] But how did he get away with it? It turns out that regulations at that time had what became known as the "Daschle loophole." A lobbyist wasn't officially considered a lobbyist (and thus did not have to submit the filings that would spotlight their activities) if they spent less than 20 percent of their work time lobbying and avoided contact with legislators.

That loophole contains an essential word: "legislators." That means lobbyists that have contact with executive branch policymakers are not subject to the same rules.

For example, Congress frequently surrenders rulemaking authority to executive branch entities within the broader scope of pieces of legislation. Consider the alphabet soup of federal regulatory organizations: CDC,

FCC, FTC, FAA, FDA, EPA...Smash three letters together, and there's a good chance you'll get a government bureaucracy that has some kind of rulemaking authority. And you can lean on them without being called a lobbyist.

You can also lean on presidential campaigns. When WikiLeaks dumped a trove of emails from John Podesta (Hillary Clinton's 2016 campaign chairman), the batch included correspondence between Podesta and Daschle. Before officially registering as a lobbyist for Aetna, Daschle emailed Podesta regarding the proposed merger between Aetna and Humana (a proposal Clinton had criticized on the campaign trail). Daschle attempted to set up a meeting to help soften the candidate's rhetoric. (Apparently, corporate America thought it was crucial to court Hillary Clinton—never mind, we covered that already.)

Six months later, Daschle decided to register as a lobbyist and report such correspondence, but when he clicked Send on his chummy email to Podesta, he had no such restrictions. It feels icky, but it was all perfectly legal.

Still, Congress continues to struggle to restrict this type of activity and slow the spin of the revolving door. Even Senator Ted Cruz and Representative Alexandria Ocasio-Cortez—not exactly ideological pals—both called for a lifetime ban on lobbying for former members of Congress. It's not a new idea, though even with bipartisan support, it has failed to gain the traction legislation needs to become law.

Most recently, Senator Jon Tester (D-MT), Senator Michael Bennet (D-CO), and (now former) Senator Cory Gardner (R-CO) introduced it in the Close the Revolving Door Act of 2019. The bill languished in committee until one of the sponsors, Gardner, lost his reelection bid in 2020.

Guess what Gardner has been up to lately? In June 2021, he joined the board of advisors for Michael Best Strategies. A lobbying firm.[24] You can't make this stuff up.

Slush Funds

Believe it or not, as late as 1989, some members of Congress were still allowed to personally keep millions of dollars in campaign cash when they retired. For the last quarter of a century or so, this gambit has been strictly illegal. But that doesn't mean a politician's war chest has to be refunded to the donor or given to charity (although that is an option... for *suckers*). For one thing, they can set up their own nonprofit foundation, name it after themselves (for example, the Evan and Susan Bayh Foundation[25]), do good deeds, and take the credit.

The most obvious example of this is the aforementioned Clinton Foundation (now the Bill, Hillary and Chelsea Clinton Foundation), established in 1997—a name that conjures all sorts of images, including foreign governments like Qatar gaining access to a once (and presumed future) president.[26] But even if you put aside the optics and allegations, the Clinton Foundation also demonstrates how messy this business can be and how ostensibly charitable activities can result in profit for the principal.

Consider a 2011 memo written by longtime Clinton aide Doug Band and reported on by *USA Today*, which demonstrates how Bill Clinton's personal wealth was tied to the foundation: "Independent of our fundraising and decision-making activities on behalf of the Foundation, we have dedicated ourselves to helping the President secure and engage in for-profit activities—including speeches, books, and advisory service engagements," Band wrote. "In that context, we have in effect served as agents, lawyers, managers and implementers to secure speaking, business and advisory service deals. In support of the President's for-profit activity, we also have solicited and obtained, as appropriate, in-kind services for the President and his family for personal travel, hospitality, vacation and the like."[27]

But the Bidens and Clintons aren't representative of most former law-makers, so I hesitate to spend too much time on them. The truth is, they are simply a concentrated microcosm of the revolving door writ large.

Back to your average retired member of Congress who leaves office with leftover campaign money. A December 2021 piece in *Roll Call* noted that more than twenty of the lawmakers who had announced they were leaving Congress after the 117th Congress "will hit the exits with nearly $53 million in combined leftover political cash, including in their cam-paign accounts and separate leadership PACs."[28] We are talking about tens of millions of dollars effectively being transferred every couple of years from political donors to retiring politicians to oversee and use—even if they can't personally use the money as a salary or to pay off their mortgage.

"The question comes up: What can politicians do with the left-over PAC money, and the answer is pretty much whatever they want," declared Dave Levinthal, communications director for the Washington, DC–based Center for Responsive Politics back in 2010, according to ABC News.[29]

Even former politicians who don't go into lobbying (or become a "strategic advisor") can still retain significant influence—based on the campaign cash they have left over. This money can be used to influence other politicians or (increasingly) to fund the lifestyle of a former politi-cian who still controls it.

The new trend is for former lawmakers to form a leadership PAC where they can draw on a personal slush fund to build their post-electoral political fiefdom and continue to live the lifestyle to which they have become accustomed. Take, for example, the case of former representa-tive Ileana Ros-Lehtinen (R-FL), who has used her old campaign cash to buy meals, lodging, and even Disney World tickets. According to Axios, "The former congresswoman told the FEC all of those expenses covered legitimate political activities related to her support for other candidates and were not for personal use."[30] Because the FEC declined to pursue the case when they deadlocked in a three-to-three vote (the commission is currently split along party lines), there is now precedent for the loophole to continue until or unless Congress closes it.

But even if that happens, ex-lawmakers will still have plenty of other ways to cash in on their networks, experience, and influence.

Who says you can't take it with you?

Chapter 10

Don't Eat the Rich

Take dead aim on the rich boys. Get them in the crosshairs and take them down. Just remember, they can buy anything, but they can't buy backbone. Don't let them forget that.
> —*Herman Blume (portrayed by Bill Murray)*
> *in* **Rushmore**

By now, you're probably convinced that in modern America, the rich get elected and the elected get rich (and get even richer after leaving office). Moreover, suppose I have done my job. In that case, you are probably aware of at least the perception that our elected officials are more interested in feathering their nests than they are in public service; you recognize that this priority is corrosive to our nation.

So what do we do? Try to fix it, obviously. But we have to be wise about this. We live in a fallen world. No political reform can fix that. As James Madison said, men are not angels. So we need rules to incentivize good behavior and punish bad behavior.

In a healthy culture, people's interests converge with the institution's and society's interests. The key is to institute policies that mitigate our human nature and reward civilized and ethical behavior. This keen insight was taken from our nation's creation—unlike utopian regimes that believe they can change human nature on their way to reimagining the world.

As author and Fordham Law professor Zephyr Teachout writes in *Corruption in America*, "the framers built their bulwarks against corruption through structural rules."[1] One example of what she was talking about was the prohibition on accepting gifts or "emoluments" from foreign countries. Such rules are not only designed to prevent quid pro quo bribery but also to preempt and prevent a culture of corruption. Teachout writes that "A *system* was corrupt when the public power was excessively used to serve private ends instead of the public good," and that "A *person* was corrupt when they use public power for private ends."[2] When we look at politicians' misappropriation of campaign funds and insider trading in Congress, it is clear that we have both a systemic *and* an individual problem. What so many of our political leaders are doing to enrich themselves may not always (or even usually) be illegal, but it *is* corrupt.

America's Founders were students of history. They were obsessed with Rome and why the Republic fell. And as the description of historian Ramsay MacMullen's *Corruption and the Decline of Rome* puts it, "Rome's fall was the steady loss of focus and control over government as its aims were thwarted for private gain by high-ranking bureaucrats and military leaders."[3] As H. W. Brands notes in his book *The First American*, after the Revolutionary War, Benjamin Franklin believed that Great Britain's "'great disease'...was the large number and emoluments of her political offices; her downfall the 'avarice and passion' these aroused in her public officials....As long as riches [were] attached to [the] office, Britain would suffer."[4] There are many reasons why nations fail, but the perception that the game is rigged for the ruling class is certainly one of them.

Again, the desire to accumulate wealth and power is entirely human and, to some degree, unavoidable. But a healthy culture that is bolstered by what Teachout refers to as "prophylactic rules" can preempt, diminish, and manage these urges. We should be thankful that the Founders created a system that aspires to do that. However, as times (and technology) change, so must we adapt. In a sense, this is an arms race against the forces of barbarism. Because the world is not static, we must constantly be vigilant in finding ways to curb our carnal nature. This great experiment is, as Ben Franklin famously said outside of Independence Hall in 1787, "A republic, if you can keep it."

Can we keep it? It's worth asking whether the reforms have kept pace with the temptations, especially at the upper echelons of politics. The following are some new (or never-really-been-tried) reform ideas that deserve our attention, if not our support.

Ban Stock Trading for Congress and Their Families

The most obvious thing we can do is to ban stock trading for members of Congress and their families. This step has been necessitated by the failure of past reforms to curb the practice. The STOCK Act, passed in 2012, already banned insider trading for members of Congress, but this act was inherently hard to police—even in cases with curious trades. Most politicians who end up in trouble over questionable stock trades tell us that someone else manages their transactions. In some cases, this is a spouse; in other cases, it's a financial professional.

And the truth is, many are probably telling the truth. Good investment advisors will naturally buy energy and defense companies before a military escalation for investment purposes, and their clients benefit. But questions remain, including:

1. Are the elected feeding information to the discretionary investment advisors?

2. If the elected official gave an advisor this investment discretion, why not just close the loop and go to full blind trust?

3. Don't the optics matter?

Regarding the optics, as Emma Lydon, managing director of P Street, the sister organization to the Progressive Change Campaign Committee, told me: "The second you're asking the public to trust that you're not breaking the law, you're losing."[5] Theoretically, a blind trust should assuage our concerns, but that stopgap measure has not diminished the appearance of impropriety to the degree it has been voluntarily tried.

It's time to ban members of Congress and their immediate families from owning and purchasing individual stocks. Now, some people argue that such a ban would have the effect of causing the best and brightest to opt out of public service. Take Senator Tommy Tuberville (R-AL) for example. "I think [a ban is] ridiculous. They might as well start sending robots up here," he told *The Independent*. "I think it would really cut back on the amount of people that would want to come up here and serve."[6]

Others disagree. "I mean, give me a break, it's total garbage,"[7] said former governor and congressman Mark Sanford (R-SC) when I raised the excuse for doing nothing.

Of course, implementing this sort of policy should be done in a thoughtful manner. "In some cases, lawmakers might enter Congress with existing, difficult-to-liquidate assets that predate their government service," writes Josh Barro,[8] adding that "these are harder cases, and we would need a framework for dealing with these situations that does not discourage successful people from serving in government." But aside from such accommodations, individual stocks should be banned, though after divestment, members should still be allowed to hold mutual funds. (Generally speaking, these are risk-averse and broad-based portfolios that include hundreds of stocks. For this reason, it would be nearly impossible for a politician's conflict of interest to result in more than marginal financial gains.)

Increase Transparency

After almost two decades in city management—including stints as assistant city manager in Plano, Texas, as well as city manager in Garland, DeSoto, Farmersville, and Sundown—my friend Ron Holifield founded Strategic Government Resources to help train and mentor local leaders. When I talked with Ron about some of the problems in national politics, including (but not limited to) the appearance of congressional insider trading, he told me that many of the problems we see in Congress are addressed in the codes of ethics that most local governments have already implemented. These codes stress loyalty to the interests of the citizens first, as well as preserving integrity and independence. What is more, in many places, violating a code of ethics results in a misdemeanor.

I prodded Ron for more information, and he sent me an article about Mission, Texas, from July 2, 2022, which includes this idea: "A longstanding item labeled 'disclosure of conflict of interest' will be near the top of each meeting agenda, which the city posts at least seven days before a meeting. If there is an agenda item in which a vendor or an elected official has a conflicting interest, it will be stated on the agenda and put on public record."[9]

Imagine a scenario where members of Congress must disclose all potential conflicts of interest *before* voting on any bill. Imagine a scenario where politicians tell us about their investments before voting on something that might make them richer. "This particular step is fairly rare but powerful," Ron said.

In a perfect world, compromised politicians might even be forced to recuse themselves. Indeed, the House Ethics Manual *already* states that "Every Member...shall vote on each question put, unless he has a direct personal or pecuniary interest in the event of such question."[10] The catch is the part about "direct personal" interest. As C. Simon Davidson, a lawyer who wrote a regular column about congressional ethics, noted, "while a Member should not vote on bills in which he has a direct interest as an individual, he may vote on bills that affect him as a member of a class."

Being a stockholder theoretically makes you a member of a *class*. As you can see, this is a huge loophole that allows politicians to vote for their own self-interest with impunity. Still, requiring members to publicize their potential conflicts of interest before voting would be a step forward. That's probably also a pipe dream.

Ban Politicians from Hiring Their Families

In chapter 5, I talked about how politicians spread the wealth around. One way is to pay members of their family to work on their campaigns. While family members should certainly be allowed to volunteer on a campaign, there really is no reason they should view this as a profitable endeavor. In 2022, Representative Pat Fallon (R-TX) introduced the Family Integrity to Reform Elections (FIRE) Act, which would ban such payments, including those made by political committees affiliated with the candidate. "Americans are sick of politicians abusing their voters' hard-earned money," said Fallon, according to the *New York Post*. "This modern-day spoils system must end. My bill shines light on shady campaign finance practices while punishing those who take advantage of these funds to enrich their families."[11]

The bill had real teeth. Anyone who violated the proposed law would receive "a fine of either $100,000 for each violation or twice the amount paid to the family members—whichever is greater—and/or imprisonment for up to two years."[12]

But we should go further and also ban *presidential* nepotism. As the *Boston Globe* opines, "Congress should pass a bill to make explicit that the president cannot appoint a relative to any official government post, even if they forgo a salary. In the event that a president's relative is widely perceived to be the best qualified for a certain role, that appointment should require a waiver from Congress so that the candidate can be evaluated on their merits."[13]

Pay Congress More

You heard me right. It sounds counterintuitive to pay politicians more money—especially in a book titled *Filthy Rich Politicians* (and especially since many of the proposed reforms are geared toward reducing perks). After all, the annual salary of a member of Congress is already $174,000, which greatly exceeds that of the average American. Members of Congress also receive a generous allowance to help cover their office and travel expenses. What is more, although members of Congress do not (despite internet memes) enjoy free health care, their benefits are commensurate with those enjoyed by private sector employees working for a large company.[14] The biggest perk may be that "In the Capital region only, they may receive free medical outpatient care at military facilities," as Snopes noted.[15]

So why do I believe members of Congress should be paid more? First, as journalist Matthew Yglesias has noted, "Congressional pay has been declining in inflation-adjusted terms since the mid-1960s, even while incomes for other professional occupations have risen."[16] Second, there is a natural temptation for politicians, who must rub elbows with the rich (to raise campaign cash), to aspire to that same lifestyle. Unless we are going to throw out our current campaign finance system and go to public campaign financing (an idea that, regardless of the merits, seems unlikely any time soon), a salary that is too low could have the unintended consequence of incentivizing corruption. And third, a salary that is too low would end up dissuading highly qualified individuals from going into public service.

In early 2022, Texas representative Dan Crenshaw, a Republican, was asked by a podcaster about his stock trades and whether he supported banning members of Congress from owning individual stocks. *Vox* reported that Crenshaw claimed to be "neutral" on the idea, but then he said, "If you want only millionaires and billionaires to run for Congress, then keep making sure we can't raise our pay. Just keep in mind that no one will run for Congress because you have no way to better yourself."[17]

One way to better yourself is to *leave*. This outcome is often salutary. The Founders didn't expect members of Congress to stick around Washington forever. However, if a salary is too low, it won't attract talented people in the first place. What is more, a salary that is too low might make it impossible for John Q. Public to serve at all. Regarding state legislatures, Morgan Cullen of the National Conference of State Legislatures writes that "Salaries should be enough to attract highly qualified candidates with a variety of diverse backgrounds and experiences, while also ensuring that everyone—rich or poor—can afford to serve."[18]

Another problem is brain drain—the attrition of knowledgeable, intelligent people. Super-rich politicians stick around Washington for fun and attention, while ambitious young politicians use politics as a springboard to an even better gig. Former senator Ben Sasse (R-NE) might be an example of both brain drain and using his perch in Washington as a stepping-stone. In October 2022, word leaked that Sasse (who had been reelected in 2020 for a six-year term) was planning to resign to become president of the University of Florida. The immediate speculation was that Sasse had taken the job for a pay increase (likely around $1 million). "US Senator is one of those weird jobs where you help control trillions but quitting often gets you a raise," observed *Bloomberg* reporter Steven Dennis.[19]

Sasse's premature departure in January of 2023 was too bad for those of us who would have loved to see Sasse translate his high-minded lectures about Edmund Burke and Alexis de Tocqueville into leading and legislating. He never really did. But for Sasse, I suspect, it all paid off. Legislating wasn't as much fun as it might have been in a more civilized era, and Sasse (who previously served as president of Midland University, "a small Lutheran school in Nebraska"[20]) was able to parlay his political experience and notoriety into a high-paying, prestigious gig. It's hard to blame him for doing what's best for him and his family, even if it's a sad commentary on our politics. (It is unlikely the next senator from Nebraska will feel the need to flee Congress for a higher-paying job. In January 2023, former Nebraska governor Pete Ricketts, a Republican who also happens to be part owner of the Chicago Cubs and the son of the founder of TD Ameritrade,[21] was appointed to replace Sasse in the US Senate.)

Being elected to Congress is *not* about bettering yourself financially. But this is the real world, and we are talking about humans. Members of Congress are expected to reside in their home districts (the expense of which varies by area) and also live much of the year near Washington, DC, which is a decidedly pricey location. In the past, members of Congress resorted to sleeping in their congressional offices or living in group homes. Each option has downsides, and neither is conducive to a politician bringing their family with them.

"Practical difficulties can ensue for less wealthy members who spend much of the year in Washington," noted Elizabeth Titus in the *Texas Tribune*.[22] "Henry Bonilla, a former Texas congressman, said some members did not want the public to know they slept in their offices and showered in the House gym." Conversely, other members "publicize such actions as a symbol of frugality that appealed to constituents back home."[23]

Regardless, most of us probably don't consider the toll associated with living in two different places, especially when one location is the nation's capital (consistently rated as one of the most expensive cities in America). "Given the travel and expenses involved, it's not a simple matter to raise a family on what a member is paid," says Yuval Levin, a senior fellow at the American Enterprise Institute. "And if you haven't already made a lot of money, and if you're the kind of person who could, you're not really inclined to run for Congress right now."[24]

End Double-Dipping

Numerous social media posts also inaccurately claim that members of Congress receive lavish pensions.[25] This myth is so pervasive that even people who run for Congress might believe it. Remember Representative George Santos (R-NY), the serial fabulist we met in chapter 3? In 2023, Santos's former friend and roommate, Gregory Morey, confided to CBS News' Caitlin Huey-Burns that Santos once told him, "If I can get elected to Congress, for just one term, I will be set with a pension and health care for the rest of my life."[26] The joke's on him. As *Newsweek* pointed out, "Members of Congress are only eligible for a pension aged sixty-two if they served for at least five years, or aged fifty if they completed twenty years in Congress. Those who completed twenty-five years of service are eligible for a pension at any age."[27] As I write this, it seems unlikely that Santos's tenure in Congress will be long enough for him to qualify. Regardless, the larger point is that congressional retirement plans are pretty much in line with what other federal employees receive.[28]

Having said that, something approaching 20 percent of members of Congress are also "double-dipping," which is to say they are able to collect their full taxpayer-funded salary, plus receive a governmental pension from their days working as an elected official in state government. In 2013, *National Journal*'s Shane Goldmacher noted that "freshman

Rep. Joyce Beatty, D-Ohio, received $253,323 from her government pension last year—a sum that, combined with her congressional salary, will make her better paid than President Obama this year."[29] One could argue that it is wrong for members of Congress to receive *two* checks from the taxpayers. That strikes me as a reasonable take. But that issue is separate from whether members of Congress should receive higher salaries.

Let Campaigns Cover Health Insurance for the Candidate

And if we're going to contemplate paying members of Congress more, perhaps we should also consider allowing political candidates to make a living wage while running for office. Chapter 3 discusses how the inability to take time off from one's job is a primary reason why ordinary working people do not tend to run for political office.

Right now, the FEC only allows candidates to pay themselves the *lower* amount of two options: the candidate's previous salary or $174,000, which is the salary for a member of Congress. This is problematic for people who made significantly less than that. One possible reform would be to allow candidates to earn more money from their campaign. The problem is that reforms sometimes have unintended consequences. Running for office is already a racket for too many (to gain attention and fame and raise their profile). Making the act of merely running for office a highly profitable endeavor would result in an influx of perennial candidates who would rather "Potemkin campaign" than get a real job. The late literary agent Lucianne Goldberg used to serve a dish at dinner parties she called "Chicken Harold Stassen." It was a reference to the former governor of Minnesota who ran *nine* failed presidential races. Goldberg's joke was that the chicken is "So bad you can't keep it down."[30] Resilience isn't always a salutary quality. I suspect every state has at least one of these guys. There are already enough of these candidates as it is.

In Maryland, where I'm from, there's a guy named Robin Ficker, who has run dozens of failed campaigns.[31] The last thing we need are more incentives for perennial candidates to turn candidacy into a full-time career.

And even for potentially viable campaigns, do we want people to view running for office as a way to cash in personally? Presumably, the voters would punish a candidate who exploits this system, but we can't count on that. During a 2000 interview, Donald Trump boasted to *Fortune*: "It's very possible that I could be the first presidential candidate to run and make money on it."[32] The reformer's job is difficult because we are balancing competing challenges.

Perhaps more troubling is that candidates cannot pay for their own health insurance with campaign funds, even though they *can* use those funds to insure campaign staffers.[33] Changing this strikes me as a commonsense compromise that should be enacted. (The FEC is considering making reforms that would potentially allow candidates to earn more money and also health insurance, and there may be some movement. As *Roll Call* noted, in recent years, the FEC has ruled that candidates can use campaign funds for child care[34] as well as for personal security—perhaps a sign of the times.)[35]

Treat Books Like Speeches

Since 1991, members of Congress have been prohibited from making money from speeches. What is more, they are prohibited from earning more than $29,595[36] in "outside earned income" above and beyond their salary. (Note: income from investments doesn't count, as it is considered "unearned"[37]). For some reason, the law exempts book deals, according to the *Washington Post*.[38] But why? One reason for prohibiting politicians from profiting off of speeches was that they could accept paid speaking engagements from people or industries hoping to curry favor.

But laundering this payment through bulk book orders isn't much different. Writing a book is also a time-consuming endeavor (trust me), so if an elected official does so primarily to boost their income, I have to wonder about their priorities.

According to the House Committee on Ethics, "In the debate preceding adoption of the [outside earned income] rule, one Member distinguished earned income as that which one earns 'by the sweat of [one's] brow.'"[39] Any author will tell you that writing a book is hard work. It may not be sweat-inducing labor, but it is work. As such, regarding members of Congress, they should be allowed to write as many books as they want. However, money earned from books (both advances and royalties) should be limited to fit within the "outside earned income/outside employment" restrictions.

Term Limits

For years, I opposed term limits. I think my reasoning was formed when Ronald Reagan told an interviewer that he wanted to "start a movement to eliminate the constitutional amendment...that limits a President to two terms." It's worth noting that Reagan did not wish this rule change to apply to himself, "but for Presidents from here on."[40] Reagan's populist premise was that we have term limits on our elected officials every two to six years in elections. Why not trust the voters?

Likewise, I was also persuaded that there would be unintended consequences. We would deprive voters of returning a highly qualified and experienced public servant to office and empower a permanent leadership class of bureaucrats, staffers, and lobbyists. Years ago, at a conservative conclave, I raised these points to a major political donor and activist who had dedicated much of his life to enacting term limits. I'll never forget his response: "I've already spent so much money and time on this cause that I can't abandon it now." I had to respect his honesty, but it's good to reevaluate our priorities every once in a while. At least I'm taking my own advice.

The last few years have led me to question my faith in the American public's ability to vet and remove truly bad actors from public office. At the same time, as I began to research and write this book, new problems (such as insider trading) became more important to me. While instituting term limits wouldn't solve the problems addressed in this book, it would mitigate the amount of damage that a politician, hell-bent on enriching himself in office, could do.

A Ten-Year Prohibition on Lobbying

According to the House Committee on Ethics, section 207 of the Ethics Reform Act of 1989 imposes a one-year "cooling-off period" on the former members, officers, and covered employees.[41] For senators, the period lasts two years—for good reason. As Public Citizen (a nonprofit consumer advocacy organization) notes, "The intent is to keep former officials and employees from tapping into their inside connections in government for private gain."[42]

Those claiming to be the most serious about "draining the swamp" want a lifetime ban on lobbying for former members. This stance is popular on both the populist left and the populist right. As Texas senator Ted Cruz tweeted in 2019, "Here's something I don't say often: on this point, I AGREE with [Representative Alexandria Ocasio-Cortez]. Indeed, I have long called for a LIFETIME BAN on former Members of Congress becoming lobbyists. The Swamp would hate it, but perhaps a chance for some bipartisan cooperation?"[43] (emphasis his).

But even if it could muster enough votes, I'm not sure a lifetime ban could survive legally. As such, I would settle on an across-the-board ten-year ban. Again, though, like every reform, this is no panacea. To paraphrase Jeff Goldblum in *Jurassic Park*, *money* finds a way.

End Pensions for Presidents

As noted in chapter 2, Harry S. Truman's poor financial state inspired Congress to eventually pass the Former Presidents Act of 1958, which provided a $25,000 annual pension for ex-presidents, as well as administrative support. Since then, however, things have changed. Anyone elected to president these days is either already a millionaire, or they possess almost unlimited earning potential after having served as president. Donald Trump, a billionaire, receives hundreds of thousands of dollars (counting his pension and benefits) annually.[44] It is at least conceivable that some future president could find themselves in need of a pension. If that happens, one should be provided. But no president who is a millionaire (and that describes every modern ex-president) should receive another check from the taxpayers.

Make Tax Rules Fair

"Congressional wealth comes from many different places, but one thing links it together: These lawmakers, unlike most of their constituents, do not draw the bulk of their income from a paycheck," according to the *Atlantic*.[45] A step that would help would be to tax capital gains at the same rate as ordinary income. The problem is the catch-22: Simply put, why would the winners want to change the game?

Consider how working people are taxed at a higher rate than people who primarily make their money off investments. As Tax Policy Center research analyst Philip Stallworth noted in 2019, "Under current law, long-term capital gains and qualified dividends are taxed at significantly lower rates than ordinary income." Now, most of us are paying that higher tax rate. But according to Stallworth's calculations, for people making $3.4 million or more (which includes many elected officials), "more than half of [their] income comes from interest, dividends, and capital gains, while only one-quarter comes from wages and benefits."[46]

Many Americans—even some on the right—see this as unfair. As Tucker Carlson told me,[47] "The way it's currently structured, the message is really clear: you're an idiot if you work for a living. You're an idiot if you work for a wage. The smart people are investing money. *But what if I don't have any money to invest?*" he asked rhetorically. "I shouldn't feel like I'm a fool, should I? *If only I'd gone into finance.* That shouldn't be the hope of every person in America with an IQ over 120. And now it is. The really smart people go into finance. Is that a good thing?"

While I was writing this book, Virginia governor Glenn Youngkin, a Republican (who earned an MBA from Harvard and worked at the global management and consulting firm McKinsey & Company before joining the multinational private equity firm Carlyle Group in 1995 as an analyst),[48] made news by donating his entire gubernatorial salary to various charities. He also made news when a lawsuit accused him of making millions of dollars in stocks and paying zero taxes on it—legally. "Under the deal, approved by the Carlyle board and code-named 'Project Phoenix,'" NBC News reported, Youngkin "began receiving $8.5 million in cash and exchanged his almost $200 million stake in the company for an equal amount of tax-free shares, according to court documents."[49]

While this deal was perfectly legal, advantaging financial speculation over physical labor is the kind of thing that causes many average Americans to conclude that the game is rigged.

Beware Unintended Consequences

None of these reforms are a panacea. However, I believe they would go a long way toward restoring confidence in the system. In today's politics—on both sides of the aisle—it seems the cool kids have settled on a false choice: we can look the other way while more and more Americans lose faith in our institutions, or we can wise up and start a revolution. I prefer the third option: to acknowledge our problems and fix them. That's the case for tax reform. Still, as noted earlier, we should be careful about what we seek to change and how we seek to change it.

Let's consider, for example, the Bipartisan Campaign Reform Act, aka McCain-Feingold, which kicked in following the 2002 elections. Although its motives were to reduce the corrupting influence of money in politics, the results were…well, look at the state of our politics today. The bill included a ban on "soft money," which is money given to political parties (and the party committees dedicated to House and Senate elections) for party building and overhead expenses. This provision weakened political parties, ultimately rendering them impotent and unable to perform their one vital role: vetting and selecting sane and decent nominees. The result would be Donald Trump winning the Republican nomination in 2016.

But that's not the only recent and virtuous-sounding reform that has backfired: In 2021, Democrats brought back the practice of earmarks, which allow members of Congress to insert pork spending into bills (you know, like the one we discussed in chapter 4 when former Speaker Dennis Hastert added an earmark to a transportation bill without telling anyone he owned land next to the highway he was funding). While eliminating earmarks (which Republicans did after they won control of Congress in the 2010 midterms) seemed like a prudent and positive reform, it soon became clear that this unseemly form of legal bribery acted as a sort of lubricant that kept the wheels of Congress moving. Democrats decided to bring it back (rebranding the practice "community project funding"), and it has been used in a bipartisan fashion. "It's my last couple of years, so I decided to make the most of it," boasted Senator Roy Blunt.[50] But there was an important distinction tacked onto President Joe Biden's 2022 $1.5 trillion omnibus spending bill. According to the *New York Times*: "Each lawmaker had to sign a form attesting that they had no personal or family connection to it."[51] After retaking the House in 2023, Republicans chose to tighten up earmarks.[52] But they wisely did not get rid of them altogether.

The Toothpick Rule

Sometimes (as was the case with the ban on soft money and the earmark ban) unintended consequences result in truly negative externalities. Other times, they are silly window dressings that result when politicians are forced to comply with onerous regulations. In these cases, they usually waste time and energy trying to abide by rules while skirting their spirit.

Take, for example, a House ethics rule adopted in 2007 that allowed members of Congress and staffers to eat only "food or refreshments of a nominal value offered other than as part of a meal"[53] at Capitol Hill holiday parties and receptions. The only real change was that instead of sitting with forks and knives, you stand and eat them with toothpicks, sticks, or your fingers. As *BizBash* described one February 2007 event hosted by a Fortune 500 company, the reception featured "tempura lobster lollipops with a tomato/tarragon aioli, and one-bite rosemary lamb chops with a pomegranate sauce."[54]

To the degree that this reform *did* change behaviors, some believe the outcome was a net negative. "The opportunity for folks to interact with members of Congress and their staffs have been greatly reduced since 2007, and I think that may help to explain in part the dysfunction we're seeing," Chris DeLacy, whose expertise includes congressional gift and travel rules, told *Roll Call*.[55] "There are very few opportunities to meet with folks outside of a fund-raiser or a 15-minute meeting."[56]

My guess is the "toothpick rule," as it is colloquially referred to, didn't make the world a significantly worse place, just a more phony place that is slightly less enjoyable. The idea that this reform was going to stem corruption is laughable.

The point is that while positive reforms are needed, we should not assume that all reforms—even nice-sounding ones—will yield positive results. America's problems, including (but not limited to) the erosion of trust in our institutions, are deep-seated. These problems didn't materialize overnight, and we aren't going to fix them with a toothpick.

Finally...

My most important piece of advice—for those who want to change the way the game is rigged for filthy-rich politicians—is to not succumb to bitterness.

At the macro level, it's dangerous to believe the game is rigged (which is why changing the reality is important). Americans have lost faith in almost every institution, and there is a growing belief that the American experiment has failed. Even with all her blemishes (many of which are recent developments), I believe that the United States is a precious miracle that must be preserved at all costs. Preserving freedom requires America to constantly adjust. Right now, tremendous problems confront us, and one of many is distrust in American politicians. The reforms outlined in this chapter will help address that distrust. It's a mistake to dwell on the problems instead of focusing on the solutions.

But if not getting bogged down in the negatives is important at the macro level, it's also important at the micro level. The person who assumes the game is rigged against them will have little incentive to work hard (considering they already believe they cannot get ahead). If anything, they will work for *political* solutions—urging the government to use coercive powers to punish the rich. But they won't attempt to start a business. And they will probably die bitter and angry.

Now let's take a person who—maybe *quixotically*—believes they can succeed if they just work hard enough. They no doubt will be happier and more likely to succeed. Given a choice between naïve trust in the

American system and cynicism toward the fat cats in the ruling class, trust is better. The person who harbors resentment, anger, and aggrievement (stoked by the very political leaders they trust) will likely be worse off than the naïve person whose heart swells with patriotism every time they see Old Glory. And who's better off if this person eventually makes enough money to send their children to college?

We all intuitively understand that politicians are disproportionately rich, but the process of researching and documenting the phenomenon really underscored the point for me. It is very rare for someone to come from nothing and make it to Congress, much less the presidency. Even in cases where someone is not born financially wealthy, most elected officials are brought up relatively privileged by class, connections, knowledge, or education. This upbringing, no doubt, impacts their worldview. Then, upon (and after) being elected, most politicians find a way to dramatically increase their wealth, enrich their families, and make sure their children get a huge head start. This cycle reinforces the notion that the game is rigged.

Our response should not be to want to seize their wealth and redistribute it, but rather to create a country where income and social mobility are such that the old saying about how "anyone can grow up to be president" is true. Rather than trying to topple the regime, we can (and should) promote and implement the reforms spelled out in this book. These reforms will incentivize good behavior and disincentivize corruption, and they will prevent politicians from using the system (and our taxpayer dollars) to feather their nests.

The financial disparity between our leaders and our neighbors is huge. Unfortunately, the ruling-class elites have a vested financial interest in refusing to promote the reforms so desperately needed to rebuild Americans' trust. In order to preserve the American system, citizens should believe that the game isn't rigged. Achieving this level of trust will require commonsense reforms. And if Americans demand transparency and accountability from their elected leaders, I believe we can restore this trust.

It is only by taking steps to reform the system that we can restore faith in our institutions and preserve American democracy for future generations.

There really is no richer inheritance we could leave them.

The Richest Twenty-Five Members of Congress

Here are the twenty-five wealthiest members of Congress, according to *Business Insider* (2021).[1] Note: The order of the rankings and amounts come from them; the brief commentary below each name is my own.

25. Representative Ralph Norman, a Republican from South Carolina: $20,679,156

Ralph Norman is a top real estate developer in South Carolina. His dad, Warren Norman, started the Warren Norman Company, a real estate development company, in 1948, and Ralph joined the firm in 1975. Norman became embroiled in controversy in 2022, when it was revealed that he had texted Donald Trump's chief of staff Mark Meadows, urging Trump to declare "marshall law" [sic] so he could remain in office before Joe Biden's inauguration.[2]

24. Representative Sara Jacobs, a Democrat from California: $21,428,125

See chapter 3.

23. Representative John Rose, a Republican from Tennessee: $23,362,065

In 1992, John Rose cofounded Transcender Corporation, which is described as a "Provider of IT practice exams designed to help IT professionals gear up for their certification exams."[3] The firm reportedly sold for $60 million in 2000 to Kaplan, the test preparation giant. He then founded Boson Software, LLC, which also does certification prep for IT professionals. According to his official congressional website, Rose remains the owner and president.

22. Representative Fred Upton, a Republican from Michigan: $24,692,218

In 1922, Fred Upton's grandfather, Frederick, cofounded the Upton Machine Company with his brother Louis and uncle Emory. In 1950, that company later became known as the Whirlpool Corporation. (Note: Upton did not run for reelection in 2022, apparently worrying that his vote to impeach Donald Trump might cause him trouble. That's right, being super rich—and the uncle of supermodel Kate Upton—isn't enough to ensure election or reelection.)

21. Representative Dean Phillips, a Democrat from Minnesota: $24,778,495

Dean Phillips is the grandson of Pauline Phillips, the "Dear Abby" advice columnist. But that's not where the bulk of the family fortune comes from. It started in 1912 when Edward J. "Eddie" Phillips (Representative Phillips's great-grandfather) started a Minneapolis liquor business, the Phillips Distilling Company.[4] And it grew when Representative Phillips's adoptive father,[5] Eddie Phillips, took over the business; he introduced Belvedere vodka to the American market in 1996[6] and invested in Talenti gelato (Talenti sold to Unilever in 2014 for an undisclosed amount). Representative Phillips was the fifth member of his family to run the family business, according to *Roll Call*,[7] and he was elected to Congress in 2018.

20. Representative Kevin Hern, a Republican from Oklahoma: $26,761,380

See chapter 3.

19. Representative Kathy Manning, a Democrat from North Carolina:
$27,202,287

The daughter of a Ford Motor Company employee and a Michigan public school teacher, Kathy Manning is a former civil rights lawyer and a philanthropist. But her vast wealth seems to derive mostly from her marriage to Randall Kaplan. Kaplan's grandfather started Kay Chemical Company, "the leading global supplier of cleaning and sanitizing products and services to the [quick-service restaurant] industry with over 40 years of experience,"[8] in Greensboro, North Carolina. The business was sold to Ecolab in 1995, but Randall stayed on as their CEO until 1999.[9] Since then, Kaplan's work has included being chairman of Elm Street Technology and being CEO of Capsule Group, LLC.

In June 2022, the conservative site the *Washington Free Beacon* reported, "Manning and her husband hold more than $1 million in Seven Bridges Multi-Strategy Fund Ltd., her financial disclosure shows. The private fund is located in the Cayman Islands, a notorious tax haven for America's elite, according to SEC filings. In 2020, Manning earned up to $100,000 from the fund, which feeds into another investment fund that holds roughly $350 million from 144 investors. An investor must put up at least $1 million to join."[10]

18. Representative Don Beyer, a Democrat from Virginia: $29,805,092

Beyer was my congressman when I lived in Northern Virginia. But even before that, he was a household name. That's because his dad, Donald Beyer Sr., bought a struggling Volvo dealership in the 1970s, turning it into a Northern Virginia behemoth.[11]

17. Representative David Trone, a Democrat from Maryland:
$32,927,094

See chapter 3.

16. Representative Jay Obernolte, a Republican from California: $39,250,014

Obernolte, who has a graduate degree in artificial intelligence from the University of California, Los Angeles,[12] founded the video game development studio FarSight Studios (formerly Farsight Technologies) back in 1988. Their franchises include "Game Party for the Wii and Xbox 360, NCAA college football games for EA, Sega Sports' NFL games for the Genesis, Backyard Sports for Atari, PlayTV for Radica/Mattel, and the Pinball Hall of Fame for Crave."[13]

15. Representative Scott Peters, a Democrat from California: $39,738,062

Scott Peters is a successful former attorney who invested a lot of his earnings.[14] But much of his wealth is no doubt attributed to his marriage to Lynn Gorguze. Gorguze is CEO of the private equity firm Cameron Holdings, which she cofounded with her father, Vincent Gorguze, former president and CEO[15] of (as their website describes it) the "global technology, software, and engineering powerhouse"[16] Emerson Electric.

14. Representative Nancy Pelosi, a Democrat from California: $46,123,051

Most of Pelosi's money comes from investments made by her husband, Paul Pelosi's, business investments. See chapter 4 on insider information.

13. Representative Suzan DelBene, a Democrat from Washington: $52,156,097

After earning her MBA at the University of Washington, DelBene helped start Drugstore.com, and she served as CEO and president of the software company Nimble Technology. Next, she spent a dozen years at

Microsoft, culminating in her role as corporate vice president of their mobile communications business.[17]

12. Representative Peter Meijer, a Republican from Michigan: $60,514,285

In 1934, Meijer's great-grandfather, a Dutch immigrant, started Meijer's Grocery using $340 worth of credit to stock the shelves. By 1991, Peter's father and uncle had taken over the business, which by then had estimated sales of $5 billion. As of 2019, the company boasted 256 stores and over $18 billion in annual revenue.[18] According to *Forbes*, "Meijer's choice to pursue a political career hasn't cost him a stake in the family fortune. According to a financial disclosure form he filed in 2019, the congressman has access to multiple trusts, including a blind family trust with more than $50 million in assets."[19]

What is amazing is that Meijer is the second wealthy Michigander to be chased out of Congress by Donald Trump. Meijer's predecessor, former representative Justin Amash, was also a conservative who, like the aforementioned super-rich Fred Upton, ran afoul of Donald Trump. Amash retired. Meijer was defeated in his 2022 Republican primary.

11. Representative Roger Williams, a Republican from Texas: $67,438,045

Roger Williams is chairman of Roger Williams Chrysler Dodge Jeep Ram. His father started the business in 1939.[20] And like a lot of car dealers, his business received funding as part of the CARES Act to help businesses and their workers deal with the impact of the COVID-19 pandemic. According to the *Dallas Morning News*, Roger Williams Chrysler Dodge Jeep in Weatherford said in a statement that "like millions of small businesses across America, our family-owned business was not immune to the economic damage caused by the government's shelter-in-place orders and the impacts of COVID-19."[21] (Not to worry, though, Williams isn't alone. Pennsylvania representative Mike Kelly, also a Republican, had dealerships that also got COVID cash, as *Salon* reported.[22] So did car dealerships owned by Representative Vern Buchanan and the aforementioned Don Beyer.[23])

10. Representative Doris Matsui, a Democrat from California: $73,872,062

After Congressman Bob Matsui of the Sacramento area died in 2005, his wife, Doris, replaced him in the House. However, her income got a huge boost in 2020 when she married Roger Sant, the cofounder and chairman emeritus of the AES Corporation, a Fortune 200 global power company.

9. Representative Trey Hollingsworth, a Republican from Indiana: $74,629,062

Hollingsworth's story starts in Clinton, Tennessee (a small town outside of Knoxville), with his developer dad, Joe. Joe Hollingsworth made his bones building homes, running a "thriving convenience store chain and sports club chain," and revitalizing a shopping center. In 2005, after he graduated from the University of Pennsylvania's prestigious Wharton School, "Hollingsworth Capital Partners was formed with Joe's son, Trey, as managing partner and majority owner."[24] In 2008, Hollingsworth expanded his business into Indiana, buying property there.

In 2016, when Representative Todd Young vacated his House seat to run for the US Senate, thirty-two-year-old Trey ran for the open seat, having lived in Indiana for less than a year.[25] To win the primary, Trey spent over $1 million of his own money, and his dad, Joe, put hundreds of thousands of dollars into a pro-Hollingsworth super PAC.[26] Hollingsworth is a fan of term limits and a critic of career politicians, and (amazingly) he decided to act like it. He did not run for reelection in 2022.[27]

8. Senator Richard Blumenthal, a Democrat from Connecticut: $85,231,232

See chapter 5.

7. Senator Mitt Romney, a Republican from Utah: $85,269,083

Mitt Romney is the son of George Romney, a former governor of Michigan, but the bulk of Mitt Romney's fortune came from his fifteen years of working at the private equity firm Bain Capital.[28] One of his most famous deals involved helping transform the office supply store Staples into a $18 billion juggernaut.[29] Other prominent deals involved the acquisition of Domino's Pizza, as well as the mattress company Sealy. But not every profitable deal was a win-win. When he ran for president in 2012, Romney was accused of "vulture capitalism" by both Democratic and Republican rivals. While Romney can point to positive examples (like Staples) where Bain helped turn struggling companies around, critics view private equity firms like Bain as a cash grab that exploits and harvests its victims. For example, during Romney's 2012 presidential campaign, Matt Taibbi wrote in *Rolling Stone* that Romney and "his private equity firm staged an epic wealth grab, destroyed jobs—and stuck others with the bill."[30]

6. Senator Mark Warner, a Democrat from Virginia: $93,534,098

See chapter 3.

5. Senator Dianne Feinstein, a Democrat from California: $96,518,036

Much of Dianne Feinstein's wealth can be attributed to her 1980 marriage to Richard Blum. The two met when she was president of the San Francisco Board of Supervisors.[31] Blum, who died in 2022, ran Blum Capital Partners and had a net worth estimated at $1 billion.[32] See chapter 5 on marrying rich.

4. Representative Vern Buchanan, a Republican from Florida:
$113,384,088

Vern Buchanan bought his first car dealership in Florida in 1992. But just as Heinz wanted fifty-seven varieties, when this erstwhile middle-class Michigan kid first ran for Congress in 2006, he boasted a diverse collection of fifty-seven companies.[33] According to the *Sarasota Herald-Tribune*, the list included "a construction company, charter jet business, boat management company, financial companies, a day spa, an offshore reinsurance company, rental properties and several pieces of real estate."[34]

"I'm a blue-collar kid whose parents worked in factories and who did better than I ever thought I would in business, and now I'm enjoying public service," Buchanan said a few years back, as reported in *Sarasota Magazine*.[35] "With my role on Ways and Means, which is the most powerful committee in Congress, where nearly $2 trillion flows through every year, I can have a tremendous impact for our district. And I say this humbly... I am Florida's most effective representative in Congress." Well, this blue-collar kid has done all right for himself; in 2017, he purchased an Ocean Alexander yacht (the cheapest one goes for $3.25 million).[36]

But it hasn't always been easy. According to *Sarasota Magazine*, "His chain of American Speedy printing shops in Michigan went bankrupt soon after he resigned and he was sued by former franchise owners. In 1999, after rebuilding his business reputation in Sarasota, Buchanan was frozen out of a deal to develop the Ritz-Carlton, Sarasota, after other developers questioned whether Buchanan had overstated his assets."[37]

3. Representative Darrell Issa, a Republican from California:
$115,850,012

Issa made his money through a car alarm business. See chapter 3.

(Note: I am writing this at a fancy hotel in Florida where many members of Congress go to hold fund-raising events for lobbyists. We had breakfast today at the hotel's restaurant, and we sat next to Issa's table. My wife would not allow me to interrupt his family's meal to ask him how to hot-wire a car.)

2. Representative Michael McCaul, a Republican from Texas: $125,880,292

Business Insider estimates McCaul's wealth at $125,880,292, with the bulk of it coming from his wife, Linda McCaul. Linda's father, Lowry Mays, is CEO of Clear Channel Communications. McCaul's "dramatic rise in net worth appears to be the product of generational wealth transfer," reports *New York* magazine.[38] See chapter 5 on marrying rich.

1. Senator Rick Scott, a Republican from Florida: $200,327,223

With a net worth of over $200 million, Florida senator Rick Scott is the richest member of Congress.[39] But his life didn't start so charmed. Scott's mother divorced his abusive father when Scott was born "so my brother and I could have a better life." His mother considered putting him up for adoption, but she eventually married a man who would later adopt Scott and become the only father he ever knew. Scott grew up in public housing, joined the navy, used the GI Bill to pay for college, and opened a donut shop.

But Scott really made his money by cofounding two health-care companies, an experience he used to gain notoriety opposing Obamacare. Then he parlayed that notoriety (and all the cash he made) into a successful run for Florida governor. A few years later, in 2018, he spent $64 million of his own money to win a US Senate seat in Florida, according to *Roll Call*.[40] Next, Scott chaired the National Republican Senatorial

Committee during the 2022 cycle; there, he drew the ire of Senate Minority Leader Mitch McConnell by announcing a plan that would make everyone—even poor people—pay income tax. Scott was also dinged in August 2022 for "spending part of his congressional recess on a luxury yacht in Italy with his family after criticizing President Biden for vacationing in Delaware," *Axios* reported.[41]

The Ten Richest US Presidents

Note: This list was compiled by 24/7 Wall St.[42] The amounts are adjusted for inflation to December 2018.

10. **Bill Clinton**, 42nd president (1993–2001)
    Peak net worth: $75.9 million

9. **Herbert Hoover**, 31st president (1929–1933)
    Peak net worth: $83 million

8. **Lyndon B. Johnson**, 36th president (1963–1969)
    Peak net worth: $109.3 million

7. **James Madison**, 4th president (1809–1817)
    Peak net worth: $113.3 million

6. **Andrew Jackson,** 7th president (1829–1837)
    Peak net worth: $132.6 million

5. **Theodore Roosevelt**, 26th president (1901–1909)
    Peak net worth: $139.7 million

4. **Thomas Jefferson**, 3rd president (1801–1809)
    Peak net worth: $236.8 million

3. **George Washington**, 1st president (1789–1797)
    Peak net worth: $587 million

2. **John F. Kennedy**, 35th president (1961–1963)
    Peak net worth: $1.1 billion

1. **Donald J. Trump**, 45th president (2017–2021)
    Peak net worth: $3.1 billion

Appendix

$$ § § § $$

The above list reinforces major themes from *Filthy Rich Politicians*, including inherited wealth, marrying into money, and the ability to become wealthy after having served in office.

The top five richest presidents on this list (Trump, Kennedy, Washington, Jefferson, and Roosevelt) all inherited great wealth. That doesn't mean they didn't also work and expand their financial empire (most did). But let's be honest. They got a leg up.

Let's take Donald Trump, for example. "By age 3, Mr. Trump was earning $200,000 a year in today's dollars from his father's empire," according to the *New York Times*.[43] "He was a millionaire by age 8. By the time he was 17, his father had given him part ownership of a 52-unit apartment building. Soon after Mr. Trump graduated from college, he was receiving the equivalent of $1 million a year from his father. The money increased over the years, to more than $5 million annually in his 40s and 50s." I guess old Fred Trump wasn't *that* bad.

Of the top 10 richest presidents, only Clinton, Hoover, Johnson, and Jackson did not inherit wealth. Johnson deserves an asterisk, because his wife was the main source of his income. Likewise, most of Clinton's wealth came after serving as president. Only Jackson and Hoover were wealthy self-made men *before* entering politics.

Acknowledgments

Someone smart once said, "Books need friends," and no truer words have ever been spoken. Writing is a collaborative process (and then, the real work of promoting a book begins).

My literary agent Frank Weimann of Folio Literary Management deserves credit for the idea's genesis. Frank submitted my proposal to Kathryn Riggs, my editor at Center Street. She reviewed it and then shared it with Center Street's editorial director, Alex Pappas, a friend and former colleague of mine from my days working at the Daily Caller. And then, they both championed it! In addition to making it a reality, Kathryn and Alex helped transform the idea that ultimately blossomed into this book and also helped edit it.

Special thanks are in order to the supremely talented Kristi Speights, a professional grant editor and friend, who put in countless hours doing the heavy lifting of editing the first draft of this manuscript. Additionally, Robyn Matthews, a new friend, was a big help in tracking down and formatting the many citations found in this book.

Much credit also belongs to my friends Jim Eltringham and David Pietrusza, who were invaluable in helping research and craft *Filthy Rich Politicians*. I have known Jim for two decades (going back to our days working at the Leadership Institute), and I have known David—who is one of the best historians and authors in America—for almost one. Jim and David are two of the most talented (and funniest) people I know. Getting to work with pals on this book was a thrill. I am also grateful to my friend Bill Scher for reading the manuscript and helping smooth out some rough edges. For more than a dozen years now, Bill and I have been doing a weekly podcast called *The DMZ.* I have probably spent more time talking to him than anybody else on earth, save for my wife. This is to say that, aside from being a great writer in his own right, Bill knows me about as well as anyone—which makes him an invaluable collaborator on any major project.

Speaking of friends, I am also especially grateful for the help from those who know much more about investing in the stock market than I do; Adam Dresher and David Bahnsen were especially helpful with the sections on the stock market. David was generous with his time, trading phone calls and emails and generally making sure I didn't write anything entirely stupid. Adam deserves much praise for tirelessly walking me through such topics as options and IPOs. I'll never forget sitting in Adam's home in Scottsdale, Arizona, and watching him try to explain the Black-Scholes model's standard deviation chart on a dry-erase board as my eyes glazed over. (It's not you, it's me.)

My friends Jamie Weinstein, Yuval Levin, Ron Holifield, Tevi Troy, Jeff Mayhugh, Tom Ricks, Nick Givas, Daniel Lippman, Stephen Kent, Chris Meekins, Cory Lisk, Frederick M. Hess, Dr. David A. Foltz, and Dr. Denis J. Woods also deserve special thanks for their guidance and support. I am also eternally grateful to Batya Ungar-Sargon for generously agreeing to write the foreword to this book.

Some of the topics I explore at greater length here are an outgrowth of my writing at the *Daily Beast.* So thank you to the *Beast*—especially editor-in-chief Tracy Connor, senior opinion editor Anthony L. Fisher, and senior editor Harry Siegel—all of whom edited my columns while I wrote this book.

I can't tell you how important it is to have a steady gig to balance out the vagaries of the book-writing industry. I am also grateful for the flexibility my job offers. This is now the second book I have written where the writing process did not entail taking a book leave. Does this make me the Cal Ripken of political commentary? That's for you to decide.

Acknowledgments

Last (but not least), thank you to my beautiful and loving wife, Erin DeLullo; our wonderful children, Burke and Becket Lewis; and my awesome mom, Hope Lewis, for your love and support. Thank you, Erin, for sticking with me "for richer or poorer." And thank you, Mom, for sacrificing to give me what felt like a solid middle-class lifestyle. (Among your many sacrifices, I will never forget those $100 Air Jordans you bought me in 1986!)

It takes a village to raise a child—and to write a book. Here's hoping this book makes us all Filthy Rich.

Notes

Introduction

1. Jay-Z raps this line in a 2005 remix of Kanye West's song "Diamonds from Sierra Leone," which is featured on Kanye's *Late Registration* album. https://genius.com/Kanye-west-diamonds-from-sierra-leone-remix-lyrics.
2. Carmen Reinicke, "56% Of Americans Can't Cover a $1,000 Emergency Expense with Savings," CNBC, January 20, 2022, https://www.cnbc.com/2022/01/19/56percent-of-americans-cant-cover-a-1000-emergency-expense-with-savings.html.
3. Joshua M Sanchez, "This Is How to Button Your Suit Jacket the Right Way," *Esquire*, February 26, 2015, https://www.esquire.com/style/mens-fashion/advice/a33367/how-to-button-suit-jacket.
4. Alyssa Fisher, "Ivanka Talks About Her Father Admitting He Was in Massive Debt in Old Clip," Forward, May 9, 2019. https://forward.com/fast-forward/424037/ivanka-trump-president-trump-samantha-bee-debt.
5. Ellis Simani, Robert Faturechi, and Ken Ward Jr., "How These Ultrawealthy Politicians Avoided Paying Taxes," *ProPublica*, November 4, 2021, https://www.propublica.org/article/how-these-ultrawealthy-politicians-avoided-paying-taxes.
6. Tim McGraw, "I Like It, I Love It," *All I Want*, 1995.

Chapter 1

1. F. Scott Fitzgerald, "The Rich Boy," *Red Book* (January and February 1926), https://www.gutenberg.net.au/fsf/THE-RICH-BOY.txt.
2. Amy Sherman, "Yes, Congress Has Disproportionate Share of Millionaires, but Claim's Numbers Are Off," *PolitiFact*, January 22, 2020, https://www.politifact.com/factchecks/2020/jan/22/facebook-posts/yes-congress-has-disproportionate-share-millionair.
3. Dan Burrows, "Millionaires in America 2020: All 50 States Ranked," *Kiplinger*, May 28, 2020, https://www.kiplinger.com/slideshow/investing/t006-s001-millionaires-america-all-50-states-ranked/index.html.
4. According to a 2020 report from Phoenix Marketing International (https://www.kiplinger.com/slideshow/investing/t006-s001-millionaires-america-all-50-states-ranked/index.html), "a record 6.71% (or 8,386,508 out of 125,018,808 total U.S. households) can now claim millionaire status." It's important to note that "to be considered a millionaire by the standards of wealth research, a household must have investable assets of $1 million or more, excluding the value of real estate,

employer-sponsored retirement plans and business partnerships, among other select assets." Dan Burrows, "Millionaires in America 2020: All 50 States Ranked," *Kiplinger*, May 28, 2020, https://www.kiplinger.com/slideshow/investing/t006-s001-millionaires -america-all-50-states-ranked/index.html.

5. Note: It's impossible to perfectly compare the net worth of members of Congress and average citizens, but this comparison is also not exactly apples and oranges. Members of Congress have many tricks they use to hide their wealth. When it comes to members of Congress, OpenSecrets calculates net worth by summing the filer's assets and then subtracting any listed liabilities. In addition, OpenSecrets also notes that "the ethics law does not require filers to report property, including personal residences, that is not held for investment purposes and does not produce income." OpenSecrets, "About the Personal Finances Data & OpenSecrets' Methodology," n.d., https://www.opensecrets .org/personal-finances/methodology.

6. U.S. Bureau of Labor Statistics, "May 2021 National Occupational Employment and Wage Estimates United States," n.d., https://www.bls.gov/oes/current/oes_nat.htm.

7. Karl Evers-Hillstrom, "Majority of Lawmakers in 116th Congress Are Millionaires," OpenSecrets, April 23, 2020, https://www.opensecrets.org/news/2020/04/majority-of -lawmakers-millionaires.

8. Dan Kopf, "The Typical US Congress Member is 12 Times Richer Than the Typical American Household," *Quartz*, February 12, 2018, https://qz.com/1190595/the -typical-us-congress-member-is-12-times-richer-than-the-typical-american-household.

9. Kristen Bialik, "For the Fifth Time in a Row, the New Congress Is the Most Racially and Ethnically Diverse Ever," Pew Research Center, February 8, 2019. https://www .pewresearch.org/fact-tank/2019/02/08/for-the-fifth-time-in-a-row-the-new-congress -is-the-most-racially-and-ethnically-diverse-ever.

10. Casey Burgat and Charles Hunt, "Congress in 2019: The 2nd Most Educated and Least Politically Experienced House Freshman Class," Brookings, December 28, 2018, https://www.brookings.edu/blog/fixgov/2018/12/28/congress-in-2019-the-2nd-most -educated-and-least-politically-experienced-house-freshman-class.

11. This book focuses on *American* politicians, but it should be noted that the phenomenon of filthy-rich politicians is not unique to us. While I was writing this book, Rishi Sunak was elected to serve as prime minister of Great Britain, and British tabloids promptly dubbed him "Rishi Rich." According to the *New York Times*, "His wife, a fashion designer, is the daughter of the billionaire founder of the technology company Infosys. Mr. Sunak's foes have pointed to his penchant for wearing suits that cost 3,500 pounds, about $4,300. They [the tabloids] have noted that he wears Prada, once showing up at a construction site in a pair of that brand's loafers—cost, £490. The couple also have homes in London; his parliamentary constituency in Yorkshire, England; and in Santa Monica, Calif."

12. https://www.washingtonpost.com/business/economy/growing-wealth-widens -distance-between-lawmakers-and-constituents/2011/12/05/gIQAR7D6IP_story.html

13. Peter Atencio (@Atencio), "Actor bios in the 60s and 70s: He was an amateur boxer and truck driver before joining the merchant marines and was discovered by a producer in Cuba where he was in jail for assault. Actor bios today: His dad was an

investment banker and his mom was a model. He attended Yale." Twitter, September 19, 2022, https://twitter.com/Atencio/status/1571966743500980224.

14. Peter Whoriskey, "Growing Wealth Widens Distance between Lawmakers and Constituents," *Washington Post*, December 26, 2011, https://www.washingtonpost.com/business/economy/growing-wealth-widens-distance-between-lawmakers-and-constituents/2011/12/05/gIQAR7D6IP_story.html.

15. Ballotpedia, "Personal Gain Index (U.S. Congress)," n.d., https://ballotpedia.org/Personal_Gain_Index_(U.S._Congress).

16. https://www.pewresearch.org/politics/2015/11/23/6-perceptions-of-elected-officials-and-the-role-of-money-in-politics/

17. "6. Perceptions of Elected Officials and the Role of Money in Politics," Pew Research Center, November 23, 2015, https://www.pewresearch.org/politics/2015/11/23/6-perceptions-of-elected-officials-and-the-role-of-money-in-politics.

18. "User Clip: Pat Buchanan Acceptance Speech," C-SPAN, August 12, 2000, https://www.c-span.org/video/?c4499901/user-clip-pat-buchanan-acceptance-speech.

19. "User Clip: Pat Buchanan Acceptance Speech."

20. Jeffrey M. Jones, "Confidence in U.S. Institutions Down; Average at New Low," Gallup, July 5, 2022, https://news.gallup.com/poll/394283/confidence-institutions-down-average-new-low.aspx.

21. "1. Trust in government: 1958–2015," Pew Research, November 23, 2015, https://www.pewresearch.org/politics/2015/11/23/6-perceptions-of-elected-officials-and-the-role-of-money-in-politics.

22. Ezra Klein, "Why a Middle-Class Lifestyle Remains Out of Reach for So Many," July 17, 2022, https://www.nytimes.com/2022/07/17/opinion/inflation-prices-affordability.html.

23. https://www.washingtonexaminer.com/news/you-should-be-ashamed-critics-unleash-on-pelosi-for-showing-off-freezer-loaded-with-ice-cream.

24. Emma Colton, "'You Should Be Ashamed': Critics Unleash on Pelosi for Showing off Freezer Loaded with Ice Cream," *Washington Examiner*, April 16, 2020, https://www.washingtonexaminer.com/news/you-should-be-ashamed-critics-unleash-on-pelosi-for-showing-off-freezer-loaded-with-ice-cream

25. Colton, "'You Should Be Ashamed.'"

26. James Gordon, "Left-Wing Dems Blame Nancy Pelosi's Refrigerator Filled with $12-a-Pint Ice Cream in Her Multi-Million Dollar Home for Putting Off Ordinary Americans Voting Democrat," *Daily Mail*, November 11, 2020, https://www.dailymail.co.uk/news/article-8939861/Left-wing-Democrats-claim-Pelosis-expensive-ice-cream-drawer-voters-lockdown-crisis.html.

27. https://www.politico.com/f/?id=00000175-b4b4-dc7f-a3fd-bdf660490000.

28. Selena Fragassi, "How Much Is New Democrat House Leader Hakeem Jeffries Worth?" GOBankingRates.com, November 30, 2022. https://www.gobankingrates.com/net-worth/politicians/hakeem-jeffries-net-worth.

Chapter 2

1. Harry S. Truman Library and Museum, July 1, 1954, https://www.trumanlibrary.gov/node/404594.

2. C. James Taylor, "John Adams: Life before the Presidency," UVA Miller Center, n.d., https://millercenter.org/president/adams/life-before-the-presidency.

3. Tom Kertscher, "Were the Founding Fathers 'Ordinary People'?" PolitiFact, July 2, 2015, https://www.politifact.com/article/2015/jul/02/founding-fathers-ordinary-folk/.

4. Michelle Fields, "Barons of the Beltway: Inside the Princely World of Our Washington Elite—and How to Overthrow Them" (Crown Forum, 2016), 20.

5. Steve Inskeep, "How Jackson Made a Killing in Real Estate," *Politico*, July 4, 2015, https://www.politico.com/magazine/story/2015/07/andrew-jackson-made-a-killing-in-real-estate-119727.

6. Michael Burlingame, "Abraham Lincoln: Life before the Presidency," UVA Miller Center, n.d., https://millercenter.org/president/lincoln/life-before-the-presidency.

7. https://www.nytimes.com/1998/06/14/weekinreview/june-7-13-abraham-lincoln-deadbeat.html.

8. Harry E. Pratt, "Personal Finances of Abraham Lincoln," Lincoln Monographs, n.d. https://quod.lib.umich.edu/l/lincoln2/5250244.0001.001/1:17.4.

9. Edmund Morris, *The Rise of Theodore Roosevelt* (Coward, McCann & Geoghegan, 1979).

10. Morris, *The Rise of Theodore Roosevelt*.

11. Morris, *The Rise of Theodore Roosevelt*.

12. John W. Schoen, "Top 10 Richest U.S. Presidents," CNBC, August 12, 2016, https://www.cnbc.com/2016/08/12/top-10-richest-us-presidents.html#slide=3.

13. https://www.moaf.org/exhibits/checks_balances/franklin-roosevelt/fdr-family.

14. James Barron, "Remembering the House F.D.R. Built (Well, His Mother Did)," *New York Times*, November 29, 2018, https://www.nytimes.com/2018/11/29/nyregion/roosevelt-house-nyc.html.

15. https://www.moaf.org/exhibits/checks_balances/franklin-roosevelt/fdr-family.

16. Barron, "Remembering the House F.D.R. Built."

17. Kelly O'Donnell, "Out of Office, Trump Has Received over $342,000 in Benefits," NBC News, August 24, 2022, https://www.nbcnews.com/meet-the-press/meetthepressblog/office-trump-received-342000-benefits-rcna44641.

18. "Remarks of senator john f. Kennedy at the Gridiron Club, Washington, D.C., March 15, 1958," John F. Kennedy Presidential Library and Museum, https://www.jfklibrary.org/archives/other-resources/john-f-kennedy-speeches/washington-dc-19580315.

19. Craig Fehrman, "'I Would Rather Win a Pulitzer Prize Than Be President,'" *Politico*, February 11, 2020, https://www.politico.com/news/magazine/2020/02/11/john-f-kennedy-pulitzer-obsession-consumed-him-113452.

20. David R. Stokes, *JFK's Ghost: Kennedy, Sorenson, and the Making of Profiles in Courage* (Lyons Press, 2021), 79.

21. Richard L. Berke, "More Wealth Than Meets the Eye Lies behind Frugal Dukakis Image," *New York Times*, July 6, 1988, https://www.nytimes.com/1988/07/06/us/more-wealth-than-meets-the-eye-lies-behind-frugal-dukakis-image.html.

22. Berke, "More Wealth Than Meets the Eye."

23. "Perot Spent $56 Million of Own, $4.5 Million in Loans on Race," *Los Angeles Times*, December 5, 1992, https://www.latimes.com/archives/la-xpm-1992-12-05-mn-1144-story.html.

24. "Perot Spent $56 Million."

25. This point is also made in Chuck Klosterman's 2022 book, *The Nineties*. On p. 61, Klosterman writes that "it's impossible to imagine the arc of that election without Perot's presence."

26. According to Britannica, "As of 2015, more than 1,600 [servicemen who were designated 'missing in action'] were still 'unaccounted-for.'" https://www.britannica.com/topic/Vietnam-War-POWs-and-MIAs-2051428.

27. Tierney Sneed, "Exclusive Clip: Perot Driven by 'Personal Dislike,' Bush 41 Says," *U.S. News and World Report*, September 10, 2013, https://www.usnews.com/news/blogs/washington-whispers/2013/09/10/exclusive-clip-perot-driven-by-personal-dislike-bush-41-says.

28. "Kerry Would Be Third-Richest U.S. President If Elected," *Forbes*, October 29, 2004. https://www.forbes.com/2004/02/13/cx_da_0213kerry.html.

29. Albert Salvato, "Ohio Recount Gives a Smaller Margin to Bush," *New York Times*, December 29, 2004, https://www.nytimes.com/2004/12/29/politics/ohio-recount-gives-a-smaller-margin-to-bush.html.

30. Kenneth P. Vogel, "McCain Family Owns 8 Properties," *Politico*, August 21, 2008, https://www.politico.com/story/2008/08/mccain-family-owns-8-properties-012700.

31. https://www.businessinsider.com/barack-obama-michelle-obama-net-worth-2018-7#the-obamas-entered-the-white-house-with-a-13-million-net-worth-in-2008-that-has-since-grown-to-at-least-70-million-according-to-international-business-times-1.

32. https://www.washingtonpost.com/blogs/election-2012/post/rick-perry-doubles-down-on-vulture-capitalist-criticism-of-mitt-romney/2012/01/11/gIQAziWqqP_blog.html.

33. https://www.politico.com/story/2012/06/fear-factors-what-worries-mitt-backers-077046.

34. Devin Dwyer, "Mitt Romney Ordered $55,000 'Phantom Park' Car Elevator, Designer Says," ABC News, May 25, 2012, https://abcnews.go.com/blogs/politics/2012/05/mitt-romney-ordered-55000-phantom-park-car-elevator-designer-says.

35. Daniella Diaz, "Trump: 'I'm Smart' for Not Paying Taxes," CNN, September 27, 2016, https://www.cnn.com/2016/09/26/politics/donald-trump-federal-income-taxes-smart-debate/index.html.

36. https://www.newsweek.com/dave-chappelle-snl-opening-monologue-read-full-jokes-1759195.

37. Eugene Scott, "Trump: 'I Just Don't Want a Poor Person' in Cabinet Economic Jobs," CNN, June 22, 2017, https://www.cnn.com/2017/06/22/politics/donald-trump-poor-person-cabinet/index.html.

38. Daniel Strauss, "Donald Trump's New Pitch: I'm So Rich I Can't Be Bought," *Politico*, July 28, 2015, https://www.politico.com/story/2015/07/donald-trumps-so-rich-i-cant-be-bought-120743.

39. https://www.forbes.com/sites/michelatindera/2020/10/22/how-the-bidens-earned-167-million-after-leaving-the-white-house/?sh=3e4aab5e1e42

40. Tom Kertscher, "Fact-Checking Joe Biden's Claim That He Was among the Poorest in Government," PolitiFact, October 30, 2019, https://www.politifact.com/factchecks/2019/oct/30/joe-biden/fact-checking-joe-bidens-claim-hes-among-poorest-g.

41. Lukas Mikelionis, "Vintage Biden Clip Resurfaces Showing Him Falsely Claiming He Was in 'Top Half of My Class' in Law School," Fox News, May 4, 2019, https://www.foxnews.com/politics/vintage-biden-clip-resurfaces-law-school.

Chapter 3

1. "Hustlin'" was Rick Ross's 2006 debut single. It was the first single from his debut album, *Port of Miami*.
2. Lance Williams, "Issa's Army Record in Doubt," *SFGate*, May 29, 1998, https://www.sfgate.com/news/article/Issa-s-Army-record-in-doubt-3087843.php.
3. https://www.newyorker.com/magazine/2011/01/24/dont-look-back-ryan-lizza.
4. Ryan Lizza, "Don't Look Back," *New Yorker*, January 16, 2011, https://www.newyorker.com/magazine/2011/01/24/dont-look-back-ryan-lizza.
5. https://www.newyorker.com/magazine/2011/01/24/dont-look-back-ryan-lizza.
6. Eric Lichtblau, "Issa's Rags-to-Riches Tale Has Some Ugly Chapters," *Los Angeles Times*, May 23, 1998, https://www.latimes.com/archives/la-xpm-1998-may-23-mn-52746-story.html.
7. https://www.newyorker.com/magazine/2011/01/24/dont-look-back-ryan-lizza.
8. Lance Williams and Carla Marinucci, "Rep. Issa Was Charged in San Jose Auto Theft," *SFGate*, June 25, 2003, https://www.sfgate.com/politics/article/Rep-Issa-was-charged-in-San-Jose-auto-theft-2568524.php.
9. "Greg Gianforte," OpenSecrets, n.d., https://www.opensecrets.org/personal-finances/greg-gianforte/net-worth?cid=N00040733&year=2018.
10. Megan Henney, "The 5 Wealthiest Members of Congress—and How They Made Their Fortune," *Fox Business*, July 6, 2020, https://www.foxbusiness.com/money/wealthiest-members-congress.
11. AP News, "Gianforte Uses $4M More of His Own Money for Campaign," October 21, 2020, https://apnews.com/article/election-2020-campaign-finance-greg-gianforte-elections-campaigns-b1cf3ea7ec7be9c80331903a82fef305.
12. "Gov. Mark R. Warner," National Governors Association, n.d., https://www.nga.org/governor/mark-r-warner/
13. Madison Hall and Angela Wang, "Meet the 25 Wealthiest Members of Congress," *Business Insider*, December 14, 2021, https://www.businessinsider.com/wealthiest-members-congress-house-senate-finances-2021-12.
14. https://www.theatlantic.com/magazine/archive/2006/05/the-man-with-the-golden-phone/304777/.
15. "Winners and Losers in the Great Cellular Giveaway," *Fortune*, November 5, 1990, https://money.cnn.com/magazines/fortune/fortune_archive/1990/11/05/74304/index.htm.
16. Paul Starobin, "The Man with the Golden Phone," *The Atlantic*, May 2006, https://www.theatlantic.com/magazine/archive/2006/05/the-man-with-the-golden-phone/304777.
17. Timothy L. O'Brien, "'McCongressman' Gets a Large Order of PPP," *Bloomberg*, July 7, 2020, https://www.bloomberg.com/opinion/articles/2020-07-07/-mccongressman-kevin-hern-gets-a-large-order-of-ppp.

18. Chris Casteel, "Hern Worth More Than Rest of State's Congressional Delegation Combined," *The Oklahoman*, January 17, 2019, https://www.oklahoman.com/story/news/columns/2019/01/27/hern-worth-more-than-rest-of-states-congressional-delegation-combined/60476037007/

19. "Multimillionaire Burger Maker with Arkansas Roots Ready to Legislate in Congress," United States Representative Kevin Hern website, February 25, 2019, https://hern.house.gov/news/documentsingle.aspx?DocumentID=39.

20. https://hern.house.gov/news/documentsingle.aspx?DocumentID=39.

21. "Rep. Kevin Hern (OK-01): Spinda Bifida," https://www.congress.gov/116/meeting/house/110820/witnesses/HHRG-116-AP00-Wstate-H001082-20200623.pdf.

22. "A Golden Opportunity," Arkansas Tech University, n.d., https://www.arkansastechnews.com/a-golden-opportunity/

23. Dylan Goforth, "The McCongressman? Out-of-State McDonald's Money Flows into the Campaign of Tulsa Restaurateur Kevin Hern," *The Frontier*, June 25, 2018, https://www.readfrontier.org/stories/mccongressman-state-mcdonalds-money-flows-campaign-restaurateur-kevin-hern.

24. https://www.nytimes.com/2023/01/05/us/politics/kevin-hern-speaker-boebert.html.

25. https://www.nytimes.com/2023/01/05/us/politics/kevin-hern-speaker-boebert.html.

26. Fredreka Schouten, "Meet the Man Who Spent $12 Million on a Congressional Race—and Lost," *USA Today*, April 27, 2016, https://www.usatoday.com/story/news/politics/onpolitics/2016/04/27/david-trone-12-million-biggest-self-funding-house-candidate-maryland/83589854.

27. Meagan Flynn, "David Trone Projected to Win Reelection in Maryland's 6th District," *Washington Post*, November 11, 2022, https://www.washingtonpost.com/dc-md-va/2022/11/11/maryland-6th-results-trone-wins-parrott.

28. Bill Turque, "David Trone Has Donated More Than $150,000 to Republicans, Database Shows," *Washington Post*, January 28, 2016. https://www.washingtonpost.com/local/md-politics/david-trone-has-donated-more-than-150000-to-republicans-database-shows/2016/01/28/962a7048-c5e3-11e5-a4aa-f25866ba0dc6_story.html.

29. https://www.politico.com/magazine/story/2014/01/roscoe-bartlett-congressman-off-the-grid-101720/.

30. https://www.sandiegouniontribune.com/news/politics/sd-me-jacobs-resume-20180327-story.html.

31. https://timesofsandiego.com/politics/2018/06/09/sara-jacobs-concedes-to-mike-levin-in-49th-district-congressional-race/.

32. https://prospect.org/politics/an-intraparty-democratic-battle-in-san-diego/.

33. https://timesofsandiego.com/politics/2020/10/03/sara-jacobs-the-generals-would-help-remove-trump-if-he-loses-wont-leave/.

34. https://www.nbcsandiego.com/news/politics/decision-2020/georgette-gomez-concedes-53rd-district-race-to-leader-sara-jacobs/2436250/.

35. Theodore Schleifer, "A Tech Billionaire Spent Millions to Elect His Granddaughter. It's Working," *Vox*, March 4, 2020, https://www.vox.com/recode/2020/3/4/21162400/irwin-jacobs-qualcomm-sara-jacobs-san-diego-congress.

36. Richard E. Neustadt, *Presidential Power: The Politics of Leadership from Roosevelt to Reagan* (John Wiley & Sons, 1960), 9.

37. https://twitter.com/Jflood111/status/1554497371341570059.

38. Bruce Springsteen, "Badlands," recorded February 25, 1978, on *Darkness on the Edge of Town*, Columbia.

39. Nicholas Carnes, "Working-Class People Are Underrepresented in Politics. The Problem Isn't Voters," *Vox*, October 24, 2018, https://www.vox.com/policy-and -politics/2018/10/24/18009856/working-class-income-inequality-randy-bryce- alexandria-ocasio-cortez.

40. Carnes, "Working-Class People Are Underrepresented in Politics."

41. https://www.politico.com/news/magazine/2023/01/19/marie-gluenskamp-perez -democrats-middle-class-00078215.

42. https://www.politico.com/news/magazine/2023/01/19/marie-gluenskamp-perez -democrats-middle-class-00078215.

43. Interview with the author on September 28, 2022.

44. https://www.vox.com/policy-and-politics/2018/10/24/18009856/working-class-income -inequality-randy-bryce-alexandria-ocasio-cortez.

45. Jaclyn Diaz, "The First Gen Z Member of Congress Was Denied a D.C. Apartment Due to Bad Credit," National Public Radio, December 9, 2022.

46. Karl Evers-Hillstrom, "State of Money in Politics: The Price of Victory Is Steep," OpenSecrets, February 19, 2019, https://www.opensecrets.org/news/2019/02/state-of -money-in-politics-the-price-of-victory-is-steep.

47. https://www.britannica.com/biography/Kevin-McCarthy-politician.

48. https://www.npr.org/sections/itsallpolitics/2015/09/28/443957272/lucky-guy -kevin-mccarthy-once-won-the-lottery-now-he-might-be-speaker.

49. https://www.npr.org/sections/itsallpolitics/2015/09/28/443957272/lucky-guy -kevin-mccarthy-once-won-the-lottery-now-he-might-be-speaker.

50. https://www.cbsnews.com/newyork/news/congressman-elect-george-santos-admits -lying-about-education-work-experience-i-will-be-sworn-in/.

51. https://www.nytimes.com/2023/01/04/opinion/george-santos-jewish-heritage.html.

52. https://www.nytimes.com/2023/01/18/nyregion/george-santos-mother-911.html.

53. https://www.thedailybeast.com/openly-gay-rep-elect-george-santos-didnt-disclose -divorce-with-woman.

54. https://www.theleaderonline.com/single-post/santos-filings-now-claim-net -worth-of-11-million.

55. https://www.politico.com/news/2022/12/26/george-santos-background-ny -post-00075605.

56. https://www.nytimes.com/2023/01/17/style/george-santos-style.html.

57. https://www.newsweek.com/george-santos-symptom-political-system-that-only-lets -rich-opinion-1769802.

58. Dana Rubinstein, "Daniel Goldman, Ex-Trump Prosecutor, Tops Crowded Field in N.Y. Primary," *New York Times*, August 24, 2022, https://www.nytimes.com/2022 /08/24/nyregion/daniel-goldman-trump-ny-primary.html.

59. Molly Martinez, "'People Are Building Personal Empires': Challengers Question Sen. Hoeven's Personal Wealth ahead of Primaries," KFYR-TV, June 14, 2022, https://www.kfyrtv.com/2022/06/14/people-are-building-personal-empires-challengers-question-sen-hoevens-personal-wealth-ahead-primaries.

60. Bill Glauber, "Democratic U.S. Senate Candidate Alex Lasry Files for Extension on Statement of Economic Interests until after Aug. 9 Primary," *Milwaukee Journal Sentinel*, May 17, 2022, https://www.jsonline.com/story/news/politics/elections/2022/05/17/alex-lasry-files-extension-statement-economic-interests-until-after-democratic-primary/9800924002.

61. Vanessa Swales, "Johnson Benefited from Tax Cut, but It's Not a Loophole," Politi-Fact, April 27, 2022, https://www.politifact.com/factchecks/2022/apr/27/opportunity-wisconsin/johnson-benefitted-tax-cut-its-not-loophole.

62. Swales, "Johnson Benefited from Tax Cut."

63. Meagan Flynn, "Don Beyer's First Primary Challenger Asks Him to 'Pass the Torch,'" *Washington Post*, April 24, 2022. https://www.washingtonpost.com/dc-md-va/2022/04/24/don-beyer-opponent-virginia-congress.

Chapter 4

1. John Bartlett, *Familiar Quotations*, 10th ed. (Little, Brown and Co., 1919), 168. The entry for this quotation is available online at Bartleby.com.

2. As the *Washington Post* explains, "Because lawmakers are allowed to report their holdings and debts in broad ranges, it is impossible for the public to determine their precise net worth. They also are not required to reveal the value of their homes, the salaries of their spouses or money kept in non-interest-bearing bank accounts and their congressional retirement plan."

3. Karl Evers-Hillstrom, "Majority of Lawmakers in 116th Congress Are Millionaires," OpenSecrets, April 23, 2020, https://www.opensecrets.org/news/2020/04/majority-of-lawmakers-millionaires.

4. According to OpenSecrets, in 2008, Pelosi's net worth was an estimated $38,539,554. By 2018, it had grown to an estimated $114,662,521.

5. https://www.npr.org/2021/09/21/1039313011/tiktokers-are-trading-stocks-by-watching-what-members-of-congress-do.

6. Ryan Zickgraf, "Nancy Pelosi: 2021 Wall Street Trader of the Year," *Jacobin*, December 16, 2021, https://jacobin.com/2021/12/house-speaker-paul-stocks-insider-trading-wealth.

7. https://www.visa.ie/visa-everywhere/innovation/visa-commerce-network.html.

8. "Congress: Trading Stock on Inside Information?" CBS News, June 11, 2012, https://www.cbsnews.com/news/congress-trading-stock-on-inside-information.

9. Steven Nickolas and Charles Potters, "Call Options: Right to Buy vs. Obligation," Investopedia, September 29, 2022, https://www.investopedia.com/ask/answers/032515/what-difference-between-right-and-obligation-call-option.asp.

10. Ali Swenson, "Pelosi's Husband Invested in Tesla, but Not as Viral Post Claims," AP News, February 1, 2021, https://apnews.com/article/fact-checking-afs:Content:9949984867.

11. Camila DeChalus, "Nancy Pelosi's Husband Just Bought $2.2 Million Worth of Tesla Stock," *Business Insider*, March 23, 2022, https://www.businessinsider.com/nancy-pelosi-tesla-stock-congress-2022-3.

12. Sophie Mellor, "House Speaker Nancy Pelosi's Husband Cashed in on Big Tech Just as Congress Was Set to Pounce," *Fortune*, July 8, 2021, https://fortune.com/2021/07/08/house-speaker-nancy-pelosi-husband-paul-big-tech-stocks.

13. https://greenwald.substack.com/p/nancy-and-paul-pelosi-making-millions?fbclid=IwAR1GvW9SeguQgk7gpJ1GGrH3wZ-MmDxUsRChgE0uZN9h7ysefUu9LfqmEws.

14. https://www.businessinsider.com/congress-holding-stocks-facebook-twitter-disney-fox-news-2021-12.

15. https://www.marketwatch.com/story/nancy-pelosis-husband-buys-millions-worth-of-nvidia-stock-ahead-of-chip-manufacturing-bill-vote-11658179117.

16. Jordan Novet, "Microsoft Wins U.S. Army Contract for Augmented Reality Headsets, Worth up to $21.9 Billion over 10 Years," CNBC, March 31, 2021, https://www.cnbc.com/2021/03/31/microsoft-wins-contract-to-make-modified-hololens-for-us-army.html.

17. https://apnews.com/article/business-nancy-pelosi-congress-8685e82eb6d6e5b42413417f3d5d6775.

18. Clerk of the House or Representatives, "Periodic Transaction Report," July 14, 2022, https://disclosures-clerk.house.gov/public_disc/ptr-pdfs/2022/20021374.pdf.

19. Lydia Moynihan, "Pelosis Sold $5M in Nvidia Stock ahead of Vote on Chipmaker Subsidies," *New York Post*, July 27, 2022, https://nypost.com/2022/07/27/pelosis-sold-5m-in-nvidia-stock-ahead-of-chipmaker-subsidy-vote.

20. Alicia Parlapiano, Adam Playford, and Kate Kelly, "These 97 Members of Congress Reported Trades in Companies Influenced by Their Committees," *New York Times*, September 13, 2022, https://www.nytimes.com/interactive/2022/09/13/us/politics/congress-members-stock-trading-list.html.

21. Parlapiano, Playford, and Kelly, "These 97 Members of Congress Reported Trades."

22. Andrew Kerr, "The Stock Market Made Nancy Pelosi Rich. Now, She Wants to Ban Her Colleagues from Trading," *Washington Free Beacon*, October 5, 2022, https://freebeacon.com/democrats/the-stock-market-made-nancy-pelosi-rich-now-she-wants-to-ban-her-colleagues-from-trading.

23. Michael Brendan Dougherty and Zeke Miller, "Full Details: How Congress Insider Traders Abused the Public's Trust during the Financial Crisis," *Business Insider*, November 14, 2011, https://www.businessinsider.com/heres-how-congressmen-gamed-the-financial-crisis-to-make-big-bucks-in-the-stock-market-2011-11.

24. Peter Schweizer, *Throw Them All Out: How Politicians and Their Friends Get Rich off Insider Stock Tips, Land Deals, and Cronyism That Would Send the Rest of Us to Prison* (Houghton Mifflin Harcourt, 2011), 33.

25. "Congress: Trading Stock on Inside Information?"

26. To be clear, this is *60 Minutes'* words (not Boehner's spokesman's): https://www.cbsnews.com/news/congress-trading-stock-on-inside-information/.

27. https://www.businessinsider.com/congress-insider-trading-john-kerry-obamacare
-health-care-reform-2011-11.

28. https://www.reuters.com/article/usa-obama-congress/obama-signs-insider-trading
-bill-wants-more-curbs-on-congress-idUSL2E8F434E20120404.

29. Robert Faturechi and Derek Willis, "Senator Dumped Up to $1.7 Million of Stock
after Reassuring Public about Coronavirus Preparedness," *ProPublica*, March 19, 2020,
https://www.propublica.org/article/senator-dumped-up-to-1-7-million-of-stock
-after-reassuring-public-about-coronavirus-preparedness.

30. Michela Tindera, "The Richest Politician on Capitol Hill Is Likely Georgia's Recently
Appointed, Controversial Sen. Kelly Loeffler," *Forbes*, August 3, 2020, https://www
.forbes.com/sites/michelatindera/2020/08/03/the-richest-politician-on-capitol
-hill-is-likely-georgias-recently-appointed-controversial-senator-kelly-loeffler.

31. Annie Karni, "As Feinstein Declines, Democrats Struggle to Manage an Open
Secret," *New York Times*, May 2, 2022, https://www.nytimes.com/2022/05/02/us/politics
/dianne-feinstein-memory-issues.html.

32. Shane Harris, Greg Miller, Josh Dawsey, and Ellen Nakashima, "U.S. Intelligence
Reports from January and February Warned about a Likely Pandemic," *Washington Post*,
March 20, 2020, https://www.washingtonpost.com/national-security/us-intelligence
-reports-from-january-and-february-warned-about-a-likely-pandemic/2020/03/20
/299d8cda-6ad5-11ea-b5f1-a5a804158597_story.html.

33. Dan Mangan, "DOJ Will Not Criminally Charge Sen. Richard Burr for Stock Trades
He Made after Getting Covid Intelligence," CNBC, January 19, 2021, https://www
.cnbc.com/2021/01/19/doj-will-not-charge-sen-richard-burr-for-covid-stock-trades
.html.

34. Robert Faturechi and Derek Willis, "On the Same Day Sen. Richard Burr Dumped
Stock, So Did His Brother-in-Law. Then the Market Crashed," *ProPublica*, May 6,
2020, https://www.propublica.org/article/burr-family-stock.

35. Christina Wilkie, "Unsealed FBI Docs Reveal a Flurry of Calls and Stock Trades
by Sen. Burr in Early 2020," CNBC, September 6, 2022, https://www.cnbc
.com/2022/09/06/unsealed-fbi-docs-reveal-a-flurry-of-calls-amid-burrs-stock-trades
.html.

36. Dave Michaels, "Judge Inclined to Have Burr's Brother-in-Law Testify in SEC
Insider-Trading Probe," *Wall Street Journal*, October 29, 2021, https://www.wsj.com
/articles/judge-inclined-to-have-burrs-brother-in-law-testify-in-sec-insider-trading-probe
-11635543377.

37. Tim Mak, "Weeks before Virus Panic, Intelligence Chairman Privately Raised Alarm,
Sold Stocks," NPR, March 19, 2020, https://www.npr.org/2020/03/19/818192535
/burr-recording-sparks-questions-about-private-comments-on-covid-19.

38. https://www.nytimes.com/2020/03/19/us/politics/richard-burr-stocks-sold-coronavirus
.html.

39. Mak, "Weeks before Virus Panic."

40. Katie Shepherd, "'There Is No Greater Moral Crime': Tucker Carlson Calls for Sen.
Richard Burr's Resignation over Stock Sell-Off," *Washington Post*, March 20, 2020, https://
www.washingtonpost.com/nation/2020/03/20/coronavirus-tucker-carlson-burr.

41. Alexandria Ocasio-Cortez, Twitter post, March 19, 2020, 5:57 pm, https://twitter .com/aoc/status/1240759241847308293?lang=en.

42. In 2022, former Indiana GOP representative Stephen Buyer was charged with insider trading—but he left Congress in 2011.

43. Renae Merle, "Ex-congressman Chris Collins Sentenced to 2 Years on Insider-Trading, False-Statements Charges," *Washington Post*, January 17, 2020, https://www.washington post.com/business/2020/01/17/former-rep-chris-collins-be-sentenced-insider-trading -case.

44. Robert J. McCarthy, "Pardoned by Trump, a Contrite Collins Returns Home a Changed Man," *Buffalo News*, December 24, 2020, https://buffalonews.com/news/pardoned-by -trump-a-contrite-collins-returns-home-a-changed-man/article_4a914ae4-4608-11eb -9974-0715d91f7b6b.html.

45. McCarthy, "Pardoned by Trump, a Contrite Collins Returns Home."

46. Aruna Viswanatha, "Justice Department Closing Insider-Trading Investigations into Three U.S. Senators," *Wall Street Journal*, May 26, 2020, https://www.wsj.com/articles /justice-department-closing-insider-trading-investigations-into-three-u-s-senators -11590520934.

47. George McCain, "I'm a 17-Year-Old High School Student Who Can't Vote. Here's Why I Built a System to Track Congress' Troubling Stock Trades," *Business Insider*, July 10, 2022, https://www.businessinsider.com/congress-stock-trades-law-investing-data -2022-7.

48. Robert Faturechi and Derek Willis, "Senator Dumped up to $1.7 Million of Stock after Reassuring Public about Coronavirus Preparedness," *ProPublica*, March 19, 2020, https://www.propublica.org/article/senator-dumped-up-to-1-7-million-of-stock-after -reassuring-public-about-coronavirus-preparedness.

49. Faturechi and Willis, "Senator Dumped up to $1.7 Million of Stock."

50. Christina Wilkie, "Unsealed FBI Docs Reveal a Flurry of Calls and Stock Trades by Sen. Burr in Early 2020," CNBC, September 6, 2022, https://www.cnbc .com/2022/09/06/unsealed-fbi-docs-reveal-a-flurry-of-calls-amid-burrs-stock -trades.html.

51. Rebecca Ballhaus, Joe Palazzolo, Brody Mullins, Chad Day, and John West, "As Covid Hit, Washington Officials Traded Stocks with Exquisite Timing," *Wall Street Journal*, October 19, 2022, https://www.wsj.com/articles/covid-washington-officials -stocks-trading-markets-stimulus-11666192404.

52. Rahm Emanuel, "Let's Make Sure This Crisis Doesn't Go to Waste," *Washington Post*, March 25, 2020, https://www.washingtonpost.com/opinions/2020/03/25/lets-make -sure-this-crisis-doesnt-go-waste.

53. https://twitter.com/CNBCWEX/status/1504754872041852968.

54. https://www.youtube.com/watch?v=va5g5KhOi0o.

55. Representative Marjorie Taylor Greene (@RepMTG), "War and rumors of war is incredibly profitable and convenient. And just like that, the media now has a lie to use as the reason for our shattered economy and out of control inflation. What a sad exis- tence it must be to shill for Globalism & America Last politicians." Twitter, February 23, 2022, https://twitter.com/repmtg/status/1496490950444597250.

56. https://www.businessinsider.com/mtg-congress-stock-sale-microsoft-activision-2022-1?utm_source=facebook.com&utm_medium=social&utm_campaign=sf-bi-main.

57. Tamara Keith, "How Congress Quietly Overhauled Its Insider-Trading Law," NPR, April 16, 2013, https://www.npr.org/sections/itsallpolitics/2013/04/16/177496734/how-congress-quietly-overhauled-its-insider-trading-law.

58. https://www.citizen.org/wp-content/uploads/migration/case_documents/2017_stock_act_report.pdf.

59. Dave Levinthal, "72 Members of Congress Have Violated a Law Designed to Prevent Insider Trading and Stop Conflicts-of-Interest," *Business Insider*, October 12, 2022, https://www.businessinsider.com/congress-stock-act-violations-senate-house-trading-2021-9.

60. Walter Shaub, "Pelosi's Stock Ban Bill Isn't Just Weak, It's Dangerous," *Time*, September 30, 2022, https://time.com/6218708/congress-stock-trading-ban-bill.

61. Shaub, "Pelosi's Stock Ban Bill Isn't Just Weak."

62. Stephanie Lai and Kate Kelly, "House Puts Off Vote to Limit Lawmakers' Stock Trades, Casting Doubt on Prospects," *New York Times*, September 30, 2022. https://www.nytimes.com/2022/09/30/us/politics/stock-trading-vote-congress.html.

63. Lai and Kelly, "House Puts Off Vote."

64. https://www.cnn.com/2023/01/12/politics/congressional-stock-trading-ban-spanberger-roy-bipartisan/index.html.

65. Jack Shafer, "The Clintons, Honest Graft and Dishonest Graft," *Politico*, April 24, 2015, https://www.politico.com/magazine/story/2015/04/the-clintons-honest-graft-and-dishonest-graft-117326.

66. "How the Gores, Father and Son, Helped Their Patron Occidental Petroleum," The Center for Public Integrity, January 10, 2000, https://publicintegrity.org/politics/how-the-gores-father-and-son-helped-their-patron-occidental-petroleum.

67. Edward J. Epstein, *Dossier: The Secret History of Armand Hammer* (Carroll and Graf, 1999).

68. "How the Gores, Father and Son, Helped Their Patron."

69. Charles R. Babcock, "Gore Getting $20,000 a Year for Mineral Rights on Farm," *Washington Post*, August 15, 1992, https://www.washingtonpost.com/archive/politics/1992/08/15/gore-getting-20000-a-year-for-mineral-rights-on-farm/4232f019-92dc-4da5-af6d-733aeb655931.

70. https://www.npr.org/sections/itsallpolitics/2015/03/27/395777411/harry-reid-the-senator-who-never-forgot-the-path-he-took.

71. https://www.politico.com/story/2016/04/harry-reid-whorehouse-childhood-221962.

72. "Harry Reid," OpenSecrets, n.d., https://www.opensecrets.org/personal-finances/harry-reid/net-worth?cid=N00009922.

73. https://www.nationalreview.com/2012/08/how-did-harry-reid-get-rich-betsy-woodruff/.

74. https://www.cbsnews.com/news/sen-reid-made-11m-in-land-deal/.

75. Liam Stack, "Dennis Hastert, Ex-House Speaker Who Admitted Sex Abuse, Leaves Prison," *New York Times*, July 18, 2017.

76. Matea Gold and Anu Narayanswamy, "How Dennis Hastert Made a Fortune in Land Deals," *Washington Post*, May 29, 2015, https://www.washingtonpost.com/politics/how-dennis-hastert-made-a-fortune-in-land-deals/2015/05/29/680f357a-0628-11e5-bc72-f3e16bf50bb6_story.html.

77. https://www.npr.org/sections/thetwo-way/2016/04/27/475865637/former-house-speaker-dennis-hastert-awaits-sentencing-in-hush-money-case.

78. Michael Kranish, "The Making of Madison Cawthorn: How Falsehoods Helped Propel the Career of a New Pro-Trump Star of the Far Right," *Washington Post*, February 27, 2021, https://www.washingtonpost.com/politics/2021/02/27/making-madison-cawthorn-how-falsehoods-helped-propel-career-new-pro-trump-star-far-right.

79. Kate Ashford, "What Is Cryptocurrency?" *Forbes*, June 6, 2022, https://www.forbes.com/advisor/investing/cryptocurrency/what-is-cryptocurrency.

80. https://www.washingtonexaminer.com/news/house/madison-cawthorn-implicated-in-potential-insider-trading-scheme-experts-say.

81. Andrew Kerr, "Madison Cawthorn Reaped Profits with Crypto 'Pump and Dump' Scheme, Filing Shows," *Washington Examiner*, May 27, 2022, https://www.washingtonexaminer.com/news/house/madison-cawthorn-reaped-profits-with-crypto-pump-and-dump-scheme-filing-shows.

82. Zoë Richards, "Ethics Panel Directs Madison Cawthorn to Donate $15K for Improperly Promoting Let's Go Brandon Cryptocurrency," NBC News, December 6, 2022, https://www.nbcnews.com/politics/congress/madison-cawthorn-fined-improperly-promoting-cryptocurrency-rcna6042.

83. Alan J. Ziobrowski, James W. Boyd, Ping Cheng, and Brigitte J. Ziobrowski, "Abnormal Returns from the Common Stock Investments of Members of the U.S. House of Representatives," *Cambridge University PressBusiness and Politics* 13, no. 1 (January 20, 2017): 1–22,. https://www.cambridge.org/core/journals/business-and-politics/article/abs/abnormal-returns-from-the-common-stock-investments-of-members-of-the-us-house-of-representatives/BC6C6A524BBE96738BB94D37EF0FD1A5.

84. https://abcnews.go.com/Politics/story?id=4853292&page=1.

85. Mike Sprague, "Napolitano Uses Campaign Ruling to Make More Than $200,000 in Interest on 1998 Campaign Loan," *Daily Breeze*, February 20, 2009, https://www.dailybreeze.com/2009/02/20/napolitano-uses-campaign-ruling-to-make-more-than-200000-in-interest-on-1998-campaign-loan.

86. Jordy Yager, "Report: Members of Congress Find Ways to Keep Money in the Family," *The Hill*, March 22, 2012, https://web.archive.org/web/20120325175231/http://thehill.com/blogs/on-the-money/1007-other/217681-report-members-of-congress-keep-money-in-the-family.

87. Sprague, "Napolitano Uses Campaign Ruling."

88. Ian Millhiser, "The Supreme Court Just Made It Much Easier to Bribe a Member of Congress," *Vox*, May 16, 2022, https://www.vox.com/2022/5/16/23074957/supreme-court-ted-cruz-fec-bribery-campaign-finance-first-amendment-john-roberts-elena-kaga.

89. Federal Election Commission United States of America, "Candidate Loan Repayment Limitation Ruled Unconstitutional in *Ted Cruz for Senate, et al. v. FEC* (D.D.C.

1:19-cv-00908)," June 7, 2021, https://www.fec.gov/updates/candidate-loan-repayment
-limitation-ruled-unconstitutional-in-ted-cruz-for-senate-et-al-v-fec-ddc-119-cv-00908.

90. https://www.history.com/news/how-ulysses-grant-died-memoirs-mark-twain.

91. Sara Fritz, "Senators Vote to Cut Off Honorariums for Speeches: Congress: The 72–
24 Margin Indicates Many Do Not Expect Campaign Finance Reform Bill to Pass.
Curbs on Investment Income Are Also Approved," *Los Angeles Times*, May 22, 1991,
https://www.latimes.com/archives/la-xpm-1991-05-22-mn-2213-story.html.

92. U.S. House of Representatives Committee on Ethics, "FAQs about Outside Employment," n.d., https://ethics.house.gov/posts/faqs/outside-employment.

93. "How Much Outside Income Can a Member Earn in a Year?" Congressional Institute,
September 18, 2007, https://www.congressionalinstitute.org/2007/09/18/how-much
-outside-income-can-a-member-earn-in-a-year.

94. Paul Farhi, "The GOP's Big Bulk Book-Buying Machine Is Boosting Republicans on the
Bestseller Lists," *Washington Post*, April 16, 2021, https://www.washingtonpost.com
/lifestyle/media/gop-book-deals/2021/04/15/154f3820-9ca5-11eb-b7a8-014b14aeb9e4
_story.html.

95. David D. Kirkpatrick, "Hillary Clinton Book Advance, $8 Million, Is Near Record,"
New York Times, December 16, 2000, https://www.nytimes.com/2000/12/16/nyregion
/hillary-clinton-book-advance-8-million-is-near-record.html.

96. David, "Book Sales Boost Obama Income by $5 Million," GalleyCat, April 16, 2010,
https://www.adweek.com/galleycat/book-sales-boost-obama-income-by-5-million/12552.

97. Constance Grady, "What the Obamas' $65 Million Book Advance Actually Means," *Vox*,
March 2, 2017, https://www.vox.com/culture/2017/3/2/14779892/barack-michelle
-obama-65-million-book-deal-penguin-random-house.

98. Joseph Morton, "Sen. Ben Sasse Reports Just over $600k in Book Royalties, More
Than Three Times His Annual Salary," *Omaha World Herald*, August 14, 2019, https://
omaha.com/news/national/sen-ben-sasse-reports-just-over-600k-in-book-royalties
-more-than-three-times-his/article_af16b90a-c121-5e99-a09f-57453ba0a704.html.

99. Paul V. Fontelo, "These Senators Running for President Made $7.1 Million Writing
Books," *CQ Roll Call*, June 11, 2019, https://rollcall.com/2019/06/11/these-senators
-running-for-president-made-7-1-million-writing-books.

100. Kimberly Leonard, "Reading Pays for Members of Congress: They Just Made $1.8
Million in Book Advances and Royalties," *Business Insider*, December 15, 2021, https://
www.businessinsider.com/members-of-congress-made-18-million-as-book-authors
-in-2020-2021-12.

101. Kelsey Vlamis, "Sen. Marco Rubio—Who Called Student Debt Cancellation
'Unfair'—Said He Had $100,000 in Student Loans but Paid It Off by Writing a Book,"
Business Insider, August 28, 2022, https://www.businessinsider.com/sen-marco-rubio
-paid-off-100k-student-loans-writing-book-2022-8.

102. Vlamis, "Sen. Marco Rubio."

103. Sheryl Gay Stolberg, "Bernie Sanders, Now a Millionaire, Pledges to Release Tax
Returns by Monday," *New York Times*, April 9, 2019, https://www.nytimes.com/2019/04
/09/us/politics/bernie-sanders-millionaire-net-worth-taxes.html.

104. Zach Everson, "A Trump Political Committee Bought $158,000 Worth of Books Shortly after Jared Kushner Published His Best-Selling Memoir," *Forbes*, October 16, 2022, https://www.forbes.com/sites/zacheverson/2022/10/16/a-trump-political-committee-bought-131000-worth-of-books-four-days-later-jared-kushners-hit-the-best-seller-list.

105. https://campaignlegal.org/sites/default/files/2021-04/4-6-21%20Cruz%20personal%20use.pdf.

106. Jake Sherman and Anna Palmer, "Politico Playbook: Could Infrastructure Week Make a Comeback?" *Politico*, May 21, 2020, https://www.politico.com/newsletters/playbook/2020/05/21/could-infrastructure-week-make-a-comeback-489287.

107. Tom Benning, "Houston Rep. Dan Crenshaw's Bestselling New Book Got Boost from Purchases by House GOP Campaign Arm," *Dallas Morning News*, May 28, 2020, https://www.dallasnews.com/news/politics/2020/05/28/houston-rep-dan-crenshaws-bestselling-new-book-got-boost-from-purchases-by-house-gop-campaign-arm.

108. Elizabeth Minkel, "When Politicians Buy Their Own Books," *New Yorker*, October 19, 2011, https://www.newyorker.com/books/page-turner/when-politicians-buy-their-own-books.

109. Benning, "Houston Rep. Dan Crenshaw's Bestselling New Book."

110. https://twitter.com/betoorourke/status/1263976648505991175.

111. Benning, "Houston Rep. Dan Crenshaw's Bestselling New Book."

112. Benning, "Houston Rep. Dan Crenshaw's Bestselling New Book."

113. Roger Sollenberger, "Adam Schiff Just Made It Easier for Politicians to Take Money," *Daily Beast*, December 14, 2021, https://www.thedailybeast.com/feds-allow-adam-schiff-to-rent-email-list-to-his-book-publisher.

114. Sollenberger, "Adam Schiff Just Made It Easier."

115. C. Eugene Emery Jr., "Bernie Sanders Ad Ignores Fact That Members of Congress Can't Be Paid for Speeches," PolitiFact, April 20, 2016, https://www.politifact.com/factchecks/2016/apr/20/bernie-sanders/bernie-sanders-ad-ignores-fact-members-congress-ca.

116. Elizabeth Minkel, "When Politicians Buy Their Own Books," *New Yorker*, October 19, 2011, https://www.newyorker.com/books/page-turner/when-politicians-buy-their-own-books.

117. Richard L. Berke, "Behind Jim Wright's Book, His Friends," *New York Times*, June 12, 1998, https://www.nytimes.com/1988/06/12/us/behind-jim-wright-s-book-his-friends.html.

118. Berke, "Behind Jim Wright's Book."

119. Peter Applebome, "Gingrich Gives Up $4 Million Advance on His Book Deal," *New York Times*, December 31, 1994, https://www.nytimes.com/1994/12/31/us/gingrich-gives-up-4-million-advance-on-his-book-deal.html.

120. Jay Root, "Cuomo Can Keep $5.1 Million in Covid Book Money, Judge Says," *New York Times*, August 16, 2022, https://www.nytimes.com/2022/08/16/nyregion/cuomo-covid-book-money.html.

121. "Gov. Andrew Cuomo's Once Highly Anticipated Book Sold Only 71 Copies the Last Week of July," *Business Insider*, August 11, 2021, https://www.businessinsider.com/cuomos-highly-anticipated-book-sold-71-copies-last-week-july-2021-8.

122. U.S. House of Representatives Committee on Ethics, "Statutes and Rules Governing Disclosure of Financial Interests," n.d., https://ethics.house.gov/financial-disclosure/statutes-and-rules-governing-disclosure-financial-interests.

Chapter 5

1. "Here Are All the Campaigns Barbara Bush Took Part in for Her Family," CBS News, April 20, 2018, https://www.cbsnews.com/news/here-are-all-the-campaigns-barbara -bush-took-part-in-for-her-family.

2. https://www.vulture.com/article/what-is-a-nepotism-baby.html.

3. Scott Bomboy, "Presidential Nepotism Debate Goes Back to the Founders' Time," National Constitution Center, November 21, 2016, https://constitutioncenter.org /blog/presidential-nepotism-debate-goes-back-to-the-founders-time.

4. Peter Schweizer, *Secret Empires: How the American Political Class Hides Corruption and Enriches Family and Friends*, (HarperCollins, 2018), 14.

5. Martin Waldron, "Johnson, Virtually Penniless in 1937, Left a Fortune Valued at $20-Million," *New York Times*, January 28, 1973, https://www.nytimes.com/1973/01/ 28/archives/johnson-virtually-penniless-in-1937-left-a-fortune-valued-at.html.

6. Jan Jarboe Russell, "Hits and Mrs.," *Texas Monthly*, September 1999, https://www .texasmonthly.com/articles/hits-and-mrs/.

7. Patricia Brennan, "'Lady Bird,'" *Washington Post*, December 9, 2021, https://www .washingtonpost.com/archive/lifestyle/tv/2001/12/09/lady-bird/87ace3f5-e844-4386 -96f7-16ada29e9226.

8. Jack Shafer, "The Honest Graft of Lady Bird Johnson," *Slate*, July 16, 2007, https:// slate.com/news-and-politics/2007/07/how-lady-bird-and-lyndon-baines-johnson -came-by-their-millions.html.

9. Michael Barnes, "Former TV News Anchor and LBJ-Family Insider Neal Spelce Spins Intriguing Yarns in New Memoir," *Austin American-Statesman*, February 5, 2022, https://www.statesman.com/story/news/history/2022/02/05/lbj-family-insider-and -tv-anchor-neal-spelce-entertains-new-memoir/6568677001.

10. Jan Jarboe Russell, "Hits and Mrs.," *Texas Monthly*, September 1999. https://www .texasmonthly.com/articles/hits-and-mrs.

11. Dan Amira, "How the Richest Member of Congress Got That Way," *New Yorker*, August 19, 2011, https://nymag.com/intelligencer/2011/08/michael_mccaul_richest _mmber_of_congress.html.

12. Amira, "How the Richest Member of Congress Got That Way."

13. "How America's Richest Members of Congress Made Their Money," Love Money, n.d., https://www.lovemoney.com/gallerylist/76380/how-americas-richest-members -of-congress-made-their-money.

14. James R. Hagerty, "Richard Blum Made a Bundle on a Circus and Battled Poverty," *Wall Street Journal*, March 4, 2022, https://www.wsj.com/articles/richard-blum -made-a-bundle-on-a-circus-and-battled-poverty-11646406058.

15. Hagerty, "Richard Blum Made a Bundle."

16. Alex Traub, "Richard Blum, Political Donor and Husband of Senator Feinstein, Dies at 86," *New York Times*, February 28, 2022, https://www.nytimes.com/2022/02/28 /us/politics/richard-blum-dead.html.

17. https://twitter.com/ethan_harsell/status/1606561403237986304.

18. Reuters, "Fact Check: Senator Mitchell McConnell's Net Worth Increase Is due to Family Inheritance in 2007," March 3, 2021, https://www.reuters.com/article

/uk-factcheck-mcconnell-inheritance-wife/factchecksenator-mitchell-mcconnellsnet
-worth-increase-is-due-to-family-inheritance-in2007-idUSKCN2AV1WM.

19. Glenn Kessler, "How Did Mitch McConnell's Net Worth Soar?" *Washington Post*, May 22, 2014, https://www.washingtonpost.com/news/fact-checker/wp/2014/05/22/how -did-mitch-mcconnells-net-worth-soar.

20. "'It's a Long Tradition in RI,' Whitehouse Defends Family's Membership in All-White Club," June 21, 2021, GoLocalProv, https://www.golocalprov.com/news/its -a-long-tradition-in-ri-whitehouse-defends-familys-membership-in-all-whi.

21. Ted Nesi, "Sen. Whitehouse's Beach Club Says Accusations of All-White Membership Are 'Inaccurate And False,'" WPRI, June 23, 2021, https://www.wpri.com/news /local-news/east-bay/baileys-beach-club-says-accusations-of-all-white-membership -are-inaccurate-and-false.

22. David Corn, "Why the Hell Isn't Jared Kushner's $2 Billion Saudi Payment a Big Scandal?" *Mother Jones*, April 20, 2022, https://www.motherjones.com/politics/2022/04 /why-the-hell-isnt-jared-kushners-2-billion-saudi-payment-a-big-scandal.

23. Philip Bump, "Millennials, Meet Roger Clinton: Hillary's Brother-in-Law Who Just Got Arrested Once Again," *Washington Post*, June 6, 2016, https://www.washingtonpost .com/news/the-fix/wp/2016/06/06/millennials-meet-roger-clinton-hillarys-brother-in -law-who-just-got-arrested-once-again.

24. Peter Carlson, "The Relatively Charmed Life of Neil Bush," *Washington Post*, December 28, 2003, https://www.washingtonpost.com/archive/lifestyle/2003/12/28/the -relatively-charmed-life-of-neil-bush/388db316-f6b9-456e-8720-b4b2bf60a8ab.

25. Wolfgang Saxon, "Donald Nixon, 72, Dies in California," *New York Times*, June 30, 1987, https://www.nytimes.com/1987/06/30/obituaries/donald-nixon-72-dies-in -california.html.

26. Kenneth Reich, "Donald Nixon, Brother of Ex-President, Dies," *Los Angeles Times*, June 30, 1987, https://www.latimes.com/archives/la-xpm-1987-06-30-me-1152-story.html.

27. Reich, "Donald Nixon, Brother of Ex-President, Dies."

28. Amanda Becker, "Report: Members Use Positions for Profit," *CQ Roll Call*, March 22, 2012, https://rollcall.com/2012/03/22/report-members-use-positions-for-profit.

29. Interview with the author on September 19, 2022.

30. Editorial Staff, "Editorial: Another crony gets the top job at the Charleston County Airport," January 28, 2020, https://www.postandcourier.com/opinion/editorials/editorial -another-crony-gets-the-top-job-at-the-charleston-county-airport/article_b9b923f2-41d5 -11ea-8286-e30979f428d2.html.

31. Aida Ahmed, "Sen. Harry Reid's Son Josh Named Henderson City Attorney," *Las Vegas Sun*, November 29, 2011, https://lasvegassun.com/news/2011/nov/29/sen-harry-reids -son-josh-named-henderson-city-atto.

32. https://www.cbsnews.com/news/why-is-congress-a-millionaires-club/.

33. Michael Mahoney, "Truth Check: Kander Ads Target Blunt's Ties to Lobbyists," KMBC, August 16, 2016, https://www.kmbc.com/article/truth-check-kander-ads-target-blunt -s-ties-to-lobbyists/3695826.

34. Mahoney, "Truth Check: Kander Ads Target Blunt's Ties to Lobbyists."

35. Juliet Eilperin, "Lobbyist Curbs Role over Tie to Rep. Blunt," *Washington Post*, September 9, 2003, https://www.washingtonpost.com/archive/politics/2003/09/09/lobbyist-curbs-role-over-tie-to-rep-blunt/5532d973-ac1a-4916-9c37-2fe052f0c355.

36. Democratic Senatorial Campaign Committee, "New DSCC Ad: Washington's Been Good to Roy Blunt, but Roy Blunt Hasn't Been Good to Missouri," September 16, 2016, https://www.dscc.org/news/new-dscc-ad-washingtons-good-roy-blunt-roy-blunt-hasnt-good-missouri.

37. Eric Garcia, "Ad Hammers Blunt for Family Lobbying Ties: Draws Contrast with Challenger Jason Kander's Military Record," *CQ Roll Call*, September 13, 2016, https://rollcall.com/2016/09/13/ad-hammers-blunt-for-family-lobbying-ties.

38. Garcia, "Ad Hammers Blunt."

39. Kelley Gillenwater, "Weeks: Manchin Puts 'Dark Cloud' over WVU," *Times West Virginia*, September 18, 2008, https://www.timeswv.com/news/weeks-manchin-puts-dark-cloud-over-wvu/article_782e0712-d583-5839-bb10-c571a6bdfd2e.html.

40. Jayne O'Donnell, "Family Matters: EpiPens Had High-Level Help Getting into Schools," *USA Today*, September 20, 2016, https://www.usatoday.com/story/news/politics/2016/09/20/family-matters-epipens-had-help-getting-schools-manchin-bresch/90435218.

41. Jen Wieczner, "The Truth about Mylan CEO's 'Heather Bresch Situation' and Her MBA," *Fortune*, August 26, 2016, https://fortune.com/2016/08/26/epipen-mylan-ceo-interview-heather-bresch-mba.

42. Matt Egan, "How EpiPen Came to Symbolize Corporate Greed," CNN Business, August 29, 2016, https://money.cnn.com/2016/08/29/investing/epipen-price-rise-history/index.html.

43. Ben Popken, "Mylan CEO's Pay Rose over 600 Percent as EpiPen Price Rose 400 Percent," NBC News, August 23, 2016, https://www.nbcnews.com/business/consumer/mylan-execs-gave-themselves-raises-they-hiked-epipen-prices-n636591.

44. Popken, "Mylan CEO's Pay Rose over 600 Percent."

45. Tara Suter, "Manchin Received Large Campaign Contributions from Daughter's Company amid EpiPen Scandal," OpenSecrets, September 21, 2021, https://www.opensecrets.org/news/2021/09/manchin-large-campaign-contributions-epipen-scandal.

46. Graham Bowley and Robin Pogrebin, "A Gallery Sells Hunter Bidens. The White House Says It Won't Know Who's Buying," *New York Times*, August 13, 2021, https://www.nytimes.com/2021/08/13/arts/design/hunter-biden-art-white-house.html.

47. Edward-Isaac Dovere, "The Sanders and Biden Families Have Been Cashing In for Years," *The Atlantic*, March 2, 2020, https://www.theatlantic.com/politics/archive/2020/03/bernie-sanders-joe-biden-enriched-their-families/607159.

48. https://nypost.com/2021/10/18/maxine-waters-campaign-paid-daughter-81k-in-fy-2021/.

49. Chuck Neubauer and Ted Rohrlich, "Capitalizing on a Politician's Clout," *Los Angeles Times*, December 19, 2004, https://www.latimes.com/archives/la-xpm-2004-dec-19-me-waters19-story.html.

50. Seth Maxon, "Bobby Rush Son Sentenced for Sex with Inmates," *HuffPost*, November 15, 2008, https://www.huffpost.com/entry/bobby-rush-son-sentenced_n_135001.

51. Gabe Kaminsky, "Democrat Congressman Used Campaign Funds to Pay His Wife and Ex-Con Son Thousands, Records Reveal," Daily Caller, June 26, 2022,. https://dailycaller.com/2022/06/26/bobby-rush-son-wife-thousands-democrats-campaign-funds.

52. Henry Rodgers, "FEC Records Show Democratic Rep. Jahana Hayes Used Campaign Funds to Pay Family Thousands of Dollars," Daily Caller, February 1, 2022, https://dailycaller.com/2022/02/01/fec-records-jahana-hayes-campaign-funds-family-david-crenshaw-asia-clermont.

53. Cameron Cawthorne and Joe Schoffstall, "Clyburn Inc.: South Carolina Dem Showers Family Members with over $200K from Campaign Funds," Fox News, April 19, 2022, https://www.foxnews.com/politics/clyburn-inc-south-carolina-dem-showers-family-members-with-over-200k-from-campaign-funds.

54. Eric Lipton, "Study Shows House Members Profit," *New York Times*, March 22, 2012, https://www.nytimes.com/2012/03/22/us/politics/study-shows-how-house-members-and-families-reap-benefits.html.

55. Kaminsky, "Democrat Congressman Used Campaign Funds."

56. Dovere, "The Sanders and Biden Families Have Been Cashing In for Years."

57. Dovere, "The Sanders and Biden Families Have Been Cashing In for Years."

58. Dovere, "The Sanders and Biden Families Have Been Cashing In for Years."

59. Dovere, "The Sanders and Biden Families Have Been Cashing In for Years."

60. https://www.foxnews.com/politics/pac-aligned-with-ocasio-cortez-paid-6g-her-boyfriend-for-marketing-work.

61. Joe Schoffstall, "Ilhan Omar's Husband's Firm Quietly Raking in Payments Again from Committee Linked to 'Squad' Member," Fox News, April 14, 2022, https://www.foxnews.com/politics/ilhan-omar-husband-firm-payments-committee-squad-member.

62. Brittany Gibson, "Abrams' Campaign Chair Collected Millions in Legal Fees from Voting Rights Organization," *Politico*, October 24, 2022, https://www.politico.com/news/2022/10/24/stacey-abrams-fair-fight-action-00061348.

63. https://www.politico.com/news/2022/10/24/stacey-abrams-fair-fight-action-00061348.

64. Associated Press, "Former Congressman William Jefferson Who Hid $90,000 in His Freezer Could Face 20 Years in Jail," *NY Daily News*, August 5, 2009, https://www.nydailynews.com/news/world/congressman-william-jefferson-hid-90-000-freezer-face-20-years-jail-article-1.395138.

65. Jonathan Tilove, "Exhibits in Jefferson Trial Reveal Payments to Daughters' Colleges," *NOLA*, June 10, 2009, https://www.nola.com/news/article_5bdb1748-6cf1-5687-986e-0b9d7bc26dba.html.

66. https://www.politico.com/news/magazine/2023/01/19/marie-gluenskamp-perez-democrats-middle-class-00078215.

67. Stephanie Mencimer, "How Matt Gaetz Used Daddy's Money to Become Trump's Favorite Congressman," *Mother Jones*, September–October 2019, https://www.motherjones.com/politics/2019/07/how-matt-gaetz-used-daddys-money-to-become-trumps-favorite-congressman.

68. Mencimer, "How Matt Gaetz Used Daddy's Money."

69. Mencimer, "How Matt Gaetz Used Daddy's Money."

70. Michela Tindera and Hank Tucker, "Matt Gaetz's Surprising Family Wealth," *Forbes*, April 3, 2021, https://www.forbes.com/sites/michelatindera/2021/04/03/inside -the-30-million-gaetz-family-fortune/?sh=2f039cbd6d40.

71. Tindera and Tucker, "Matt Gaetz's Surprising Family Wealth."

72. Seema Mehta, Ryan Menezes, and Maloy Moore, "How Eight Elite San Francisco Families Funded Gavin Newsom's Political Ascent," *Los Angeles Times*, September 7, 2018, https://www.latimes.com/projects/la-pol-ca-gavin-newsom-san-francisco-money.

73. "J.B. Pritzker," *Forbes*, n.d., https://www.forbes.com/profile/jb-pritzker.

74. "J.B. Pritzker," *Forbes*.

75. Disclosure: In 2016, I was a Pritzger Fellow at the University of Chicago.

76. "Bill Haslam," *Forbes*, n.d., https://www.forbes.com/profile/bill-haslam.

77. "Update 1-Target Co-founder Bruce Dayton Dies at 97," Reuters, November 13, 2015, https://www.reuters.com/article/target-dayton/update-1-target-co-founder-bruce-dayton -dies-at-97-idINL3N13851A20151113.

78. Iric Nathanson, "The Dayton Name: A Minnesota Institution since 1903," *MinnPost*, December 10, 2010, https://www.minnpost.com/politics-policy/2010/12/dayton-name -minnesota-institution-1903.

79. Dana Rubinstein, "Daniel Goldman, Ex-Trump Prosecutor, Tops Crowded Field in N.Y. Primary," *New York Times*, August 24, 2022, https://www.nytimes.com/2022 /08/24/nyregion/daniel-goldman-trump-ny-primary.html

80. Rubinstein, "Daniel Goldman, Ex-Trump Prosecutor."

81. https://nypost.com/2023/02/11/rep-dan-goldman-has-racked-up-84-tickets-in-6-years/.

82. "John Adams to Abigail Adams, 12 May 1780," National Archives, https://founders .archives.gov/documents/Adams/04-03-02-0258.

83. https://www.cnn.com/2023/01/17/politics/biden-family-name-invs/index.html.

84. https://www.cnn.com/2023/01/17/politics/biden-family-name-invs/index.html.

85. Dovere, "The Sanders and Biden Families Have Been Cashing In for Years."

86. Matt Viser, "James Biden—Presidential Brother, Family Helper, Political Wild Card," *Washington Post*, May 31, 2022, https://www.washingtonpost.com/politics/2022/05/31 /jimmy-biden-president-brother.

87. Ben Schreckinger, *The Bidens: Inside the First Family's Fifty-Year Rise to Power* (Grand Central Publishing, 2021), 102.

88. Viser, "James Biden—Presidential Brother."

89. Viser, "James Biden—Presidential Brother."

90. Tom Winter, Sarah Fitzpatrick, Chloe Atkins, and Laura Strickler, "Analysis of Hunter Biden's Hard Drive Shows He, His Firm Took In about $11 Million from 2013 to 2018, Spent It Fast," NBC News, May 19, 2022, https://www.nbcnews.com /politics/national-security/analysis-hunter-bidens-hard-drive-shows-firm-took-11 -million-2013-2018-rcna29462.

91. https://www.cnn.com/2023/01/17/politics/biden-family-name-invs/index.html.

92. Erika Kinetz, "China Grants 18 Trademarks in 2 Months to Trump, Daughter," AP News, November 6, 2018, https://apnews.com/article/north-america-donald-trump -trademarks-voting-ivanka-trump-0a3283036d2f4e699da4aa3c6dd01727.

93. Richard Pérez-Peña and Rachel Abrams, "Trump Assails Nordstrom for 'Unfairly' Dropping His Daughter Ivanka's Line," *New York Times*, February 8, 2017, https://www.nytimes.com/2017/02/08/business/ivanka-trump-nordstrom-tj-maxx.html.

94. Kristine Phillips, "'Go Buy Ivanka's stuff,' Kellyanne Conway Said. Then the First Daughter's Fashion Sales Exploded," *Washington Post*, March 10, 2017, https://www.washingtonpost.com/news/business/wp/2017/03/10/go-buy-ivankas-stuff-kellyanne-conway-said-then-the-first-daughters-fashion-sales-exploded.

95. "Future-Proofing the Presidency," *Boston Globe*, June 2021, https://apps.bostonglobe.com/opinion/graphics/2021/06/future-proofing-the-presidency/part-3-a-sordid-family-affair.

96. David D. Kirkpatrick and Kate Kelly, "Before Giving Billions to Jared Kushner, Saudi Investment Fund Had Big Doubts," *New York Times*, April 10, 2022. https://www.nytimes.com/2022/04/10/us/jared-kushner-saudi-investment-fund.html.

97. Kirkpatrick and Kate Kelly, "Before Giving Billions to Jared Kushner."

98. Igor Derysh, "FEC Republicans Block Action on Alleged Trump Money Laundering Scheme Despite Fining Hillary," *Salon*, May 17, 2022, https://www.salon.com/2022/05/17/fec-block-action-on-alleged-money-laundering-scheme-despite-fining-hillary.

Chapter 6

1. https://www.tampabay.com/archive/2001/02/02/it-s-very-expensive-to-be-me/.

2. Rosalind S. Helderman and Jerry Markon, "FBI Looking into Relationship between McDonnells, Donor," *Washington Post*, April 29, 2013, https://www.washingtonpost.com/politics/fbi-looking-into-relationship-between-mcdonnells-donor/2013/04/29/c97fec10-b115-11e2-9a98-4be1688d7d84_story.html.

3. "Former Va. Gov. McDonnell, Wife Indicted on Federal Corruption Charges," Fox News, December 20, 2015, https://www.foxnews.com/politics/former-va-gov-mcdonnell-wife-indicted-on-federal-corruption-charges.

4. https://www.npr.org/sections/thetwo-way/2016/06/27/483711311/supreme-court-throws-out-former-virginia-governor-bob-mcdonnells-conviction.

5. Byron York, "The Ugly, Sordid, Damning Details in the Bob McDonnell Indictment," *Washington Examiner*, January 21, 2014, https://www.washingtonexaminer.com/the-ugly-sordid-damning-details-in-the-bob-mcdonnell-indictment.

6. Randy Leonard and Paul V. Fontelo, "Every Member of Congress' Wealth in One Chart," *CQ Roll Call*, March 2, 2018, https://rollcall.com/2018/03/02/every-member-of-congress-wealth-in-one-chart.

7. "Debbie Wasserman Schultz," OpenSecrets, n.d., https://www.opensecrets.org/personal-finances/net-worth?cid=N00026106&year=2016.

8. "Steve Scalise," OpenSecrets, n.d., https://www.opensecrets.org/personal-finances/steve-scalise/net-worth?cid=N00009660&year=2017.

9. Stephen Groves, "Ethics Board Keeps 'Action' Secret on Complaint against Noem," AP News, September 20, 2022, https://apnews.com/article/kristi-noem-south-dakota-872aa9adc02bdbe4c6147c671e91053e.

10. Stephen Groves, "South Dakota Investigation Weighs Noem's Use of State Plane," AP News, September 24, 2022, https://apnews.com/article/kristi-noem-south-dakota-sd-state-wire-rapid-city-pierre-c779a5ca06476a54b77376309fd8f2e5.

11. Chris Marquette, "Ethics Office: Rep. Mooney Tapped Campaign Funds for Family Vacations, Fast Food," *CQ Roll Call*, August 25, 2021, https://rollcall.com/2021/08/25/ethics-office-rep-mooney-tapped-campaign-funds-for-family-vacations-fast-food.

12. Chris Marquette, "Rep. Alex Mooney 'Likely Violated House Rules and Federal Law,' Ethics Office Concludes," AP News, May 23, 2022, https://rollcall.com/2022/05/23/rep-alex-mooney-likely-violated-house-rules-and-federal-law-ethics-office-concludes.

13. Luke Broadwater, "Ronny Jackson Used Campaign Funds for Exclusive Club, Ethics Office Alleges," *New York Times*, May 23, 2022, https://www.nytimes.com/2022/05/23/us/politics/ronny-jackson-alex-mooney-ethics-complaints.html.

14. Marquette, "Rep. Alex Mooney 'likely Violated House Rules and Federal Law.'"

15. Marquette, "Rep. Alex Mooney 'likely Violated House Rules and Federal Law.'"

16. Gregory Wallace and Sara Ganim, "Pruitt Reimbursed Himself $65,000 from Oklahoma Attorney General Campaign," CNN, May 10, 2018, https://www.cnn.com/2018/05/03/politics/epa-scott-pruitt-campaign-reimbursements.

17. Rene Marsh, Jeff Zeleny, Jeremy Diamond, Sophie Tatum, and Elizabeth Landers, "Trump Meets with Pruitt amid Mounting Controversy," CNN, April 6, 2018, https://www.cnn.com/2018/04/06/politics/pruitt-trump.

18. Matthew Yglesias, "Scott Pruitt's Ritz-Carlton Moisturizing Lotion Scandal, Explained," *Vox*, June 7, 2018, https://www.vox.com/2018/6/7/17439044/scott-pruitt-ritz-carlton-moisturizing-lotion.

19. Town of Kiawah Island, https://www.kiawahisland.org.

20. Salamander Hotels and Resorts, https://www.salamanderresort.com/about-us.

21. Scottsdale Camelback Resort, https://www.scottsdalecamelback.com.

22. Jackson Hole Mountain Resort, https://www.jacksonhole.com/grand-teton-national-park.

23. "Congressional Third Party Paid Travel," report, Open the Books, July 18, 2022, https://www.openthebooks.com/congressional-third-party-paid-travel—openthebooks-oversight-report.

24. Fredreka Schouten, "Lawmakers Accept Millions in Free Travel," *USA Today*, February 27, 2014, https://www.usatoday.com/story/news/politics/2014/02/27/free-trips-by-member-of-congress/5844975.

25. Schouten, "Lawmakers Accept Millions in Free Travel."

26. U.S. House of Representatives Committee on Ethics, "FAQs about Travel," n.d., https://ethics.house.gov/travel/faqs-about-travel.

27. "Members' Representational Allowance: History and Usage," Congressional Research Service, March 24, 2022, https://crsreports.congress.gov/product/pdf/R/R40962.

Chapter 7

1. Elvis Costello, "The Other Side of Summer," from *Mighty Like a Rose* (1991).

2. Jada Yuan, "The Met Gala Is Full of Rich People. Alexandria Ocasio-Cortez Wore a Dress with a Message: 'Tax the Rich,'" *Washington Post*, September 14, 2021, https://www.washingtonpost.com/lifestyle/2021/09/14/aoc-met-gala-tax-rich-dress.

3. Yuan, "The Met Gala Is Full of Rich People."

4. Annie Karni, "A.O.C.'s Met Gala Dress Triggered Strong Reactions," *New York Times*, September 15, 2021, https://www.nytimes.com/2021/09/15/style/aoc-met-gala-dress.html.

5. Sarah Spellings, "Alexandria Ocasio-Cortez Sent a Message with Her First Met Gala Appearance," *Vogue*, September 16, 2021, https://www.vogue.com/article/alexandria -ocasio-cortez-met-gala-2021.

6. Spellings, "Alexandria Ocasio-Cortez Sent a Message."

7. Andrew Ferguson, "Review: 'Like a Rolling Stone' by Jann Wenner," *Washington Free Beacon*, October 9, 2022, https://freebeacon.com/culture/triumph-of-a-limousine-liberal.

8. "About Us," Tenants Union of Washington State, n.d. https://tenantsunion.org /about.

9. Richmond Tenants Union, https://richmondtenantsunion.org.

10. "SF Tenants Union Guiding Principles," San Francisco Tenants Union, October 12, 2020, https://sftu.org/sftu-guiding-principles.

11. Ilhan Omar, "Rep. Ilhan Omar Introduces Bill to Cancel All Rent and Mortgage Payments during the COVID-19 Pandemic," April 17, 2020, https://omar .house.gov/media/press-releases/rep-ilhan-omar-introduces-bill-cancel-all-rent -and-mortgage-payments-during.

12. Ayanna Pressley (@AyannaPressley), "It's absolutely time to #CancelRent," Twitter, May 2, 2020, https://twitter.com/AyannaPressley/status/1256622742503292928.

13. Ayanna Pressley (@AyannaPressley), "11 days until rent is due again. It's past time to cancel rent & mortgage payments." Twitter, May 21, 2020, https://twitter.com /AyannaPressley/status/1263578544736698373.

14. Joe Schoffstall, "Rashida Tlaib Pocketed up to $100,000 in Rental Income during the Pandemic Despite Pushing to Cancel Rent," Fox News, August 12, 2022, https:// www.foxnews.com/politics/rashida-tlaib-pocketed-100000-rental-income-pandemic -despite-pushing-cancel-rent.

15. Peter Hasson, "Ayanna Pressley, 'Cancel Rent' Advocate, Discloses Thousands of Dollars in Rental Income," Fox News, August 16, 2021, https://www.foxnews.com /politics/ayanna-pressley-cancel-rent-thousands-dollars-income.

16. https://www.foxnews.com/politics/squad-members-pressley-tlaib-raked-thousands -rent-pushing-cancel-payments-pandemic.

17. Ted Rall, "In Defense of Limousine Liberals," *Wall Street Journal*, June 11, 2021, https://www.wsj.com/articles/in-defense-of-limousine-liberals-11626041825.

18. John Kifner, "Kennedy Jeered on Boston Busing," *New York Times*, September 10, 1974, https://www.nytimes.com/1974/09/10/archives/kennedy-jeered-on-boston-busing -he-is-chased-from-rally-by-parents.html.

19. "Sheila Jackson Lee," OpenSecrets, n.d., https://www.opensecrets.org/personal-finances /sheila-jackson-lee/net-worth?cid=N00005818&year=2018.

20. John-Henry Perera, "Jackson Lee Again Named 'Meanest' Congress Member," October 9, 2014, https://www.chron.com/politics/article/Washingtonian-gives-Rep-Sheila -Jackson-Lee-5812890.php.

21. Ollie A. Williams, "118 Private Jets Take Leaders to COP26 Climate Summit Burning Over 1,000 Tons of CO2," *Forbes*, November 5, 2021, https://www.forbes.com /sites/oliverwilliams1/2021/11/05/118-private-jets-take-leaders-to-cop26-climate -summit-burning-over-1000-tons-of-co2.

22. Thomas Catenacci, "John Kerry's Family Private Jet Emitted over 300 Metric Tons of Carbon since Biden Took Office," Fox News, July 19, 2022, https://www.foxnews .com/politics/john-kerrys-family-private-jet-emitted-300-metric-tons-carbon-biden -took-office.

23. Diana Budds, "Obama Blames Liberal NIMBYs for the Housing Crisis Too," *New York Curbed*, June 29, 2022, https://www.curbed.com/2022/06/obama-aia-conference -housing-crisis-liberal-nimby-yimby.html.

24. Tim Ellis, "Survey: More than Half of Americans Support Pro-Housing Policies, but Only 27% Support Density in Their Neighborhood," Redfin, October 29, 2020, https://www.redfin.com/news/support-for-housing-not-density.

25. "Our Mission," West Side Community Organization, n.d., https://www.westsideco .org/mission.

26. Rachel Holliday Smith, "City Starts Kicking Thousands of Homeless People from Hotels Back to Shelters," *The City*, June 28, 2021, https://www.thecity.nyc/housing /2021/6/28/22555011/city-starts-kicking-thousands-of-homeless-people-from-hotels -back-to-shelters.

27. Kriston Capps, "Public Housing Takes Priority in Biden Spending Bill," *Bloomberg*, October 28, 2021, https://www.bloomberg.com/news/articles/2021-10-28/what-the -latest-build-back-better-act-invests-in-housing.

28. "Maxine Waters Criticized over Luxury Mansion by Congressional Candidate Joe Collins in New Viral Ad," Joe Collins for Congress, April 6, 2021, https://www.prnewswire .com/news-releases/maxine-waters-criticized-over-luxury-mansion-by-congressional -candidate-joe-collins-in-new-viral-ad-301276799.html.

29. "Fact Sheet: President Biden Announces Student Loan Relief for Borrowers Who Need It Most," White House, August 24, 2022, https://www.whitehouse.gov/briefing -room/statements-releases/2022/08/24/fact-sheet-president-biden-announces-student -loan-relief-for-borrowers-who-need-it-most.

30. Robert Farrington, "How Much Student Loan Debt Do Members of Congress Have?," *College Investor*, June 27, 2022, https://thecollegeinvestor.com/39318/student-loan-debt -members-of-congress.

31. Brianna McGurran and Alicia Hahn, "College Tuition Inflation: Compare the Cost of College over Time," *Forbes*, March 28, 2022, https://www.forbes.com/advisor /student-loans/college-tuition-inflation.

32. "Census Bureau Releases New Educational Attainment Data," United States Census Bureau, February 24, 2022, https://www.census.gov/newsroom/press-releases/2022 /educational-attainment.html.

33. Anna Helhoski and Ryan Lane, "Student Loan Debt Statistics: 2022," *NerdWallet*, August 25, 2022, https://www.nerdwallet.com/article/loans/student-loans/student -loan-debt.

34. Helhoski and Lane, "Student Loan Debt Statistics: 2022."

35. Fatma Khaled, "Ocasio-Cortez Rejects 'Scarcity Mindset' as GOP Attacks Student Debt Relief," *Newsweek*, August 27, 2022, https://www.newsweek.com/ocasio -cortez-rejects-scarcity-mindset-gop-attacks-student-debt-relief-1737578.

36. Jeff Stein, "White House Officials Weigh Income Limits for Student Loan Forgiveness," *Washington Post*, April 30, 2022, https://www.washingtonpost.com/us-policy/2022/04/30/white-house-student-loans.

37. Clerk of the House of Representatives, "Financial Disclosure Report," April 30, 2018, https://disclosures-clerk.house.gov/public_disc/financial-pdfs/2018/10021221.pdf.

38. Jake Johnson, "AOC Says Congress Could Reverse Trump Tax Cuts to Cancel All Student Debt," *Raw Story*, August 28, 2022, https://www.rawstory.com/aoc-student-debt.

39. "Harvard's Largest-in-the-Nation Endowment Surpasses $53 billion," Boston.com, October 14, 2021, https://www.boston.com/news/college/2021/10/14/harvards-largest-in-the-nation-endowment-surpasses-53-billion.

40. Zhemin Shao, "Yale's Endowment Reaches $42.3 Billion, Posting Highest Rate of Return since 2000," *Yale Daily News*, October 14. 2021, https://yaledailynews.com/blog/2021/10/14/yales-endowment-reaches-42-3-billion-posting-highest-rate-of-return-since-2000.

41. Brandon Gillespie, "Higher Education Showered Biden, Democrats with Millions in Campaign Cash prior to Student Loan Handout," Fox News, August 24, 2022, https://www.foxnews.com/politics/higher-education-showered-biden-democrat-candidates-campaign-cash-student-loan-announcement.

42. Sarah Mervosh, "The Pandemic Erased Two Decades of Progress in Math and Reading," *New York Times*, September 1, 2022, https://www.nytimes.com/2022/09/01/us/national-test-scores-math-reading-pandemic.html.

43. https://www.cdc.gov/media/releases/2022/p0331-youth-mental-health-covid-19.html#:~:text=According%20to%20the%20new%20data,hopeless%20during%20the%20past%20year.

44. Tejal Rao, "Why Was Newsom's French Laundry Moment Such a Big Deal? Our California Restaurant Critic Explains," *New York Times*, September 14, 2022, https://www.nytimes.com/2021/09/14/us/elections/french-laundry-newsom.html.

45. Tejal Rao, "California's Luxury Dining Circuit: Delicious and Dull," *New York Times*, September 17, 2019, https://www.nytimes.com/2019/09/17/dining/napa-luxury-restaurants.html.

46. Alexandra Macon, "Inside Ivy Getty's Fantasy Wedding Weekend in San Francisco," *Vogue*, November 8, 2021, https://www.vogue.com/slideshow/inside-ivy-getty-wedding-weekend-in-san-francisco.

47. Emily Crane, "Nancy Pelosi Slammed as Hypocrite for Attending Ivy Getty's Wedding Maskless," *New York Post*, November 10, 2021, https://nypost.com/2021/11/10/nancy-pelosi-slammed-for-attending-getty-wedding-maskless.

48. Jesse O'Neill, "Celebrities Descend on Martha's Vineyard for Obama's 'Scaled Back' Bash," *New York Post*, August 7, 2021, https://nypost.com/2021/08/07/barack-obamas-birthday-bash-at-marthas-vineyard-guest-list-john-legend-chrissy-teigen-dwayne-wade.

49. Maureen Dowd, "Behold Barack Antoinette," *New York Times*, August 14, 2021, https://www.nytimes.com/2021/08/14/opinion/barack-obama-birthday.html,

50. Dowd, "Behold Barack Antoinette."

51. https://www.realclearpolitics.com/video/2021/09/28/va_gov_candidate_mcauliffe_i _dont_think_parents_should_be_telling_schools_what_they_should_teach.html.

52. It's worth noting that some Democrats, such as Jared Polis, still do support charter schools. https://gazette.com/opinion/polis-steps-up-for-school-choice/article_6df32bca -ce4b-11ec-be22-7f4e5d616b5f.html.

53. Ana Ceballos, "Buttigieg Talks Florida Environment, Schools," *Daily Commercial,* June 11, 2019, https://www.dailycommercial.com/story/news/politics/state/2019/06/11 /buttigieg-talks-florida-environment-schools/4933192007.

54. Corey A. DeAngelis and Tommy Schultz, "2020 Democrats Are School Choice Hypocrites," Cato Institute, December 4, 2019, https://www.cato.org/commentary /2020-democrats-are-school-choice-hypocrites.

55. Valerie Strauss, "Elizabeth Warren Calls for Billions of New Dollars to Reform Pre-K–12 Schools and Fight Privatization. Here's How She Plans to Pay for It," *Washington Post,* October 21, 2019, https://www.washingtonpost.com/education/2019/10/21/elizabeth -warren-calls-billions-new-dollars-reform-prek-schools-fight-privatization-heres-how-she -plans-pay-it.

56. D'Angelo Gore, "Warren Misleads on Her Kids' Schooling," FactCheck.org, November 27, 2019, https://www.factcheck.org/2019/11/warren-misleads-on-her-kids-schooling.

57. Jennifer Garrett, "How Members of Congress Practice School Choice," Heritage Foundation, June 13, 2000, https://www.heritage.org/education/report/how-members -congress-practice-school-choice-0.

58. Jonathan Tamari, "John Fetterman's Parents Gave Him Money into His 40s. Republicans Say That Undercuts His Blue-Collar Image," *Philadelphia Inquirer,* August 3, 2022, https://www.inquirer.com/politics/election/republicans-target-john-fetterman-blue -collar-image-20220803.html&outputType=app-web-view.

59. Ana Calderone, "Inside the New Jersey Mansion Dr. Oz and His Wife Lisa Built from Scratch 20 Years Ago," *People,* February 10, 2020, https://people.com/home/inside -the-new-jersey-mansion-dr-oz-and-his-wife-lisa-built-from-scratch-20-years-ago.

60. Anders Anglesey, "Dr. Oz Steelers Gaffe at Trump Rally Sparks Mockery Online," *Newsweek,* November 6, 2022, https://www.newsweek.com/dr-oz-pittsburgh-steelers-gaffe -trump-rally-sparks-mockery-online-1757284.

61. Chuck Ross, "Fetterman Opposes School Vouchers for the Poor. He Sends His Kids to One of PA's Priciest Prep Schools," *Washington Free Beacon,* August 26, 2022, https://freebeacon.com/democrats/fetterman-opposes-school-vouchers-for-the-poor -he-sends-his-kids-to-one-of-pas-priciest-prep-schools.

62. Tamara Keith and Domenico Montanardo, "Colorado's Governor Treated COVID Differently Than Many Democrats. It May Pay Off," NPR, March 10, 2022, https:// www.npr.org/2022/03/10/1085838500/colorados-governor-treated-covid-differently -than-many-democrats-it-may-pay-off.

63. George F. Will, "Why Colorado Gov. Jared Polis Could Answer Democrats' 2024 Prayers," *Washington Post,* September 14, 2022, https://www.washingtonpost.com/opinions /2022/09/14/democrat-jared-polis-presidential-potential-2024.

64. Will, "Why Colorado Gov. Jared Polis."

65. Ellis Simani, Robert Faturechi, and Ken Ward Jr., "How These Ultrawealthy Politicians Avoided Paying Taxes," *ProPublica*, November 4, 2021, https://www.propublica.org/article/how-these-ultrawealthy-politicians-avoided-paying-taxes.

66. Ernest Luning, "Polis Fires Back at GOP Attack over Income Taxes, Calls on Stapleton to Release Tax Records," Colorado Politics, September 11, 2018, https://www.coloradopolitics.com/news/polis-fires-back-at-gop-attack-over-income-taxes-calls-on-stapleton-to-release-tax/article_57da6566-b8dc-574f-ad11-cf008ccd5c83.html.

67. "Jared Polis," OpenSecrets, 2017, https://www.opensecrets.org/personal-finances/jared-polis/net-worth?cid=N00029127&year=2017.

68. "Jared Polis," OpenSecrets, 2014, https://www.opensecrets.org/personal-finances/net-worth?year=2014&cid=N00029127.

69. Simani, Faturechi, and Ward, "How These Ultrawealthy Politicians Avoided Paying Taxes."

70. Valerie Richardson, "Jared Polis, Who Led Charge for Trump's Tax Returns, Refuses to Release His Own," *Washington Times*, September 12, 2018, https://apnews.com/article/2b93eb2c94e7753e9b538e99f86a25f1.

71. Simani, Faturechi, and Ward, "How These Ultrawealthy Politicians Avoided Paying Taxes."

72. Jason Lemon, "Marjorie Taylor Greene Brags about $25K in Fines for Refusing to Wear Masks: 'Stand Up,'" *Newsweek*, October 9, 2021, https://www.newsweek.com/marjorie-taylor-greene-brags-about-25k-fines-refusing-wear-masks-stand-1637296.

73. https://www.newsweek.com/ilhan-omar-calls-marjorie-taylor-greene-hypocrite-cult-leader-over-masked-airplane-photo-1630463.

Chapter 8

1. https://books.google.com/books?id=h1o5EAAAQBAJ&pg=PR14&lpg=PR14&dq=Well,+Lyndon,+you+may+be+right+and+they+may+be+every+bit+as+intelligent+as+you+say,+but+I%E2%80%99d+feel+a+whole+lot+better+about+them+if+just+one+of+them+had+run+for+sheriff+once&source=bl&ots=c4sTsAzVc7&sig=ACfU3U0y9gqyhr3dNL6UUzRCuirjvpZ0iw&hl=en&sa=X&ved=2ahUKEwj6yK3Q4d78AhVLj4kEHThLCPoQ6AF6BAgfEAM#v=onepage&q=Well%2C%20Lyndon%2C%20you%20may%20be%20right%20and%20they%20may%20be%20every%20bit%20as%20intelligent%20as%20you%20say%2C%20but%20I%E2%80%99d%20feel%20a%20whole%20lot%20better%20about%20them%20if%20just%20one%20of%20them%20had%20run%20for%20sheriff%20once&f=false.

2. Elizabeth Warren, "Unsafe at Any Rate," *Democracy*, Summer 2007, https://democracyjournal.org/magazine/5/unsafe-at-any-rate.

3. Nicole Darrah, "'I Am Angry': Warren Blasts 'Extremist' Supreme Court after Roe Opinion Leaks," *Yahoo! News*, May 3, 2022, https://news.yahoo.com/roe-wade-elizabeth-warren-angry-extremist-supreme-court-181430932.html.

4. https://www.theatlantic.com/ideas/archive/2022/01/ivy-league-apologists-january-6-gop-elitism-populsim/621153/.

5. Soo Rin Kim and Libby Cathey, "Obama-Era Officials Return to White House Worth Millions," ABC News, March 21, 2021, https://abcnews.go.com/US/obama -era-officials-return-white-house-worth-millions/story?id=76582015.

6. Kim and Cathey, "Obama-Era Officials Return to White House."

7. Kim and Cathey, "Obama-Era Officials Return to White House."

8. https://www.marketwatch.com/story/incoming-biden-chief-of-staff-zients-is-nearly -wealthy-enough-to-buy-the-entire-white-house-11674474535.

9. Chad Day, Luis Melgar, and John McCormick, "Biden's Wealthiest Cabinet Officials: Zients, Lander, Rice Top the List," *Wall Street Journal*, March 23, 2021, https:// www.wsj.com/articles/bidens-wealthiest-cabinet-officials-zients-lander-rice-top-the-list -11616500809.

10. Alex Thompson, "Lander Held On to Vaccine Maker Stock Months into Tenure," *Politico*, February 9, 2022, https://www.politico.com/news/2022/02/09/lander-vaccine -stock-ethics-00007100.

11. https://www.theatlantic.com/ideas/archive/2022/01/ivy-league-apologists-january -6-gop-elitism-populsim/621153/.

12. Abigail Johnson Hess, "It Costs Over $70,000 a Year to Go to Harvard—but Here's How Much Students Actually Pay," CNBC, April 6, 2019, https://www.cnbc.com /2019/04/05/it-costs-78200-to-go-to-harvardheres-what-students-actually-pay.html.

13. "AP Was There: Bush's Bum Rap on 'Amazing' Barcode Scanner," AP News, December 4, 2018, https://apnews.com/article/george-hw-bush-north-america-us-news-newspapers -politics-61f29d10e27140b0b108d8e12b64b839.

14. Dan Nakaso, "Obama's Grandmother Blazed Trail," ABC News, n.d., https://abcnews .go.com/Politics/story?id=4608394.

15. Ronald Radosh, "Steve Bannon, Trump's Top Guy, Told Me He Was 'a Leninist,'" *Daily Beast*, April 13, 2017, https://www.thedailybeast.com/steve-bannon-trumps-top -guy-told-me-he-was-a-leninist.

16. Jennifer Senior, "American Rasputin," *The Atlantic*, June 6, 2022, https://www.theatlantic .com/magazine/archive/2022/07/steve-bannon-war-room-democracy-threat/638443.

17. Colleen Bell, "Spooked by the Demos: Aristotle's Conception of the Good Citizenry against the Mob," *Problematique*, Spring 2007, https://www.yorku.ca/problema/Issues /Problematique1102.pdf.

18. Disclosure: My wife was a fundraising consultant for Hillyer's 2013 campaign for Congress in Alabama.

19. Quin Hillyer, "Sen. John Kennedy's Full-Trump Mode Is Just His Latest Stage Persona," *Washington Examiner*, December 2, 2019, https://www.washingtonexaminer.com /opinion/sen-john-kennedys-full-trump-mode-is-just-his-latest-stage-persona.

20. Jason Zengerle, "Ted Cruz: The Distinguished Wacko Bird from Texas," *GQ*, September 22, 2013, https://www.gq.com/story/ted-cruz-republican-senator-october-2013.

21. https://www.theatlantic.com/ideas/archive/2022/01/ivy-league-apologists-january-6 -gop-elitism-populsim/621153/.

22. Kate Taylor, "Walmart Accidentally Sparks Battle with Sen. Josh Hawley, after a Social Media Staffer Calls Him a '#soreloser' on the Company's Twitter Account,"

Business Insider, December 31, 2020, https://www.businessinsider.in/retail/news/walmart-accidentally-sparks-battle-with-sen-josh-hawley-after-a-social-media-staffer-calls-him-a-soreloser-on-the-companys-twitter-account/articleshow/80037077.cms.

23. https://www.nbcnews.com/meet-the-press/meetthepressblog/hawley-reiterates-wont-run-president-rcna57235.

24. ·Kimberly Leonard, "With $319,000 of Net Worth, Ron DeSantis Is the Anti-Donald Trump When It Comes to His Own Money, New Records Show," *Business Insider,* June 15, 2022, https://www.businessinsider.com/ron-desantis-net-worth-is-just-319000-2022-6.

25. Paul V. Fontelo, "Maybe They're Too Rich for Congress?" *CQ Roll Call,* February 27, 2018, https://rollcall.com/2018/02/27/maybe-theyre-too-rich-for-congress.

Chapter 9

1. "Hillary Rodham Clinton," United States Senate Public Financial Disclosure Reports for Annual and Termination Reports, 2000, https://pfds.opensecrets.org/N00000019_00.pdf.

2. Dan Merica, "Hillary Clinton in 2001: We Were 'Dead Broke,'" CNN, June 9, 2014, https://www.cnn.com/2014/06/09/politics/clinton-speeches.

3. Robert Yoon, "$153 Million in Bill and Hillary Clinton Speaking Fees, Documented," CNN, February 6, 2016, https://www.cnn.com/2016/02/05/politics/hillary-clinton-bill-clinton-paid-speeches.

4. "Who Can Beat Hillary Clinton?" *Politico,* November 11, 2015, https://www.politico.com/magazine/story/2015/11/who-can-beat-hillary-clinton-213346.

5. Nick Gass, "Sanders Slams Clinton: 'I Don't Get Personal Speaking Fees from Goldman Sachs,'" *Politico,* January 17, 2016, https://www.politico.com/blogs/live-from-charleston-sc/2016/01/hillary-clinton-goldman-sachs-speaking-fees-217920.

6. Rosalind S. Helderman and Philip Rucker, "Plans for UCLA Visit Give Rare Glimpse into Hillary Clinton's Paid Speaking Career," *Washington Post,* November 26, 2014, https://www.washingtonpost.com/politics/plans-for-ucla-visit-give-rare-glimpse-into-hillary-clintons-paid-speaking-career/2014/11/26/071eb0cc-7593-11e4-bd1b-03009bd3e984_story.html.

7. Helderman and Rucker, "Plans for UCLA Visit Give Rare Glimpse."

8. Rosalind S. Helderman, Tom Hamburger, and Steven Rich, "Clintons' Foundation Has Raised Nearly $2 Billion—and Some Key Questions," *Washington Post,* February 18, 2015, https://www.washingtonpost.com/politics/clintons-raised-nearly-2-billion-for-foundation-since-2001/2015/02/18/b8425d88-a7cd-11e4-a7c2-03d37af98440_story.html.

9. Helderman, Hamburger, and Rich, "Clintons' Foundation Has Raised Nearly $2 Billion."

10. https://www.nytimes.com/2008/12/19/us/politics/w19clinton.html.

11. Matthew Belloni, "Ted Sarandos and Nicole Avant Are Redefining Power for the 21st Century," *Town and Country,* October 21, 2020, https://www.townandcountrymag.com/society/a34349138/ted-sarandos-nicole-avant-netflix-power-couple.

12. Michela Tindera, "How the Bidens Earned $16.7 Million after Leaving the White House," *Forbes*, October 22, 2020, https://www.forbes.com/sites/michelatindera/2020/10/22 /how-the-bidens-earned-167-million-after-leaving-the-white-house.

13. Timothy P. Carney, "Joe Biden Also Profited off the Secret Service. It Was Also Wrong," American Enterprise Institute, February 10, 2020, https://www.aei.org/op-eds /joe-biden-also-profited-off-the-secret-service-it-was-also-wrong.

14. Tindera, "How the Bidens Earned $16.7 Million."

15. https://www.washingtonpost.com/politics/once-the-poorest-senator-middle-class-joe -biden-has-reaped-millions-in-income-since-leaving-the-vice-presidency/2019/06 /25/931458a8-938d-11e9-b570-6416efdc0803_story.html.

16. Jonathan Tamari, "Penn Has Paid Joe Biden More Than $900K since He Left the White House. What Did He Do to Earn the Money?" *Philadelphia Inquirer*, July 12, 2019, https://www.inquirer.com/news/joe-biden-penn-salary-lectures-20190712.html.

17. Matt Viser, "Once the Poorest Senator, 'Middle Class Joe' Biden Has Reaped Millions in Income since Leaving the Vice Presidency," *Washington Post*, June 25, 2019, https://www.washingtonpost.com/politics/once-the-poorest-senator-middle-class-joe -biden-has-reaped-millions-in-income-since-leaving-the-vice-presidency/2019/06 /25/931458a8-938d-11e9-b570-6416efdc0803_story.html.

18. Alan Zibel, "Revolving Congress: The Revolving Door Class of 2019 Flocks to K Street," Public Citizen, May 30, 2019, https://www.citizen.org/article/revolving-congress.

19. "Former Members," OpenSecrets, n.d., https://www.opensecrets.org/revolving/top .php?display=Z.

20. John Breshnahan, Anna Palmer, and Jake Sherman, "Shuster Admits Relationship with Airline Lobbyist," April 16, 2017, https://www.politico.com/story/2015/04/bill -shuster-admits-personal-relationship-with-lobbyist-117054.

21. Mike Stuckey, "Tauzin Aided Drug Firms, Then They Hired Him," NBC News, March 22, 2006, https://www.nbcnews.com/id/wbna11714763.

22. Isaac Arnsdorf, "Daschle Is Officially a Lobbyist Now," *Politico*, March 29, 2016, https://www.politico.com/story/2016/03/tom-daschle-officially-lobbyist-221334.

23. C. Davidson McGuire Woods, "Are Lobbyists Banned from House and Senate Gyms? A Question of Ethics," *CQ Roll Call*, June 23, 2015, https://rollcall.com/2015/06/23 /are-lobbyists-banned-from-house-and-senate-gyms-a-question-of-ethics.

24. Ernest Luning, "Cory Gardner Lands Job with Top National Lobbying Firm," *Colorado Politics*, June 23, 2021, https://www.coloradopolitics.com/quick-hits/cory-gardner -lands-job-with-top-national-lobbying-firm/article_856d5db8-d43a-11eb-a425-c3795188 c2ce.html.

25. https://www.buzzfeednews.com/article/andrewkaczynski/evan-bayhs-foundation -moved-from-indiana-to-dc-after-he-left.

26. Rosalind S. Helderman, "Hacked Emails Show Extent of Foreign Government Donations to Clinton Foundation," *Washington Post*, October 16, 2016, https://www.washingtonpost .com/politics/hacked-emails-show-extent-of-foreign-government-donations-to-clinton -foundation/2016/10/16/ce871a82-9319-11e6-a6a3-d50061aa9fae_story.html.

27. Eliza Collins, "Memo Shows Bill Clinton's Wealth Was Tied to Clinton Foundation," *USA Today*, October 27, 2016, https://www.usatoday.com/story/news/politics

/onpolitics/2016/10/27/memo-shows-bill-clintons-wealth-tied-clinton-foundation
/92842822.

28. Kate Ackley, "Taking It with Them: Members Leaving with Money in the Bank," *CQ Roll Call*, December 8, 2021, https://rollcall.com/2021/12/08/taking-it-with-them -members-leaving-with-money-in-the-bank.

29. Rich Blake, "Senators and House Members Can Keep Campaign Funds on the Way Out," ABC News, March 25, 2020, https://abcnews.go.com/Business/campaign -finance-senators-house-members-campaign-funds-retire/story?id=10203316.

30. Lachlan Markay, "Congress Gets New Spending Loophole," *Axios*, March 30, 2022, https://www.axios.com/2022/03/31/congress-gets-new-spending-loophole.

Chapter 10

1. Zephyr Teachout, *Corruption in America: From Benjamin Franklin's Snuff Box to Citizens United* (Harvard University Press, 2014), 4.

2. Teachout, *Corruption in America*, 38.

3. Ramsay MacMullen, *Corruption and the Decline of Rome* (Yale University Press, 1988).

4. H. W. Brands, *The First American: The Life and Times of Benjamin Franklin* (Anchor, 2000) 622.

5. Interview with the author on November 1, 2020.

6. https://www.independent.co.uk/news/world/americas/us-politics/tommy-tuberville -stock-ban-congress-b2011612.html.

7. Interview with the author on September 19, 2022.

8. Josh Barro, "Members of Congress Should Not Trade Stocks," *Business Insider,* January 18, 2017, https://www.businessinsider.com/members-congress-trading-stocks-2017-1.

9. Lea Juarez, "Mission City Council to Disclose Conflict of Interest Publicly," *Progress Times*, July 22, 2022, https://www.progresstimes.net/2022/07/22/mission-city-council -to-disclose-conflict-of-interest-publicly.

10. U.S. House of Representatives Committee on Ethics, "Member Voting and Other Official Activities," n.d., https://ethics.house.gov/outside-employment-income/member -voting-and-other-official-activities.

11. Callie Patterson, "GOPers Push Ban on Lawmakers Paying Family on Campaigns," *New York Post*, June 13, 2022, https://nypost.com/2022/06/13/gopers-push-ban-on -lawmakers-paying-family-on-campaigns.

12. Patterson, "GOPers Push Ban on Lawmakers Paying Family."

13. https://apps.bostonglobe.com/opinion/graphics/2021/06/future-proofing-the-presidency /part-3-a-sordid-family-affair/.

14. Stephanie Larsen, "Do Members of Congress Enjoy Free Health Care?" Snopes, March 15, 2017, https://www.snopes.com/fact-check/members-congress-health-care.

15. Larsen, "Do Members of Congress Enjoy Free Health Care?"

16. Matthew Yglesias, "Banning Former Members of Congress from Lobbying Won't Fix the Revolving Door," *Vox*, June 3, 2019, https://www.vox.com/2019/6/3/18647228 /aoc-ted-cruz-lobbying-ban.

17. William Kim, "Crenshaw on Congress Trading Stocks: 'You Have No Way to Better Yourself,'" *Texas Signal*, January 27, 2022, https://texassignal.com/crenshaw-on -congress-trading-stocks-you-have-no-way-to-better-yourself.

18. Morgan Cullen, "Most Legislative Salaries Lag behind the Private Sector, but Raising Them Can Cause a Political Firestorm," National Conference of State Legislatures, January 2011, https://www.ncsl.org/research/about-state-legislatures/pay-problem.aspx.

19. Steven Dennis (@StevenTDennis), "US Senator is one of those weird jobs where you help control trillions but quitting often gets you a raise." Twitter, October 6, 2022, https://twitter.com/StevenTDennis/status/1578144070484230144.

20. Carl Hulse, "Nebraska's Ben Sasse Plans to Resign from Senate for University Post," *New York Times*, October 6, 2022, https://www.nytimes.com/2022/10/06/us/nebraska-senator-sasse-university-florida-president.html.

21. "Ricketts Family," *Forbes*, n.d., https://www.forbes.com/profile/ricketts/?sh=ed3b882 cef7b.

22. Elizabeth Titus, "Must You Be a Millionaire to Serve in the People's House?" *Texas Tribune*, November 11, 2011, https://www.texastribune.org/2011/11/11/poorest-texas-congressmen-tout-house-diversity.

23. Titus, "Must You Be a Millionaire…?"

24. Interview with the author on July 19, 2022.

25. "Fact Check: Inaccurate Claims about Salaries for U.S. Presidents in Retirement, Congress Members, Army Soldiers and Senior Citizens," Reuters, August 13, 2020, https://www.reuters.com/article/uk-factcheck-inaccurate-salaries-pres-co/fact-check-inaccurate-claims-about-salaries-for-u-s-presidents-in-retirement-congress-members-army-soldiers-and-senior-citizens-idUSKCN2561QY.

26. https://www.newsweek.com/george-santos-wanted-win-election-lifetime-healthcare-ex-roommate-1775242.

27. https://www.newsweek.com/george-santos-wanted-win-election-lifetime-healthcare-ex-roommate-1775242.

28. Sudiksha Kochi, "Fact Check: Post Exaggerates Benefits for Members of Congress," *USA Today*, April 22, 2022, https://www.usatoday.com/story/news/factcheck/2022/04/22/fact-check-congressional-health-care-retirement-benefits-exaggerated/7274655001.

29. Shane Goldmacher, "Nearly One in Five Members of Congress Gets Paid Twice," *Yahoo! News*, June 28, 2013, https://news.yahoo.com/nearly-one-five-members-congress-gets-paid-twice-060314402.html.

30. Jonah Goldberg, "That's No Icon, That's My Mom," *The Dispatch*, October 28, 2022, https://thedispatch.com/newsletter/gfile/thats-no-icon-thats-my-mom.

31. Bruce DePuyt, "Robin Ficker Is Disbarred; Pledges His Gubernatorial Bid Will Continue," *Maryland Matters*, March 4, 2022, https://www.marylandmatters.org/2022/03/04/robin-ficker-is-disbarred-pledges-his-gubernatorial-bid-will-continue.

32. Jerry Useem, "What Does Donald Trump Really Want?" *Fortune*, April 3, 2000, https://fortune.com/2000/04/03/what-does-donald-trump-really-want.

33. Kate Ackley, "FEC Reviewing Rules on Salaries, Benefits for Candidates," *CQ Roll Call*, June 29, 2019, https://rollcall.com/2021/06/29/fec-reviewing-rules-on-salaries-benefits-for-candidates.

34. Eric Garcia, "FEC Rules Candidates Can Use Campaign Cash for Child Care," *CQ Roll Call*, May 10, 2018, https://rollcall.com/2018/05/10/fec-rules-candidates-can-use-campaign-cash-for-child-care.

35. Kate Ackley, "FEC: Lawmakers May Use Campaign Money for 'Bona Fide' Bodyguards," *CQ Roll Call*, March 25, 2021, https://rollcall.com/2021/03/25/fec-lawmakers -may-use-campaign-money-for-bona-fide-bodyguards.

36. U.S. House of Representatives Committee on Ethics, "FAQs about Outside Employment," n.d., https://ethics.house.gov/posts/faqs/outside-employment.

37. "How Much Outside Income Can a Member Earn in a Year?" Congressional Institute, September 18, 2007, https://www.congressionalinstitute.org/2007/09/18/how-much -outside-income-can-a-member-earn-in-a-year.

38. Farhi, "The GOP's Big Bulk Book-Buying Machine Is Boosting Republicans."

39. U.S. House of Representatives Committee on Ethics, "The Outside Earned Income Limitation Applicable to Members and Senior Staff," n.d., https://ethics.house.gov /outside-employment-income/outside-earned-income-limitation-applicable-members -and-senior-staff.

40. Irvin Molotsky, "Reagan Wants End of Two-Term Limit," *New York Times*, November 29, 1987, https://www.nytimes.com/1987/11/29/us/reagan-wants-end-of-two-term -limit.html.

41. U.S. House of Representatives Committee on Ethics, "Post-Employment Restrictions," n.d., https://ethics.house.gov/outside-employment-income/post-employment-restrictions.

42. https://www.citizen.org/news/editorial-board-alert-defense-secretary-shouldnt-undo -mccain-law-restricting-lobbying/.

43. Ted Cruz (@tedcruz), "Here's something I don't say often: on this point, I AGREE with @AOC Indeed, I have long called for a LIFETIME BAN on former Members of Congress becoming lobbyists. The Swamp would hate it, but perhaps a chance for some bipartisan cooperation?" Twitter, May 30, 2019, https://twitter.com/tedcruz /status/1134166282071412741.

44. Kelly O'Donnell, "Out of Office, Trump Has Received over $342,000 in Benefits," NBC News, August 24, 2022, https://www.nbcnews.com/meet-the-press/meetthepressblog /office-trump-received-342000-benefits-rcna44641.

45. Noah J. Gordon, "How Did Members of Congress Get So Wealthy?" *The Atlantic*, September 9, 2014, https://www.theatlantic.com/politics/archive/2014/09/how-did -members-of-congress-get-so-wealthy/379848.

46. Philip Stallworth, "'Let Me Tell You about the Very Rich. They Are Different From You And Me,'" Tax Policy Center, March 18, 2019, https://www.taxpolicycenter.org /taxvox/let-me-tell-you-about-very-rich-they-are-different-you-and-me.

47. "Tucker Carlson on Working-Class Americans," *Matt Lewis and the News*, January 20, 2015, https://www.mattklewis.com/matt-lewis-and-the-news/tucker-carlson.

48. Gregory S. Schneider, "Inside Virginia GOP Gubernatorial Candidate Glenn Youngkin's Long Career at Carlyle," *Washington Post*, August 3, 2021, https://www .washingtonpost.com/local/virginia-politics/glenn-youngkin-fortune-carlyle-virginia /2021/08/02/aeeebab4-efc5-11eb-81d2-ffae0f931b8f_story.html.

49. Gretchen Morgenson, "An Unusual Deal Gave Virginia Gov. Glenn Youngkin $8.5 Million in Cash and Tax-Free Status to His Almost $200 Million in Stock, a Lawsuit Says," NBC News, August 11, 2022, https://www.nbcnews.com/news/unusual -deal-gave-virginia-gov-glenn-youngkin-85-million-stock-paid-0-rcna42091.

50. Luke Broadwater, Emily Cochrane, and Alicia Parlapiano, "As Earmarks Return to Congress, Lawmakers Rush to Steer Money Home," *New York Times*, April 1, 2022, https://www.nytimes.com/2022/04/01/us/politics/congress-earmarks.html.
51. Broadwater, Cochrane, and Parlapiano, "As Earmarks Return to Congress."
52. https://thehill.com/business/budget/3879156-house-gop-tightens-up-on-earmarks/.
53. Michele Marchetti, "Interpreting Toothpick Rule," *BizBash*, May 25, 2007, https://www.bizbash.com/catering-design/tabletop/media-gallery/13472887/interpreting-toothpick-rule.
54. Marchetti, "Interpreting Toothpick Rule."
55. Kate Ackley, "Partying within the Rules," *CQ Roll Call*, December 4, 2013, https://rollcall.com/2013/12/04/partying-within-the-rules-k-street-files.
56. Ackley, "Partying within the Rules."

Appendix

1. Hall and Wang, "Meet the 25 Wealthiest Members of Congress."
2. https://www.newsweek.com/ralph-norman-accused-sedition-over-trump-marshall-law-text-1766621.
3. "Transcender" PitchBook, n.d., https://pitchbook.com/profiles/company/153602-29.
4. "Join Our Team," Phillips Distilling Co., n.d., https://phillipsdistilling.com/careers/join-our-team.
5. "Biography," Representative Dean Phillips (website), n.d., https://phillips.house.gov/dean.
6. luxuriousmagazine.com/luxurious-beverage-month-belvedere-vodka/.
7. Simone Pathe, "Vodka and Gelato Tycoon Challenging Minnesota's Erik Paulsen," *CQ Roll Call*, May 16, 2017, https://rollcall.com/2017/05/16/vodka-and-gelato-tycoon-challenging-minnesotas-erik-paulsen.
8. "Kay Chemical Company," EcoLab, n.d., https://www.ecolab.com/about/our-businesses/kay-chemical.
9. Justin Catanoso, "Kaplan Moves from Chemicals to Car Washes," *Triad Business Journal*, June 7, 1999. https://www.bizjournals.com/triad/stories/1999/06/07/tidbits.html.
10. Collin Anderson, "'Tax the Rich'? North Carolina Dem Stashes More Than $1 Mil in Cayman Islands Fund," *Washington Free Beacon*, June 4. 2022. https://freebeacon.com/democrats/tax-the-rich-north-carolina-dem-stashes-more-than-1-mil-in-cayman-islands-fund.
11. Drew Hansen, "Donald Beyer Sr., Founder of the Falls Church Auto Empire, Dies at 93," *Washington Business Journal*, December 28, 2017, https://www.bizjournals.com/washington/news/2017/12/28/donald-beyer-sr-founder-of-the-falls-church-auto.html.
12. "About," Jay Obernolte (website), n.d., https://obernolte.house.gov/about.
13. Farsight Studios, n.d., http://farsightstudios.com.
14. Joe Perticone, "How the 15 Richest Members of Congress Made Their Money," *Business Insider*, February 6, 2019, https://www.businessinsider.com/how-richest-members-congress-made-money-house-senate-2019-2#10-scott-peters-32-million-6.
15. *The San Diego Union-Tribune*, "Vincent Gorguze," n.d. https://www.legacy.com/us/obituaries/sandiegouniontribune/name/vincent-gorguze-obituary?id=18091726
16. Emerson, n.d. https://www.emerson.com/en-us.

17. "Full Biography," U.S. Congresswoman Suzan DelBene (website), n.d., https://delbene .house.gov/about/full-biography.htm.

18. Deniz Cam, "Meet the Michigan Congressman—and Billionaire's Son—Who Voted to Impeach Trump," *Forbes,* January 16, 2021, https://www.forbes.com/sites/denizcam /2021/01/16/peter-meijer-michigan-congressman-and-billionaires-son-who-voted -to-impeach-trump.

19. Cam, "Meet the Michigan Congressman."

20. "Auto Dealers Honor Roger Williams with Legends Award," *Fort Worth Business Press,* April 27, 2018, https://fortworthbusiness.com/opinion/auto-dealers-honor-roger-williams -with-legends-award.

21. Tom Benning, "Car Dealership Owned by Texas Rep. Roger Williams Received Loan through Coronavirus Relief Fund for Small Businesses," *Dallas Morning News,* May 1, 2020, https://www.dallasnews.com/news/politics/2020/05/01/car-dealership -owned-by-texas-rep-roger-williams-received-loan-through-coronavirus-relief-fund-for -small-businesses.

22. Jon Skolnik, "GOP Congressmen Reap Millions in Federal Loans for Personal Car Dealerships," *Salon,* September 25, 2021, https://www.salon.com/2021/09/25/congress men-reap-millions-in-loans-for-personal-car-dealerships.

23. "PPP Loan Data—Don Beyer Motors, Inc, Falls Church, VA," FederalPay.org, n.d., https://www.federalpay.org/paycheck-protection-program/don-beyer-motors-inc-falls -church-va.

24. "History Founder," Hollingsworth Companies, n.d., https://hollingsworthcos.com /about/history/founder.

25. Maureen Groppe, "Businessman Trey Hollingsworth, His Dad Spend Heavily on Indiana 9th District Seat," *Indianapolis Star,* April 16, 2016, https://www.indystar .com/story/news/politics/2016/04/16/businessman-and-his-father-spending-heavily -9th-district-seat/83124920.

26. Groppe, "Businessman Trey Hollingsworth, His Dad Spend Heavily."

27. Amelia Pak-Harvey, "Indiana Congressman Trey Hollingsworth Won't Seek Reelec-tion in 2022," *Indianapolis Star,* January 12, 2022, https://www.indystar.com/story /news/politics/2022/01/12/trey-hollingsworth-wont-seek-reelection-indianas-9th -district-seat/9188625002.

28. Grace Wyler, "This Is How Mitt Romney Actually Made All His Money," *Business Insider,* December 14, 2011, https://www.businessinsider.com/how-mitt-romney-made -his-money-2011-12.

29. Wyler, "This Is How Mitt Romney Actually Made All His Money."

30. Matt Taibbi, "Greed and Debt: The True Story of Mitt Romney and Bain Capital," *Rolling Stone,* August 29, 2012, https://www.rollingstone.com/politics/politics-news /greed-and-debt-the-true-story-of-mitt-romney-and-bain-capital-183291.

31. James R. Hagerty, "Richard Blum Made a Bundle on a Circus and Battled Pov-erty," *Wall Street Journal,* March 4, 2022, https://www.wsj.com/articles/richard-blum -made-a-bundle-on-a-circus-and-battled-poverty-11646406058.

32. Traub, "Richard Blum, Political Donor and Husband of Senator Feinstein, Dies at 86."

33. Jeremy Wallace, "Buchanan Earned His Millions; Will He Earn a Seat in Congress?" *Herald-Tribune*, October 30, 2005, https://www.heraldtribune.com/story/news/2005/10/30/buchanan-earned-his-millions-will-he-earn-a-seat-in-congress/28505450007.

34. Wallace, "Buchanan Earned His Millions."

35. David Hackett, "Six-Term Republican Congressman Vern Buchanan Walks a Tightrope in the Age of Trump," *Sarasota Magazine*, September 26, 2018, https://www.sarasotamagazine.com/news-and-profiles/2018/09/vern-buchanan.

36. Hackett, "Six-Term Republican Congressman Vern Buchanan Walks a Tightrope."

37. Hackett, "Six-Term Republican Congressman Vern Buchanan Walks a Tightrope."

38. Amira, "How the Richest Member of Congress Got That Way."

39. Hall and Wang, "Meet the 25 Wealthiest Members of Congress."

40. Griffin Connolly, "Rick Scott Spent Record $64 Million of His Own Money in Florida Senate Race," *CQ Roll Call*, December 10, 2018, https://rollcall.com/2018/12/10/rick-scott-spent-record-64-million-of-his-own-money-in-florida-senate-race.

41. Jonathan Swan, Josh Kraushaar, and Alayna Treene, "Rick Scott's Ill-Timed Italian Vacation," August 23, 2022, https://www.axios.com/2022/08/23/rick-scott-senate-republicans-vacation-italy.

42. Michael B. Sauter, "America's 12 Wealthiest Presidents," 24/7 Wall St., March 13, 2020, https://247wallst.com/special-report/2019/02/05/americas-12-wealthiest-presidents-2.

43. David Barstow, Susanne Craig, and Russ Buettner, "Trump Engaged in Suspect Tax Schemes as He Reaped Riches from His Father," *New York Times*, October 2, 2018, https://www.nytimes.com/interactive/2018/10/02/us/politics/donald-trump-tax-schemes-fred-trump.html.

Index

Index

About the Author

Matt Lewis is a senior columnist at the Daily Beast and the author of *Too Dumb to Fail: How the GOP Betrayed the Reagan Revolution to Win Elections (and How It Can Reclaim Its Conservative Roots)*. A frequent guest on MSNBC's *Morning Joe* and a former CNN political contributor (from 2016 to 2020), Matt has provided political commentary on HBO's *Real Time with Bill Maher*, CBS News's *Face the Nation*, C-SPAN, PBS's *NewsHour*, and ABC's *Nightline*, to name a few. Matt's writing has appeared in outlets such as the *Wall Street Journal*, *GQ*, the *Washington Post*, *The Week*, *Roll Call*, *Politico*, *The Telegraph*, *The Independent*, and *The Guardian*—and he has been quoted or cited by major media outlets including *New York* magazine, the *Washington Post*, the *New York Times*, the *New York Post*, and the Associated Press. Matt previously served as senior contributor for the Daily Caller and, before that, as a columnist for AOL's *Politics Daily*. Matt currently hosts his own podcast and YouTube show, *Matt Lewis and the News*, which features interviews with some of America's top thinkers, authors, and newsmakers. He also cohosts *The DMZ* on Bloggingheads.tv. Matt grew up in Frederick County, Maryland, and graduated from Shepherd College (now Shepherd University) in Shepherdstown, West Virginia. He lives with his family in the eastern panhandle of West Virginia.